Rev. RALp

cottage 6

D0985113

PHILIPPIANS

AN EXPOSITIONAL COMMENTARY

JAMES MONTGOMERY BOICE

PHILIPPIANS

AN EXPOSITIONAL COMMENTARY

JAMES MONTGOMERY BOICE

ZONDERVAN PUBLISHING HOUSE
GRAND RAPIDS, MICHIGAN

CONTENTS

Preface

PREFACE

When I first came to Tenth Presbyterian Church in Philadelphia, in the spring of 1968, to the pulpit already made illustrious by Dr. Donald Grey Barnhouse and his successor, Dr. Mariano Di Gangi, I chose Paul's letter to the Philippians as the basis for a series of Sunday morning studies that eventually came to occupy myself and the congregation for more than the first year of my ministry. The choice was deliberate. For Philippians is at once so simple and so profound that I knew it could speak with power to Christians at all levels of their spiritual maturity and could, at the same time, call the attention of many non-believers to all of the essential doctrines of the Christian faith. In the short scope of only 104 verses most of the major doctrines of Christianity are covered. And there are also many profound statements of Christian hope, joy, love, aspiration, and confidence in Philippians. In developing this commentary on Philippians I have occasionally used my own literal translation of the epistle and other related Bible passages.

For a time, shortly after the studies were begun, some of the messages were aired over a local Philadelphia radio program known as "Time and Eternity." Then, in 1969, the opportunity came for a wider radio ministry over the twenty-year-old "Bible Study Hour." Once again the book of Philippians was chosen. The studies were completed on the "Bible Study Hour" in the spring of 1970, and have since proved a blessing to many persons through a preliminary printing in the small booklets that are made available monthly to supporters of the radio program.

No one who is at all versed in popular evangelical literature or in more academic studies of Philippians will fail to recognize the great debt which I bear to other authors. Quite often this is indicated by direct quotation. At other times it is by a similarity of theme or by passing reference. The greatest debt is that which I bear to Dr. Donald Barnhouse who has been the human channel for the greater part of that insight which God has given me into Scripture. His published works are a mine of biblical knowledge, and I have drawn upon his ten-volume *Romans* commentary extensively, as well as *The Invisible War, God's Methods for Holy Living*, and other works. It has also been a privilege to work through such valuable commentaries as those of H. C. G. Moule, F. W. Beare, and J. A. Motyer, and on occasion I quote particularly well written passages from them. Insights by C. S. Lewis, John Stott, H. A. Ironside, Watchman Nee, and others also lie behind these studies.

I wish to thank the following publishing firms for permission to quote material for which they hold the copyright: Abingdon Press (E. Stanley Jones, *Abundant Living*, 1942); Adam & Charles Black (F. W. Beare, *A Commentary on the Epistle to the Philippians*, 1959); Channel Press (Frank E. Gaebelein, *The Practical Epistle of James*, 1955); Christian Literature Crusade (Watchman Nee, *Sit, Walk, Stand*, 1957); Christian Publications (A. W. Tozer, *The Pursuit of God*, 1948); Wm. B. Eerdmans Publishing Co. (J. R. W. Stott, *Basic Christianity*, 1958); Harcourt, Brace & World (C. S. Lewis, *Surprised by Joy*, 1955); Harvard University Press (Epictetus, *The Discourses*, trans. by W. A. Oldfather, 1961); Johns Hopkins Press (William Foxwell Albright, *From the Stone Age to Christianity*, 1957); Inter-Varsity Press (J. A. Motyer, *Philippian Studies: The Richness of Christ*, 1966); Loizeaux Bros. (H. A. Ironside, *Philippians*, 1922; *Random Reminiscences*, 1939); The MacMillan Company (C. S. Lewis, *Mere Christianity*, 1958); Pickering & Inglis (Handley C. G. Moule, *Philippian Studies: Lessons in Faith and Love*, n.d.); Fleming H. Revell (R. A. Torrey, *The Bible and Its Christ*, 1904-1906); and Zondervan Publishing House (Donald Grey Barnhouse, *The Invisible War*, 1965).

I also wish to thank the Session and congregation of Tenth Presbyterian Church who permit me to spend much of my time in this type of Bible study and writing. May all that is of God abide and bear much fruit, as He has promised. May all that is of the author alone be quickly forgotten.

JAMES MONTGOMERY BOICE

Philadelphia, Pa.

PHILIPPIANS

AN
EXPOSITIONAL
COMMENTARY

JAMES MONTGOMERY BOICE

1.

The Joyful Letter

(Introduction to Philippians)

BETWEEN 1963 AND 1966, when I was studying at the University of Basel in Switzerland, my wife and I were invited to attend a Bible study group that met on Friday evenings. It was a small group at first, but it grew. And by the time we had gone through Acts and Romans together and through several other books of the Bible, the numbers had doubled and several people had become Christians. Along with the Bible study went a growth in personal commitment to Christ and a concern for others.

In time the group began to meet on Sunday mornings. A church was founded, and the original Bible study which was in English was supplemented by another conducted in German. Soon there was a noon group for secretaries. Over the years people left the church to return to their homes in various parts of the world, and they founded groups there. At last count I knew of eleven such Bible study groups, all of which grew out of the original group in Basel. And I know that through them many more are coming to a deeper knowledge of the Scriptures.

I firmly believe that what happened in such a graphic way in Switzerland will happen wherever the Bible is studied seriously and applied to daily life. I believe that three things will happen. First, there will be conversions to Jesus Christ. Second, there will be growth in personal commitment and holiness on the part of Christians. And third, there will be an expanding concern for others. Moreover, I am confident that these things will also happen in your life as you use this book to explore Paul's great and very personal letter to the Philippians.

A JOYOUS BOOK

The letter to the Philippians is one of the most joyous books in the Bible. All the way through the letter Paul speaks of joy, of inner

13

happiness — sixteen times in four brief chapters — and he does it in
such an artless way that we know that the one who advised the Philippians to "rejoice in the Lord always" had himself found the true
source of joy. He had not only learned in whatever state he was to be
content; He had learned to rejoice in whatever state he was. He over-
flowed with rejoicing.

Throughout the centuries, from the time that Paul first wrote this
letter, Philippians has been cherished for its deep expression of Christian sentiment. A Canadian commentator has written that "the springs
and aspirations of the Christian life, its hopes and its resources, are
here unfolded for us in a manner that has contributed mightily to the
whole shape and character of Christian piety from the beginning"
(F. W. Beare, *The Epistle to the Philippians,* p. 33). And Christians
have always known this. Some of the most beloved verses in the Bible
are to be found in this book. "For me to live is Christ, and to die is
gain" (1:21). "That I may know him, and the power of his resurrection, and the fellowship of his sufferings, being made conformable
unto his death" (3:10). "For I have learned, in whatever state I am,
in this to be content" (4:11). "I can do all things through Christ,
who strengtheneth me" (4:13). "But my God shall supply all your
need according to his riches in glory by Christ Jesus" (4:19).

The book of Philippians is also noteworthy for its great doctrinal
statements. This letter is not intended as a doctrinal treatise, as are
Romans and Galatians, but it is filled nonetheless with doctrine. Paul
thought doctrine. Consequently, great expressions of Christian truth
fall like ripe fruit from his pen. At times this seems to happen almost
incidentally. Thus, the entire argument of Romans is found in one
verse of the third chapter, where Paul writes of his desire to be found
in Christ, "not having mine own righteousness, which is of the law,
but that which is through the faith of Christ, the righteousness which
is of God by faith" (3:9). The sum of his teaching about the resurrection in I Corinthians 15 is found in Philippians 3:20, 21: "For . . .
Christ . . . shall change our lowly body, that it may be fashioned like
his glorious body, according to the working by which he is able even
to subdue all things unto himself." Moreover, the greatest doctrinal
passage about Christ in the entire Bible is found in this book, in the
section that tells how Christ laid aside His preincarnate glory to take
the form of a man (2:5-11).

THE MIND OF PAUL

In a very special way the book of Philippians also reveals the mind
of Paul. Paul's mind was filled with peace, and he rejoiced in the
preaching of the Gospel. We must remember, of course, that Paul

was writing this letter during the last years of his life while facing the prospect of imminent execution for his stand for Jesus Christ. He was in prison in Rome. And except for Timothy, a few old friends, and Epaphroditus, who was soon to carry the letter back to the church in Macedonia, Paul was alone.

It is not generally recognized how poorly Paul had been received in Rome. When we read the book of Romans we think that the church that had received this letter would owe undying gratitude to the man who wrote it; but although this should have been true, it was certainly not the case. Luke tells us that when Paul arrived in Rome as a prisoner, many of the Christians went out to meet him, just as we might go to the airport to meet a celebrity. But then Paul went to prison. Two years passed, perhaps more. The pastors were jealous of Paul, and they neglected him for that reason. And when the pastors forgot their duty, the people forgot it also. In time Paul was almost forgotten. The proof of this lies in the fact that when Onesiphorus, a visitor to Rome, tried to find Paul some years later, no one could tell him where Paul was. It was only by careful searching that this faithful Christian found him.

Now, of course, Paul does not say all this. But that is the way it was. Paul wrote to the Philippians that there were jealous Christians in Rome, Christians who preached Christ out of "envy and strife," hoping to add "affliction" to his bonds. He alludes to the friction in other books. He says that most of the Christians had deserted him. And in II Timothy he tells of the difficulty Onesiphorus had in finding him. Paul says, "The Lord give mercy unto the house of Onesiphorus; for he often refreshed me, and was not ashamed of my chain, but, when he was in Rome, he sought me out *very diligently*, and found me" (II Tim. 1:16, 17). Think of it — the great apostle in a dirty Roman prison, deserted by most of his friends, and almost forgotten. And yet he writes with joy, rejoicing in the riches that belong to all believers in Christ.

PAUL'S SECRET

Why did Paul have joy in a place and at a time like that? And why do so few of us have it in affluent America? What was Paul's secret? What was the key which he had found? The secret is a simple one. It is this: Paul had filled his mind with Christ. I have read some-where, and I believe it is true, that the human mind cannot think of two things at once. You cannot be thinking about the pain in your back in the same moment in which you are thinking about crepes suzette. Similarly, you cannot be thinking about your problems in the same moment that you are thinking about Jesus Christ. This Paul knew. He knew it theoretically and he knew it practically. Consequently, he had filled his mind with Christ.

We see this most noticeably in the number of times Paul speaks the name of Christ. Did you know that the name of "Christ" or "Jesus Christ" occurs seventeen times in the first chapter alone, and that this represents a frequency of more than once for every two verses? Paul speaks of joy many times. This is significant. But it is greatly overshadowed by the number of times he mentions Jesus. Paul longed to know Jesus, and he longed to know Him well. He had achieved many things humanly speaking. He had been a rabbi. He knew the law. But he counted all these things as loss "for the excellency of the knowledge of Christ Jesus."

Oh, how much Christians need to learn this. There is so much bickering in Christian circles, so much complaining, so much unhappiness. But this was never meant to be. Christians were meant to be filled with Christ and, being filled with Christ, also to be filled with love and joy and peace — in short with all of the virtues that are the result of the life of Christ within the Christian.

Maybe you feel that this is only an ideal, something possible for Paul and for other outstanding Christians, but not for you. But I am not sure that I can agree with that at all. We are able to fill our minds with material things; we can also fill our minds with Christ. I have seen our daughter so preoccupied with chocolate candy that she will be led to ask for some merely by seeing something that is painted brown. In the same way, we should be so preoccupied with Christ that we see Him in everything — in nature, in human relationships, in our triumphs, and also in our sorrows. To be filled with Christ is the secret of real Christian living. It is the secret of true happiness.

The Mind of Christ

It is true, then, that the letter to the Philippians is important as an opening into the mind of Paul. But what is much more important, it is also an open door into the mind of Christ. It tells us what He thought of as He came to earth; it tells us why He came.

Few sections of the Bible give us a comparable picture. There is nothing like this in the great doctrinal books. They tell us the meaning of Jesus' coming and the significance of His life and ministry, His death and resurrection. But they do not tell us much about the working of Christ's mind. These insights are not really given in the gospels either, for these are a record of what Jesus said and did and almost never a record of His own thoughts.

How much more satisfying is the account in Philippians. It is personal. It is positive. And it is world-embracing. Paul tells us that Jesus "thought it not robbery to be equal with God, but made himself of no reputation, and took upon him the form of a servant, and was made in the likeness of men; and, being found in fashion as a man, he humbled himself and became obedient unto death, even the death of the cross" (2:6-8).

These verses tell us that Christ's coming to earth involved two things: humility and obedience. Humility is one of those virtues about which we talk a good deal but achieve very little. In practice, humility consists in two parts: first, relinquishing what we have; and second, receiving something that is generally regarded as inferior. Many of us only relinquish something if we think we are getting something better in return, like a girl who gives up a boy friend only if someone more handsome has been asking her for a date. Most of us do not relinquish anything at all. We hoard things and constantly try to add to what we have.

Paul tells us that Jesus did neither. Instead of hoarding what rightfully belonged to Him, Jesus laid it all aside — His power and honor, even His omniscience — and took the form of a man.

Do you know how animal dealers sometimes catch monkeys? It is an excellent illustration of the truth in this verse. Monkeys are greedy creatures and can be caught by a combination of curiosity, greed, and ingenuity. The animal trainers take a number of narrow-mouthed jars, place some shiny beads in them and then anchor them firmly to the ground by means of a length of rope. The monkeys come upon the jars, see the shiny beads, and immediately stick their hands through the narrow mouths to grab a fistful of beads. Of course, when they grasp the beads it is necessary for them to make a fist. And because a fist is of greater diameter than the unclenched hand, it is impossible for the monkeys to withdraw their hands again. Does this mean that they drop the beads and try to figure out another way to get them? Not at all! The monkeys cling to the baubles until their captors come, place them in cages, and then release them by breaking the bottles. Unfortunately, most of us are like monkeys, sometimes in more ways than one. We become fascinated by some imagined prize; and we refuse to let it go, even if it destroys us. Jesus was not like this. The Bible says that Jesus did let go. He relaxed His hand. He became a man and died for our salvation.

Secondly, Paul says that Christ's emptying of Himself also involved obedience, obedience to the Father. Christ died in obedience to the wishes of the Father. Did you ever think that it was obedience that carried our Lord to the cross? It was love that did it, of course. For we read that Christ "loved" us and "gave himself" for us (Gal. 2:20).

But it was also obedience, an obedience that did not always come easily, as His struggle in Gethsemane shows. Christ was obedient. And for this God has "highly exalted him, and given him a name which is above every name, that at the name of Jesus every knee should bow . . . and that every tongue should confess that Jesus Christ is Lord."

THE GOAL OF EVERY CHRISTIAN

We have looked at the mind of Christ and the mind of Paul. But what about your mind? Does Philippians speak of it? Yes, it does. For in the very section that speaks so wonderfully of the mind of Christ, Paul writes, "Let this mind be in you, which was also in Christ Jesus" (2:5). The mind of Christ and the mind of the believer should be one. Jesus is the pattern; we should be like Him. For Jesus that meant emptying Himself in obedience to God the Father. For us it means centering our lives upon Christ.

There is an illustration of this in the realm of astronomy. For thousands of years before Copernicus men thought that the moon, the sun, the planets, and the stars revolved around the earth. This was the Ptolemaic system. And it was a good system, much better than most people of our day imagine. It could foretell the hours of sunrise and sunset. It could chart the general alteration of the heavens. But it was wrong. Moreover, because the sun is the center of our solar system and not the earth, as Ptolemy imagined, it was inevitable that the Ptolemaic system would have defects. Simply speaking, it had two defects. First, it was not always accurate, particularly in charting the position of the planets. Under the strain of providing corrections for these movements, the system eventually broke down. Second, it did not allow for progress. New discoveries always went against it. Moreover, it was only under the system of Copernicus that Newton's theories of gravity could be developed. And it is only under this system that the flight of space ships beyond the earth is possible.

Do you see the application? You live within a spiritual solar system that is as fixed as the one that fills our heavens. Christ is the center of this system, but many people today, perhaps even you, imagine that they are the center of the system. As far as they can see the system works quite well. They serve themselves and generally get what they desire. If they work hard enough for a home, they will get it, particularly if circumstances are with them. If they work hard enough at their job and have ability, they can count on a certain measure of success. Like the proverbial Englishman, they are self-made men who worship their creator.

But this man-centered system has defects, just as the Ptolemaic system of astronomy had. In the first place, it is not quite accurate. It predicts a certain measure of success, but it does not account for failure or for the inevitable letdown when the person actually gets the thing for which he has been working. Similarly, the system of the natural man does not allow for progress. Man is limited, and any system that makes man the center of life is limited also.

It is not this way for Christians, for those who see things the way God wants all men to see them. Before God, man is abased and Christ exalted. Christ is the center of the system, the center of the spiritual universe. The Bible tells us that in this system there is infinite progress, for it is based on reality and on the nature of an infinite God. Do you know where you stand before God? Will you accept Christ's place within this system?

2.

Of Servants and Saints

(Philippians 1:1)

SPACE IS AT A PREMIUM in journalism. If an editor has two writers, each with equal insight and each maintaining an identical position, the best writer is the one who can express his thought in the shortest space. A writer who can do in one column what another man can only do in two is twice as good a writer as the first from the journalist's point of view. I believe that if the apostle Paul were living today, he would make a very good journalist. Of course, his editor would have to shorten his copy in places because Paul does go off on excursions now and then. But when he is writing carefully, one or two verses can be as condensed as any passage of Scripture. And one or two sentences can convey relationships that will take volumes to analyze.

To some extent this is true of the verse before us. Paul begins his letter as any writer in antiquity would begin a letter. He starts with his name and the name of the one who is with him. He identifies himself for the benefit of his readers. And he includes their name, identifying them, and offering a prayer on their behalf. Paul writes: "Paul and Timothy, the servants of Jesus Christ, to all the saints in Christ Jesus who are at Philippi, with the bishops and deacons."

But Paul is more than an ancient writer. He is also a Christian, and more than that, a Christian theologian. Hence, when he writes these things, he writes them not as mere civilities — as you or I would say, "Dear John" or "Dear Lois," "Sincerely and cordially" or "With kind regards" — but he writes them to communicate Christian truth and to teach the deepest and most significant Christian relationships.

A SERVANT OF JESUS CHRIST

When Paul introduces himself and Timothy as "servants of Jesus Christ," he uses a word that literally means a "slave." Paul wanted to say that he was Christ's slave and that he wished to serve Him as any obedient servant serves his master. No doubt Paul was also implying that what was true for himself should also be true for any Christian. He taught that we "are not our own"; we are "bought with a price." Therefore, we are to glorify God in our body and in our spirit which are God's (I Cor. 6:20).

It is a spiritual law that no one can become a servant of Jesus Christ until he realizes that by nature he is a slave to sin. In antiquity there were three ways by which a person could become a slave. He could become a slave by conquest, by being vanquished in a war between opposing armies. Thus, to give an example, many of those who took part in the Athenian invasion of Sicily became slaves of the Sicilians when the Greeks were defeated at Syracuse in 413 B.C. Second, a person could become a slave by birth. Any child born of slaves automatically became a slave as well. Third, a man could become a slave because of debt. Many poor people sold their children into slavery in order to pay a debt, and many became slaves themselves for this same reason. This was so common, in fact, that the Jewish people even had a law to lessen the forces of custom. Every fifty years, in the year of Jubilee, those who had become slaves because of debt were automatically set free. These laws are spelled out in the twenty-fifth chapter of Leviticus.

It is striking against this background that the Bible teaches that all men have become slaves to sin in ways similar to those by which a person could become a physical slave in antiquity. The Bible teaches that men are born in sin. David writes, "Behold, I was shaped in iniquity, and in sin did my mother conceive me" (Ps. 51:5). This verse has nothing to do with any supposed sinfulness of the sex act, as some branches of the Christian Church have taught. For sex is not sinful, but good. It merely teaches that there was never a moment of his life when David was not a sinner, and there was never a part of him that was free from its contamination. The Bible also teaches that we are slaves by conquest. Sin rules over us, so that we cannot do the things we would. Hence David prays for deliverance from presumptuous sins, asking that they not have "dominion" over him (Ps. 19:13). And Solomon speaks of the sinner being bound by "the cords of his sins" (Prov. 5:22). Then, too, we are sinners by debt. For this reason Paul speaks of the wages of sin, telling us that the account can only be paid by "death" (Rom. 6:23).

Paul knew that he had been a slave to sin in each of these ways. And every person must realize the same thing in some form before he can taste God's deliverance. A person must know that he is sick before he will go to see the doctor. In the same way a person must know that he is enslaved spiritually before he will turn to the One who alone can set him free.

Just as there were several ways of becoming a slave in ancient times, so were there several ways of becoming free from slavery. A man could earn his freedom. He could buy it. Or it could be given to him by someone able to pay the price of his redemption. Three ways! But although there were several ways of becoming free from slavery in ancient times, in spiritual terms there is only one way of deliverance and that is to be bought by the One who alone can pay sin's price. No one will ever buy his own salvation. Our acts of righteousness are debased coinage in the sight of God. No one will ever earn his salvation. We can do nothing to merit God's grace. But what we cannot earn and cannot buy God will give freely on the basis of the sacrifice of Christ. The Bible says that "the wages of sin is death," but it also teaches that Jesus paid that price on Calvary. It declares that "there is, therefore, now no condemnation to them who are in Christ Jesus" (Rom. 8:1). This is a great deliverance, and Paul knew it personally.

Someone who has not experienced this redemption from sin will want to argue that this is merely an exchange of slavery, an exchange of slavery to one master for slavery to another. But this is far from an accurate picture. No Christian would ever compare the two except in terms of a total allegiance. It is true that we have been slaves to sin, as all men are, and that we are now servants of Christ. But the second service is not at all like the first. It is a bondage of love and gratitude, a relationship that we could compare quite closely to marriage. If you are married, you know that a person is not autonomous in marriage. You are not free to do anything you want — to marry another, to leave the home, to abandon the spouse. But you are free — free to serve, free to give, free to love your family. It is thus that Christ rules us. It is thus that He rules you. He is your Lord; you are His bride. He is the master; you are His to do His bidding. This will never be slavery. It is the way of joy and peace and of genuine spiritual satisfaction.

JESUS CHRIST — JEHOVAH

One other truth needs to be seen in this phrase: the ease with which Paul substitutes the name of Jesus for the name of God — Jehovah. This phrase is not unique with Paul. When he refers to himself and to Timothy as "servants of Jesus Christ," he is not coining a phrase in order to define the relationship. He is borrowing a phrase from the Old Testament and giving it specifically Christian content.

The student of the New Testament cannot forget that all of the great Old Testament figures were called servants of God, "servants of Jehovah." The opening verses of Joshua speak of "Moses, my servant," and in Judges 2:8 Joshua himself is called the "servant of the Lord." David is called "my servant" or "his servant" several times in the Psalms (78:70; 89:3, 20). One finds the phrase "my servants" or "his servants the prophets" (Ezra 9:11; Jer. 7:25; Dan. 9:6; Amos 3:7). This phrase was familiar to Paul and to all the Jewish people. How significant then that Paul substitutes his name for those of the servants of God in Old Testament times and the name of Jesus for the name of Jehovah. Paul did not teach a new religion. He did not teach a new God or a new and contradictory revelation. The God who had spoken in old times through the prophets was speaking in Paul's day through Jesus Christ and through the testimony given to Him by the apostles and ministers of the gospel. Who is He? He is the God and Father of our Lord Jesus Christ and is one with Him. When we serve Jesus we serve the Father also.

SAINTS IN CHRIST JESUS

Next we read of the "saints in Christ Jesus," those to whom the apostle Paul is writing. These were the Christians at Philippi. They were not special Christians. They were people like you and me. Hence, the title applies to us, as it does to every Christian. Paul writes to the saints at Rome, to the saints at Corinth, to the saints at Ephesus, and so on. In every case he means believers.

A great deal of trouble has been caused for many seeking to understand what the Bible says about being a saint by the erroneous assumption that the word refers to personal holiness. It does nothing of the sort. The one who is a saint in the biblical sense will strive to be holy, but his holiness, however little or however great it may be, does not make him a saint. He is a saint because he has been set apart by God.

The biblical word for saint refers to consecration. This meaning is very evident in the Old Testament where the Bible speaks of the sanctification of objects. In Exodus 40 Moses is instructed by God to sanctify the altar and the laver in the midst of the tabernacle. Moses was to make saints of them. Clearly, the chapter does not refer to any intrinsic change in the stones of the altar or of the laver but to the fact that they had now been set apart to a special use by God. Jesus prayed for the disciples in John 17 saying, "I sanctify myself, that they also might be sanctified through the truth" (John 17:19). This does not mean that Jesus made Himself more holy, for He was holy. It does mean that He separated Himself to a special task, the task of providing salvation for all men by His death.

In the same way the Bible teaches that those who are Christians have been set apart by God. These constitute "a chosen generation, a royal priesthood, a holy nation, a people of his own," that they should show forth the praises of Him who has called them out of darkness "into his marvelous light" (I Pet. 2:9). If you are a Christian, God has set you apart in this way. David was an adulterer, but before God he was a saint. For God had set him apart unto Himself. Jeremiah was a rebellious prophet, but before God he was a saint. For God had set him apart unto Himself. The church at Philippi contained a woman who was a merchant, one who was a slave girl, and a man who was a violent soldier. Yet these were saints in Christ. Are you a Christian? If so, you are a saint, and so am I — regardless of our station in life. And we are so, not because of what we have done, but because we have been separated unto God in Jesus.

An excellent illustration of this truth comes from the life of the late Dr. Harry Ironside of Chicago. During the early days of his ministry before there were airplanes, Dr. Ironside used to travel many miles by train. On one of these trips, a four-day ride from the west coast to his home in Chicago, the Bible teacher found himself in the company of a party of nuns. They liked him because of his kind manner and for his interesting reading and exposition of the Bible. One day Dr. Ironside began a discussion by asking the nuns if any of them had ever seen a saint. They all said that they had never seen one. He then asked if they would like to see one. They all said, yes, they would like to see one. Then he surprised them greatly by saying, "I am a saint; I am Saint Harry." And he took them to verses of the Bible such as this one to show that it was so.

So it is with us. Your name may sound funny when you preface it with the title "saint." But you may rest assured that it does not sound funny to God — whether you are a Saint George, a Saint Lucy, or a Saint Harriet. God knows us all by name. And it is He who calls us saints in Christ Jesus.

BISHOPS AND DEACONS

Finally, Paul also mentions the church officers: the bishops, who were the pastors of the local congregations, and the deacons, who were the officers elected to care for the needy and to help meet the needs of the sick. These labored with the local believers in the spread of the Gospel and the strengthening of Christians.

It has often been taught by higher critics of the New Testament that the pastoral letters — I and II Timothy and Titus — cannot have been written by Paul because they give evidence of a more highly developed church structure than was possible in Paul's time. They speak of the offices of bishop and deacon, and these are supposed to have been of a later development in church history. How significant in the light of this criticism is the fact that the same offices occur in the book of Philippians, a book which only the most foolhardy of scholars would deny to be written by Paul and one which by even the most critical rating must be dated before the years A.D. 65, and probably by A.D. 60 or 61.

Moreover, the office of overseer (the literal meaning of bishop) is reflected in the Dead Sea Scrolls, all of which date from before A.D. 70 and many of which are considerably older. On this point William F. Albright has written:

> The repudiation of the Pastoral Epistles of Paul, now commonly assigned by critical scholars to the second quarter of the second century A.D., becomes rather absurd when we discover that the institution of overseers or superintendents (*episkopoi,* our bishops) in Timothy and Titus, as well as in the earliest extra-biblical Christian literature, is virtually identical with the Essene institution of *mebaqqerim* (sometimes awkwardly rendered as 'censors'). W. F. Albright, *From the Stone Age to Christianity* (Baltimore: Johns Hopkins Press, 1957), p. 23.

If anything, the evidence seems to show that the offices of bishop and deacon, far from being an invention of the post-apostolic church, were actually always present and in a completely artless way. The offices did not exist because of a rigid revelation from God or because of a carefully developed theory of the structure of the church. They existed because they were needed. If the church was to be guided, there must be those who could oversee the work. These were bishops, overseers. If the poor were to be helped, there must be men entrusted with that work. These became known as deacons. All of these worked together as believers in the furtherance of Christian work.

I believe that the most important word in this phrase is the small word "with." Many who hold office want to dominate those who are in their charge. They want to be "over" them, or at least to go "before" them in terms of prestige or honor. But it should not be so with Christians. Paul says that the officers of the congregation worked *with* the believers, and he subordinates his own role and that of Timothy by picturing both of them as the servants of all.

That is the secret of forward progress in the life of a Christian congregation. The saints must be servants. And there must be a division of labor coupled with a working together in Christ for the furtherance of the Gospel and the strengthening of other believers. This was God's way of blessing the little church at Philippi. And it is God's way of blessing your church and mine. You do not need to be a deacon, a presbyter, or an elder. But you can work together with God's saints for spiritual ends. Moreover, God wants you to do it. God wants you to witness to Christ together and to work with others to help those who need your material and spiritual assistance.

3.

Grace and Peace

(Philippians 1:2)

IN THE SECOND VERSE of Philippians Paul writes, "Grace be unto you, and peace, from God, our Father, and from the Lord Jesus Christ." These words convey a warm Christian greeting. And yet, they sound strange to modern ears, largely because few in our day know what grace or peace means. If grace means anything at all to most people, it may indicate charm, good manners, or attractiveness. And peace may refer only to peace as an alternative to warfare. Actually the words mean much more. In Paul's usage they refer to the deepest of spiritual realities.

A COMMON GREETING

The words which Paul used to greet the church at Philippi were actually quite common in Paul's day. The word translated "grace" was a normal Gentile address. It meant "greetings." We know this from the use of the word in the thousands of Greek papyri that have been found in the Near East by archaeologists and from letters written by officials of the Roman empire. An ancient letter might begin like this one from the emperor Claudius to the people of Alexandria in Egypt: "Tiberius Claudius Caesar Augustus Germanicus Imperator, Pontifex Maximus, holder of the tribunician power, consul designate, to the city of Alexandria greetings." The last word is like Paul's word for grace. Similarly, the common greeting among the Jewish people was "peace" (shalom). One of the kings of Persia used this form of address to write to the people of Jerusalem under Ezra (Ezra 4:17). And this was the common word of greeting in Jesus' day.

At the same time, however, it is important to note that the words are transformed in Paul's hands so that they carry Christian meanings. The normal Gentile greeting in Greek was cherein, a verb; but Paul uses the noun form of the same root, charis. The difference is slight, but there is a great change in meaning. For in Christian speech Paul's

27

word, *charis*, was always associated with the grace of God. The emperor Claudius was merely sending greetings to the citizens of Alexandria. Paul was saying, "God's grace be with you." In a similar way, although the word itself is unchanged, peace cannot be understood merely as a common salutation. In Paul's mouth it must always have some reference to the fruits of justification, the result of the reconciliation of the Christian man with God.

A great New Testament scholar Johannes Weiss wrote of these two words, "The fact that these terms connect themselves with the ordinary Greek and Hebrew greetings does not exclude the employment of 'grace' in its specifically Christian and Pauline sense in which it denotes the unmerited divine operation of love, which is the source and principle of all Christian salvation. Similarly, 'peace' is not to be understood primarily in the technical sense of Romans 5:1, as the firstfruit of justification; but we may be sure that, in Paul's mind, the whole state of tranquility and general well-being which was implied in 'peace' attached itself at the root to the fact of reconciliation with God."

Unmerited Grace

The first greeting that Paul has for the Christians at Philippi, then, is grace, and he uses it with its full Christian meaning. Grace! God's grace! The unmerited favor of God toward humanity.

It seems unnecessary to have to emphasize that grace is unmerited, for that is the definition of grace. Yet we must emphasize it. For man always imagines that God loves him for what he is intrinsically. We imagine that God has been gracious to us because of what we have done — because of our piety, because of our good deeds, because of our repentance, because of our virtue. But God does not love us because of that. And God is not gracious to us because of that. Paul says that "God commendeth his love toward us in that, while we were yet sinners, Christ died for us" (Rom. 5:8). Christ died for men who were hideous in His sight because of sin. And we are like that. You are like that, and so am I. If we are ever to understand the grace of God, we must begin with the knowledge that God has acted graciously toward us in Christ entirely apart from human merit.

There is a wonderful illustration of the nature of grace in the life of John Newton. John Newton had been raised in a Christian home in England in his very early years. But he was orphaned at the age of six and lived with a non-Christian relative. There Christianity was mocked, and he was persecuted. At last, to escape the conditions at home, Newton ran away to sea and became an apprentice seaman in the British Navy. He served in the Navy for some time. At last he deserted and ran away to Africa. He tells in his own words that he went there for just one purpose: and that was "to sin his fill."

In Africa he joined forces with a Portuguese slave trader, and in his home he was very cruelly treated. At times the slave trader went away on expeditions, and the young man was left in charge of the slave trader's African wife, the head of his harem. She hated all white men and took out her hatred on Newton. He tells that she exercised such power in her husband's absence that he was compelled to eat his food off the dusty floor like a dog.

At last the young Newton fled from this treatment and made his way to the coast where he lit a signal fire and was picked up by a slave ship on its way to England. The captain was disappointed that Newton had no ivory to sell, but because the young man knew something about navigation he was made a ship's mate. He could not keep even this position. During the voyage he broke into the ship's supply of rum and distributed it to the crew so that the crew became drunk. In a stupor Newton fell into the sea and was only saved from drowning by one of the officers who speared him with a harpoon leaving a fist-sized scar in his thigh.

Toward the end of the voyage near Scotland the ship on which Newton was sailing encountered heavy winds. It was blown off course and began to sink. Newton was sent down into the hold with the slaves who were being transported and told to man the pumps. He was frightened to death. He was sure that the ship would sink and that he would drown. He worked the pumps for days, and as he worked he began to cry out to God from the hold of the ship. He began to remember verses he had been taught as a child. And as he remembered them he was miraculously transformed. He was born again. And he went on to become a great preacher and a teacher of the Word of God in England. It was this John Newton who wrote:

> Amazing grace! how sweet the sound,
> That saved a wretch like me!
> I once was lost, but now am found;
> Was blind, but now I see.

Newton was a great preacher of grace, and it is no wonder. For he had learned what Paul knew and what all Christians eventually learn: grace is of God, and it is always unmerited. It is to the undeserving — and hence to you and to me — that the offer of salvation comes.

ABOUNDING GRACE

Grace is unmerited, and that is true. But grace is also abounding. Romans 5:20 says that "where sin abounded, grace did much more abound." At one time I came across an item in the Washington *Evening Star* that told of a young man who had suddenly become a millionaire. The young man had been working as a four-dollar-a-day waiter in Clearwater, Florida, and had suddenly inherited a three million dollar share of his father's lumber business. The headline story read: "$4-a-day Waiter Turns Millionaire." Suppose now that on the day before the settlement of his father's estate the owner of the restaurant had decided, entirely on his own initiative and without any real reason on the part of the young man, to increase the young man's salary from four dollars a day to five dollars a day. That would have been grace. It would not have been required. It would have been entirely unmerited. But it would have been a very small thing. In place of this, however, the young man received three million dollars. Instead of a small raise he experienced what we might call "grace abounding."

It is the same in the economy of God. God tells us that we have not the slightest claim upon Him. We deserve hell at His hands, and anything He might do for us is grace however insignificant. But God's grace is not insignificant. And it certainly does not stop with a single act. It is not a dollar-a-day grace. It is a grace that has made us millionaires in Christ.

Moreover, the Bible teaches that God's grace will go on overflowing throughout this life until the moment of our bodily resurrection, and indeed throughout eternity. Paul writes in II Corinthians 4:14, 15: "Knowing that he who raised up the Lord Jesus shall raise up us also by Jesus, and shall present us with you. For all things are for your sakes, that the abundant grace might through the thanksgiving of many redound to the glory of God." It was of grace that the worlds were hung in space and the earth was disposed for human life. Grace caused that the mountains were created and that the world was filled with life. By grace man is made in God's image with every capacity for fellowship with Him. By grace after the fall men received the biblical revelation. By grace God chose Israel for a special purpose in history. It was of grace that the Lord Jesus came — to live a life that revealed the Father and to die for human sin. Grace leads men to trust in Christ. Grace sent the Holy Spirit to be our teacher and our guide. Grace has preserved the Church through the centuries. Grace will bring forth the final resurrection. And grace will sustain us throughout eternity as we live in unbroken fellowship with God and grow in the knowledge of Him.

Grace unmerited! Grace abounding! It is the knowledge of such grace that inspired Paul to write: "Grace be unto you!" Yes, grace be unto you. Grace be multiplied.

Peace With God

But grace is not the only word in Paul's greeting to the Philippians. His second word is "peace." Just as grace was the common greeting for the Gentiles, so peace was the common greeting among the Jewish people. Shalom! Grace to the Gentiles, peace to the Jews. How thoughtful of Paul to combine the two in his characteristic greeting to Jewish-Gentile churches!

But just as Paul had a deeper meaning in mind for the word grace, so he had a deeper meaning in mind for the word peace. Shalom in the writings of the apostle Paul can never be understood merely as a common salutation. Peace comes from God. Grace is the unmerited and abounding favor of God toward men. Peace is the result of that favor, peace obtained at the cross of Christ. It is the result of the reconciliation of man and God through Jesus' death.

I have often marveled in studying the New Testament at the significant moments in the life of Christ where the promise of peace occurs. The promise of peace to men occurs first at the birth of Jesus in the words of the angels: "Glory to God in the highest, and on earth peace, good will toward men" (Luke 2:14). The angels taught that men would know peace through Him. Jesus speaks of peace to the disciples just before His crucifixion: "Peace I leave with you, my peace I give unto you; not as the world giveth, give I unto you. Let not your heart be troubled, neither let it be afraid" (John 14:27). Finally, the word peace is the first word that Jesus speaks to the disciples after His resurrection as they are assembled in the upper room. He said, "Peace be unto you" (John 20:19).

Peace with God! Think of it. We are not naturally at peace with God. We are at war with God, either passively or actively, and being at war with God we are also at war with each other and at war with ourselves. That is why we each experience so much misery and why there is so much unrest in the world. But God gives peace, perfect peace. And He does so in Christ. He will give you peace if you will come to Him in Jesus.

Now, of course, most of this applies largely to the unbeliever. But we must not forget that it is also to be applied to our everyday lives as Christians. Christians have trusted God for their salvation, a salvation from the penalty of sin. They must also trust Him for a daily victory over sin and for a constant provision for all needs; that alone brings the peace that passes human understanding. Paul writes a little later on in the epistle: "Be anxious for nothing, but in everything, by prayer and supplication with thanksgiving, let your requests be made known unto God. And the peace of God, which passeth all understanding, shall keep your hearts and minds through Christ Jesus" (4:6, 7). Do you know this peace of God? Or are you filled with anxiety? If you are, you need to trust completely in what God has already done for your salvation and then to learn to lay all your requests before Him. If you will do that, the peace of God will "keep your heart and mind through Christ Jesus."

GRACE BEFORE PEACE

The final point is this: grace comes before peace. Paul writes, "Grace be unto you and peace." Not "peace be unto you and grace." In God's order of things God's hand is always there before any spiritual blessing. And it is so in order that salvation might be entirely of Him.

We see this throughout Scripture. In chapters six through eight of Genesis we read of the great flood and of God's intervention to save Noah and his immediate family. We read of Noah's sacrifice and of God's promise never again to destroy the earth by water. All of these things are marvelous. But before any of them ever happened, we read of God's grace. "But Noah found grace in the eyes of the Lord" (Gen. 6:8).

The book of Genesis also tells of God's great blessing upon the life of Abraham. Abraham was to be the father of many nations. He was the first to receive the rite of circumcision. God promised that in his seed all the families of the earth would be blessed. We are told of Abraham's faith through which God accounted him as being righteous. But before any of these things — before the promise, before the sacraments, before the faith — God came to Abraham in grace calling him out of Mesopotamia into Palestine and establishing a permanent relationship with him.

Exodus tells of the blessing that came to Israel at Sinai and later in the promised land. The young nation received the law, and it received a kingdom. But before any of this we read of God's gracious deliverance of Israel from captivity in Egypt. Thus Moses writes, "Thou in thy mercy hast led forth the people whom thou hast redeemed" (Ex. 15:13).

So it has been in all ages. It is the story of David and Solomon, of Moses and the prophets. It is my story and yours, if you are a believer in the Lord Jesus Christ. Did you seek God? Did you find any of the fruits of salvation before God Himself was at work in your heart? Of course you did not. If you did anything at all, you ran away from God. And He had to pursue you like the hound of heaven. Men never seek God. And when men find God, it is only because God comes to them first in grace.

Grace! How wonderful! Perhaps God is coming to you in this moment. If so, you must respond to His grace. And God will pour out, not only peace, but love and joy, and He will give access into His presence, and the sure hope of life beyond the grave.

4.

A Great Fellowship

(Philippians 1:3-5)

WHAT DO YOU DO when you pray? Perhaps you will answer, "Well, I ask God for anything I really need. If I get desperate enough for something or if I end up in real trouble, I pray to God about it." Is this really what prayer is all about?

An answer to that question comes from the opening chapter of Philippians. The apostle Paul has just introduced himself to the Christians at Philippi and has greeted them in the name of Jesus Christ. Now he mentions how he prays for them. Paul writes, "I thank my God upon every remembrance of you, always in every prayer of mine for you all making request with joy, for your fellowship in the gospel from the first day until now" (1:3-5).

In Paul's mind spiritual realities always came before physical ones. He was not insensitive to material needs. At times he mentioned them. But he knew that these were always less important than spiritual things — for himself first of all and also for all Christians. Consequently, when he writes to the Philippians, he is thankful above all for their fellowship in the Gospel. Paul's prayer is a great prayer. Consequently, it is an example of prayer upon which our own prayer life may be patterned.

THANKSGIVING IN PRAYER

Isn't it interesting that the first words of Paul's prayers in his various epistles involve thanksgiving? Not only was this done in regard to this church (where there was much to be thankful about), but also in regard to the believers at Rome (Rom. 1:8) whom Paul had not yet met and to the believers at Corinth (I Cor. 1:4) who were behaving badly as Christians and causing Paul much distress.

In his prayers Paul always thanked God for the evidence of spiritual blessing among Christians. Although Paul was sensitive to the problems in his churches, he was even more sensitive to the mercies of God. He knew men's hearts. He knew that there is no good in men

34

that can satisfy God. He knew that Christians live a great deal of their lives in the flesh instead of in the Spirit. He knew that we all fall short of what God would like us to be. But Paul also was acquainted with God's grace. He gloried in God's grace. And he knew that God has provided wonderfully for His children — for their salvation and for their constant and continuing growth in the Christian life. Consequently, Paul was continually thankful for these things.

Do your prayers follow this pattern? We all laugh at the prayer that goes, "God bless me and my wife, my son John and his wife, us four and no more, Amen." And we are uneasy with the prayer that is nothing more than a string of requests — "Give me this, give me that; do it quickly, and that's that." But we often pray this way nonetheless. It should not be so. Our prayers should be spiritual prayers. And they should be filled with thanksgiving.

In many of the world's languages "giving thanks" is the basic meaning of the word for prayer. A very important Greek word for prayer is *eucharisteo,* from which we have the liturgical word Eucharist. The Eucharist is the Lord's Supper, and it refers to that aspect of the communion service that involves thanksgiving for Christ's atoning death. *Eucharisteo* means to give thanks. One of the most important Latin words for prayer is *gratia,* from which has come the French word *grace* and the English word grace. Originally it had two meanings. On the one hand it meant grace in the sense of God's unmerited favor. And that is what the word generally means in English. But *gratia* also meant thanksgiving. This meaning is preserved for us only in the "grace" that we say before a meal. In this sense grace has nothing to do with God's favor. It simply means thanksgiving.

Of course, all of this adds up to one point. For both the root meaning of the words and the example of Paul teach us that our prayers should be filled with thanksgiving. And more than this, they should be filled with thanksgiving for spiritual things. You must thank God for Christ, for His love, for the Holy Spirit, for the support of other Christians, for freedom of worship, and a host of other spiritual things. One of the standards by which you can measure your maturity in prayer is the proportion between the amount of time you spend praying to God for material things and the amount of time you spend rejoicing in Him and thanking Him for the spiritual blessings which He has given you in Christ.

FELLOWSHIP IN THE GOSPEL

The thing that Paul is most thankful for in regard to the Christians at Philippi is their fellowship with him in the Gospel "from the first day until now" (1:5).

What does this mean? The word fellowship has been so watered down in contemporary speech that it conveys only a faint suggestion of what it meant in earlier times. When we speak of fellowship today we generally mean no more than comradeship, the sharing of good times. But fellowship originally meant much more than this. It meant more than a sharing *of* something, like the fellowship of bank robbers dividing their loot. It meant a sharing *in* something, participating in something greater than the people involved and more lasting than the activity of any given moment. When the Bible uses the word it means being caught up into a communion created by God.

Let me explain it this way. British universities are not organized in the same way as our universities, with a central admissions office and various dormitories. Instead, the British university is organized by colleges within the university; and each of these has its own structure, its own admission policy, and its own distinctive traits. It governs its own students, and it has the final say about the running of the college. The affairs of the various colleges are conducted by the professors associated with that particular division of the university. They are called fellows, because they are men who fellowship together in the work of the college. Now I have been in England in the spring when the grass is green and the rain has stopped, and I have seen the fellows of the college out lounging on the greens, dressed in their academic gowns and presumably discussing Shakespeare, or Rembrandt, or Pirandello, or perhaps just the afternoon's sports. And this is fellowship in the sense that we commonly use the word. But it is not why the professors are called fellows. They are called fellows because there are also times when they leave the greens and gather for meetings that will direct the affairs of the college. In these meetings they share, not what is of interest to two or more of them, but what is held in common by them all. Their fellowship consists in their mutual interest in the college and the share they have in it.

Now this is the way the Bible regards fellowship, and it was this for which Paul was so thankful in the case of the young church at Philippi. They may have had things in common. But Paul is not speaking of these. He is thankful for their share in the Gospel of God. They had been taken up into a divine fellowship. And thus they were united, not upon a social level, but by their commitment to the truths of the Gospel.

We do not know much about the church at Philippi. We know that it was largely a Gentile church, because all of the names associated with it are Gentile names. We know that it consisted of a jailer, a violent man who would have killed himself in a crisis except he had been restrained by Paul; a slave girl who had been delivered of a spirit; a business woman who traded in purple cloth from Asia and who had been a Jewish proselyte; and others. Apparently there was little to bind them together by worldly standards. But they had one great thing in common: they had fellowship in the Gospel of God. This brought them together. Paul says that they had continued in the fellowship of the Gospel from the first day until now.

This must always be the bond between Christians. If you unite with other Christians on the basis of affluence, you will exclude the poor. If you unite along social lines, you will exclude those who do not belong to your own level of society, be it high or low. If you unite intellectually, then you will exclude either the simple or the intelligent. And however you do it, the witness of the Church will suffer. How thankful we must be that God did not establish the fellowship of His children along these lines. Our fellowship is in the Gospel of God.

FELLOWSHIP OF HIS SUFFERINGS

In two other places in this epistle, Paul again mentions fellowship. In chapter two, verse one, he speaks of the "fellowship of the Spirit." What does this mean? Well, if the fellowship of the Gospel means a mutual participation in the Gospel, the fellowship of the Spirit must mean a mutual participation in the Holy Spirit. It does not mean a fellowship between spirits, as between your spirit and mine. And it does not mean that we all receive a little bit of the Holy Spirit, like water being poured into a glass. It means that we participate in Him. As birds have their habitat in the air, and as fish have their habitat in the sea, so Christians have their habitat in the Spirit. Because we share a participation in the Holy Spirit, Paul admonishes the Philippians to strive to be of one love, of one accord, and of one mind.

In the third chapter, Paul mentions a different kind of fellowship — a fellowship in the sufferings of Christ. In one sense, none of us can suffer for sin. Only the Lord Jesus Christ could do that. But there is a sense in which we can have fellowship in His sufferings. And as we come to know something of His sufferings we also come to know something more about Him. And we come to be more like Him.

For Christians this is really the final answer to the problem of human suffering. There are many partial answers, of course, and these have been well stated many times by Christian scholars. Sometimes God's purpose in suffering is to arouse the insensitive soul to make the self-satisfied man awake to the spiritual dimension of life. And men and women are often reached for God in a moment of great mental or physical suffering who would never have responded to Him in other circumstances. If you are undergoing suffering, perhaps God has allowed it to come into your life for this reason.

Suffering also awakens us to the needs of other people. Luther would not have known the struggles of the priests of his day if he had not himself trodden a tortuous path into the full light of the Gospel. Calvin would not have known the problems of his pastors in France if he had not experienced the humiliation of being rejected in the very place where he was to do his greatest work. Thousands of believers today would not be sensitive to the needs of their neighbors, of the poor, of their friends, if they had not at some time in their lives gone through similar trials. And this may be true of you. Both of these reasons go far to explain God's purposes in permitting human sorrow.

But there is a greater reason than these, and it comes closest to explaining that for which we see no purpose. God often sends suffering simply that He may teach us something wonderful about Himself, something about His nature that is intended to awaken a new depth of experience in us. It implies Christian maturity. Without it we might never learn what is, spiritually speaking, far more important than our loss.

There is a great illustration of this principle in the story of Abraham and Isaac. Abraham was instructed to take his only son Isaac and to offer him on a mountain that God would show him, to bind him with cords and to plunge a knife into his body. What anguish Abraham must have suffered after receiving this command; what a trial it must have been to his faith and how many times he must have wished that it could have been himself instead of his son! But he carried out the command of God, and he would have plunged his knife into the heart of the boy had God not stayed his hand. Have you ever wondered why God would command such a thing? Many have asked: If God is omniscient, as He is, and hence knew what Abraham would do, why would He permit such needless torture? The point of the story, of course, is not the test itself but what Abraham learned in the process. Abraham learned what it means to sacrifice a son, and learning that, he learned something of God's character, a character that would lead God Himself to give His Son for man's salvation. This is what God revealed to Abraham in some way through the experience. And I believe that it is what Jesus referred to centuries later when he remarked that Abraham rejoiced to see Christ's day and that he saw it and was glad. Abraham saw that God would do in reality what he had only been called upon to do.

That is the way God sometimes gives suffering to Christians, to you and to me. The world may not see its purpose. And you may not see it completely at the time, or even at any time in this life. But the purpose is there, and it will be revealed to you perfectly in heaven. Suffering is never a tragedy for Christians. It is often a puzzle, but never a tragedy. And it is always an honor, for it is fellowship in the sufferings of Christ.

FELLOWSHIP WITH GOD

Paul mentions fellowship three times in this epistle to the Philippians. He points to our fellowship in the Gospel of God, our fellowship of the Holy Spirit, and our fellowship in the sufferings of Jesus Christ. In this way he teaches that we have the privilege of sharing in the full nature of God: Father, Son, and Holy Spirit. What a privilege for Christians! If you are a Christian, you already have a share in the Gospel. That fellowship is yours by virtue of your conversion to Christ. The fellowship of the Spirit is something in which you grow. It is also possible that in God's great tenderness and gentle compassion you may also touch upon the fellowship of the sufferings of our Lord.

5.

God Finishes What He Starts

(Philippians 1:6)

PHILIPPIANS 1:6 IS PERHAPS one of the three greatest verses in the Bible that teach the doctrine of the perseverance of the saints, the doctrine that no one whom God has brought to a saving knowledge of Jesus Christ will ever be lost. Paul writes, "Being confident of this very thing, that he who hath begun a good work in you will perform it until the day of Jesus Christ."

Men lack perseverance. Men start things and drop them. As men and women you and I are always beginning things that we never actually find time to finish. But God is not like that. God never starts anything that He does not finish. God perseveres. Has God begun something in your life? Have you been born again by the Spirit of God? Then you need not fear that you will ever be lost. Your confidence should not be in yourself, neither in your faith nor in your spiritual successes in earlier days, but in God. It is He who calls us as Christians, He who leads us on in the Christian life, and He who most certainly will lead us home.

A BIBLICAL TRUTH

Many other verses in Scripture support this same idea. The two passages that I regard, along with Philippians 1:6, as being the greatest expression of this theme in the entire Bible are John 10:27, 28 and Romans 8:38, 39. In John 10:27, 28, Jesus said, "My sheep hear my voice, and I know them, and they follow me. And I give unto them eternal life; and they shall never perish, neither shall any man pluck them out of my hand." In Romans 8:38, 39, Paul assures his readers, "For I am persuaded that neither death, nor life, nor angels, nor principalities, nor powers, nor things present, nor things to come, nor height, nor depth, nor any other creation, shall be able to separate us from the love of God, which is in Christ Jesus, our Lord."

The doctrine of the perseverance of the saints is also found in less formal statements in literally dozens of other passages. David writes in Psalm 138:8, "The Lord will perfect that which concerneth me." Hebrews 10:14 says, "For by one offering He hath perfected forever them that are sanctified." The Lord spoke to Jeremiah saying, "I have loved thee with an everlasting love" (Jer. 31:3). We read in II Corinthians 4:8, 9, 14, "We are troubled on every side, yet not distressed; we are perplexed, but not in despair; persecuted, but not forsaken; cast down, but not destroyed . . . knowing that he who raised up the Lord Jesus shall raise up us also by Jesus, and shall present us with you."

The doctrine is also suggested by the images that are applied to believers throughout the Bible. The saints are compared to trees that do not wither (Ps. 1:3), to the great cedars of Lebanon that flourish from year to year like the redwoods of California (Ps. 92:12), to a house built upon a rock (Matt. 7:24), to Mount Zion that cannot be moved (Ps. 125:1). All of these passages teach that the one who has been born again by God will never be lost. God never abandons His plans. God never begins a work that He does not intend to finish.

All of God

Now frankly, there are many people who do not like this teaching. And the reason they do not like it is that they like to think that men are responsible for their own salvation. They prefer to believe that men save themselves, that they are accepted by God on the basis of their good works or the use of the sacraments, and that their final salvation depends more or less on how faithful or persevering they can be. This is not biblical. And it is contradicted by every moment of the Christian's experience with God.

It is contradicted by our experience with God during the first moments of our salvation. Men do not seek God; they reject Him. And if we are saved, it is only because God comes to us first in grace. Paul wrote to the Romans that no human being will ever be justified in God's sight by his own good works, for all of his works (no matter how good they may seem in man's sight) fall short of God's standard of righteousness. Moreover, men do not seek Him. Paul writes, "There is none righteous, no, not one: There is none that understandeth, there is none that seeketh after God" (Rom. 3:10, 11). This is true of all of us. I am like that, and so are you. You do not even begin to meet God's standard of righteousness, and you do not know it unless God reveals your failure to you. You do not understand His standard. You do not seek the One who can help you. And still God comes to you, and opens your eyes, and gives you the faith to believe, and draws you to Himself.

Do you know what C. S. Lewis said about his conversion? Lewis was a brilliant British scholar who was also a thoroughgoing agnostic. Yet God sought him and found him. In his autobiography, *Surprised by Joy,* Lewis described his conversion like this: "In the Trinity Term of 1929 I gave in, and admitted that God was God, and knelt and prayed: perhaps, that night, the most dejected and reluctant convert in all England. I did not then see what is now the most shining and obvious thing; the Divine humility which will accept a convert even on such terms. The Prodigal Son, at least walked home on his own feet. But who can duly adore that love which will open the high gates to a prodigal who is brought in kicking, struggling, resentful, and darting his eyes in every direction for a chance of escape?" *

Eternity magazine once published an interesting article called "Encounter With Light" telling of a young atheistic student who had heard of C. S. Lewis and had begun corresponding with him. As this student unburdened himself of his doubts and questionings to the famous scholar, Lewis responded very simply: "I think you are already in the meshes of the net. The Holy Spirit is after you; I doubt if you'll get away." Not long afterward, this atheistic student, pursued by God for so long, finally surrendered. He had found, as C. S. Lewis himself had found, that salvation is of God. He ran, but God successfully pursued him.

Did you seek God? Of course you didn't. You resisted Him, and He had to beat down your resistance until you yielded to Him like a vanquished enemy. And if in the struggle there was a moment in which you seemed to seek Him, it was only because He was there beforehand moving you to do it.

> I sought the Lord, and afterward I knew
> He moved my soul to seek Him, seeking me;
> It was not I that found, O Saviour true;
> No, I was found of Thee.

So it is. Salvation is always of God. We love because He first loved us. We believe because He enables us to do so.

Now what is true of the first moments of our salvation is true of it all. Before you were even a gleam in the eye of your earthly father, you were beloved in the eye of your heavenly Father. And He who knew all about you even before you were born chose you and saved you; and He did so in order that one day He might make you like the Lord Jesus Christ in love, knowledge, holiness, and all his other perfections. That is why Paul can say of salvation, focusing every phrase

---

* C. S. Lewis, *Surprised by Joy* (New York: Harcourt, Brace & World, Inc., 1955), pp. 228, 229.

upon God, "For whom he did foreknow, he also did predestinate to be conformed to the image of his Son, that he might be the firstborn among many brethren. Moreover, whom he did predestinate, them he also called; and whom he called, them he also justified; and whom he justified, them he also glorified" (Rom. 8:29, 30).

Did you ever stop to wonder why God saves men in this way? The answer is given in the Bible. God has saved men in this way so that no man might boast in His presence. "For by grace are ye saved through faith; and that not of yourselves, it is the gift of God — not of works, lest any man should boast" (Eph. 2:8, 9). God will have no man in heaven boasting about how he got there. He will not let you say, "Well, I must admit that God did most of it. I was far from Him, and He called me. But there were five crises in my life in which I really showed my mettle and hung on tight. I'm really here because of my faith."

How ridiculous! This is human thinking, but God will have none of it. No one will be in heaven except saved sinners, those who deserve hell. And they will be there because salvation is entirely of God.

God never begins a thing that He does not intend to finish. And when He does it, God does it all. God does it all! — in spite of our foolishness, in spite of our running away, in spite of ourselves! We are brought to safety, not by our own efforts or our own devices, but solely by the faithfulness of our heavenly Father.

God's Purpose

Now everything that I have said thus far has been an encouragement for Christians. But there is a somber side to it as well. If you are a Christian, God has not saved you just to save you. He has saved you for a purpose. Paul says, "Being confident of this very thing, that he who hath begun a *good work* in you will keep on performing *it* until the day of Jesus Christ."

Did you ever think of this verse in that light? Not like this: "Oh, everything will be all right for me because God will certainly keep me secure until I finally get to heaven." But rather, "I know that God Almighty saved me for a purpose and that He will keep on whittling away at me until He accomplishes it in me, whether I want Him to or not." This is a somber thought, but it is certainly what the verse teaches.

Look at the verse again more closely. Paul says that God is determined to do a good work in us. What is that good work? Well, the answer is not spelled out too clearly here in Philippians 1:6, but it is spelled out very clearly in Romans 8:29. You know Romans 8:28:

"And we know that all things work together for good to them that love God, to them who are the called according to his purpose." But do you know the next verse? It tells what that purpose is. "For whom he did foreknow, he also did predestinate to be conformed to the image of his Son, that he might be the firstborn among many brethren."

Think of it. God is so delighted with Jesus Christ that He has called millions of sinful human beings to Himself in order that Jesus might reproduce Himself in them and that this universe might be populated with millions of Christs where there was only one before. This does not mean that we will become divine. We will still be His creation, the fruit of His fingers. But we will be like Him. That is the point. We will show forth His character. We will be conformed to the image of Christ.

This will mean that our growth in the character of Christ will be accompanied by growth in the knowledge of our own sinfulness. There are those who think that sanctification means becoming aware of how perfect we are becoming. But these people are hypocrites. And they discredit the faith. Sanctification means discovering how sinful we are and learning to turn to Jesus for hourly forgiveness and cleansing.

It is something like formal education. Take a student in high school who has just had a basic introduction to English literature. He has read *Macbeth* and *Julius Caesar;* he has read a few modern short stories and some modern plays — Shaw's *Pygmalion* and others. He thinks that he has a pretty good grasp of English literature. After all, he has read the best of it. It covers four hundred years. And the rest is probably not worth reading anyhow. But then he goes to college where he takes a more advanced course. And he learns that he did not really know Shakespeare so well after all. He only knew two of his tragedies; and, in addition to the other tragedies, there are also the history plays where Shakespeare's theories of kingship are most clearly seen, and the comedies which reveal another side of his outlook on life altogether, the realm of fantasy and nature, of Puck and Ariel and Falstaff. The student begins to realize how ignorant he was. If he is a good student, he also begins to realize how ignorant he *is*. And he goes on to learn, not only what Shakespeare wrote, but to master Shakespeare's background — the Holinshead Chronicles, Boethius, Chaucer, Boccaccio. And he learns to do this for other writers and other disciplines. The search is unending.

That is the way we are to go on in Christian living. When we are first born again we think that we are not too bad. We say to ourselves, "After all, I believed, didn't I? And that puts me head and shoulders above those who do not believe." But as we live with

Christ we begin to see how sinful we really are, how ignorant. And instead of saying, "Oh, I'm pretty good," we say, "Oh, I'm pretty sinful." And eventually we say, "I'm a sinful man indeed; in fact, I am the chief of sinners." That's sanctification. Dr. Donald Grey Barnhouse used to say, "There is no Christian listening to my voice who will think as well of himself five years from now as he does this morning." And that's true. It's true because God's purposes will not be thwarted, even in the sanctification of Christians.

LEANING ON GOD

Now, of course, this process has a purpose. And it is to teach us to rely on God. God does not take great pleasure in forcing us to develop low opinions of ourselves. But He knows that we will never rely on Him until we realize that we cannot rely on ourselves.

When I was very young, in grade school, I spent a number of summers at a Christian camp in Canada. One summer I spent several hours watching one of the campers learn to climb a telephone pole. This boy was one of these campers who partially pay for their vacation by working; and since the camp needed more adequate wiring, he had the job of stringing the wires. For that he had to learn to climb a pole.

Now the secret of climbing a telephone pole is to learn to lean back, allowing your weight to rest on the broad leather belt that encircles yourself and the pole, allowing your spikes to dig into the pole at as broad an angle as possible. And climbing a pole is easy — as long as you lean back. Of course, if you fail to lean back and pull yourself toward the pole, then your spikes will not dig in and you'll slip. And it isn't very pleasant to slip because the pole is covered with splinters, and these easily dig into your body.

At first my friend would not lean at all, and as a result he never got off the ground. The spikes simply would not go into the wood. It was frustrating. After a while he learned to lean back a bit and got started, but as soon as he was a few feet off the ground he became afraid that he might slip and pulled himself close to the pole. Down he would go with a bump, getting covered with splinters in the process. This practice went on in this way until he learned that he could not improve on the belt that held him and that he had to lean on it. When he learned this, he began to climb.

It is the same in the Christian life. God wants you to climb. This is His purpose in saving you. He wants you to rise to Christ's own stature. And what is more, He is going to insist on it. He is going to teach you how, to teach you to climb by resting on Him. There will be times when you will refuse to do it, when you will think that you can hold on better by grasping the pole than by leaning on the belt, and when you do you will slip spiritually and God will let you get covered with splinters. He will do it because He knows that that is the only way you will learn to trust Him. And to trust Him is the only way to climb. What is more, He will keep at you. He will not let you quit. "He that hath begun a good work in you will keep on perfecting it until the day of Jesus Christ."

Perhaps you are saying, "But that is unreasonable. God can't work like that. It must depend on me." But it is the way God works, and you will find it out sooner or later in your Christian life. Perhaps you are saying that you will run your own life, pick your own goals, choose your own purposes. Well then, God may have to break you until you learn that He is determined to accomplish His purposes in you.

But perhaps, instead, you will be willing to learn how to rely on Him, growing in grace as He molds you into the image of Christ. If this is so, then for you Philippians 1:6 will become a blessed truth rather than a bitter lesson. And you will rejoice in the certainty that "he who hath begun a good work in you will keep on performing it until the day of Jesus Christ."

6.

Fellowship That Transforms
(Philippians 1:4-8)

THERE WAS NOTHING EXCLUSIVE about the apostle Paul or about his Christian greetings. Four times in the opening verses of Philippians Paul reveals that he includes *all* of the believers in his thinking. He prays for them all (verse 4). He is confident of them all (verses 6 and 7). He speaks well of them all, being certain that they are all recipients of God's grace (verse 7). And he yearns for them all (verse 8). Paul's remarks include all Christians. For he knew that all had been brought by God into a great and indissoluble fellowship.

This is Christian brotherhood, and Paul's greeting is an example of it. It was a new thing in Paul's day. In the first Christian century the world was filled with barriers, just as it is filled with barriers in our time, barriers of race, wealth, education, and culture. There was a barrier between the Jew and the Gentile, the one fiercely proud of his religious heritage, the other equally proud of his intellectual attainments. There was a barrier between the Roman and the Greek. The Roman gloried in the strength of empire and in the glory of Roman law. The Greek looked upon the Roman as an upstart, as a member of the *nouveaux riches*. And he despised Roman culture as inferior to his own culture and as an imitation of it. The Greek thought about the Romans much as most Europeans think about Americans. He thought that he was crude and ignorant and that he had too much money for his own good. There was a barrier between the free man and the slave. There was a barrier between the patrician and the common man. All of these groups of society were bound together by the chains of Roman rule — Roman, Greek, Jew, soldier, priest, slave, plebeian. But there was no such thing as a brotherhood that joined them. There was no fellowship.

Fellowship was found first and only among Christians. Christians were one. They confessed one Lord. They knew one salvation. All of the barriers of the empire were there within the Christian Church,

47

but the Christians simply overlooked them. They met, not as antagonists, but as those who had been called out of darkness by Jesus Christ and made alive in Him. They loved one another. And the world marveled. One of the great pagan writers exclaimed, "Behold how these Christians love one another!"

Now, of course, what was true of the early church in its best days should be true of us. It should be true; sometimes, unfortunately, it is not. You may be a Christian black man, but you belong to the Church of Jesus Christ and should be welcomed as such. You may be a Christian white man, but you also belong to Christ's Church and should be welcomed as a believer by believers. The same is true whether you are rich or poor, high Church or low Church, Covenanter or Pentecostal — as long as you are a Christian. And what is more, you are to welcome other Christians as you would be welcomed. You are called upon to love all of your brethren in the Lord. You are to pray for them all, be confident of them all, speak well of them all, yearn for them all. And you are to do so even more as you grow in Christian maturity.

PRAYER FOR ALL

To look at these verses more closely is also to see how we can attain Christian fellowship today. First of all, Paul writes that he prays for the Christians at Philippi, "Always in every prayer of mine for you all making request with joy" (verse 4). This is as it should be. Christians should pray for other Christians.

Prayer is talking with God. It grows out of fellowship with God. And it is something we are told to do constantly. Colossians 4:2 says that we are to "continue in prayer." Ephesians 6:18 says that we are to pray "always with all prayer and supplication in the Spirit." Romans 12:12 says that we are to continue "diligently in prayer." This does not mean that we are to give ourselves to nothing but a constant repetition of prayers, that we are to detach ourselves from life. For one thing, all of these statements were made by Paul, and Paul was certainly an active Christian! What is more, Paul's statements are generally set in a context that includes practical suggestions for Christian activity. Paul's statements do not mean that we are to retreat from life. They simply mean that we are to cherish a constant and growing fellowship between ourselves and our heavenly Father in which all of the details of our lives are brought before Him.

This will change us if we do it. It will change the details of our lives, sometimes their whole direction. And it will change our relationships to other Christians. This is how it is. You begin by coming to God about someone you dislike, and God is glad to hear your views because He wants you to be honest with Him. And so you pray, "Oh, Lord, I just can't stand Mrs. So-and-So. She's so loud and she wears such flashy clothes; I just know she's not thinking about spiritual things during the sermon." And you go on and on, and God listens. But He also begins to work on you. And before long something comes to your attention that puts Mrs. So-and-So in a slightly different light. And you discover some evidence of God's hand in her life that you had never noticed before. And you say, "Oh, Lord, I never saw that in her before. She's really Your child and she's trying to serve You in that way." And God will smile and say, "Well, if you have discovered that, why don't you begin to pray *for* her? Because if you do, you'll begin to find other things that you don't even dream are there." And you do it. And before long you find that you are speaking to her in a friendly way, and after that you become friends. And you awake to the fact that she is really one of your sisters in the Lord. That is the power of prayer in causing Christian fellowship. God increases the fellowship by changing you.

There is one other thing that needs to be added here, and that is that prayer of this type will draw you together with other Christians so that you will pray jointly for mutual concerns. We are told that the early Christians prayed together. "They continued steadfastly in the apostles' doctrine and fellowship, and in breaking of bread, and in prayers" (Acts 2:42). I believe that ninety percent of all the divisions between true believers in this world would disappear entirely if Christians would learn to pray specifically and constantly for one another.

CONFIDENCE IN GOD

Paul also says that he is confident for them all. We read in verse seven, "Even as it is right for me to think this of you all." What does he mean by "this"? Well, he is referring to what he has just said in verse six: "Being confident of this very thing, that he who hath begun a good work in you will keep on performing it until the day of Jesus Christ." Paul not only prayed for all of the Christians at Philippi. He also was confident for them all, for he knew that God was at work in them and would certainly accomplish His purposes in their lives.

How clearly this strikes at the heart of attitudes that divide us from other Christians. We separate ourselves from other believers because we believe that they are on the wrong track and we are on the right one. They belong to a denomination that is going astray. Or they do things that we regard as worldly. Or they interpret some biblical doctrine differently from the way we do. And we completely lose sight of the fact that God is as much at work in them as He is in us. Oh that we might have confidence in God's work in other Christians. If we did, we would not see them as those from whom to separate ourselves, lest we be contaminated, but as those from whom we can learn and whom we can help along in the Christian way.

PARTAKERS OF GRACE

The third statement in which Paul mentions all of the believers refers to God's grace. He says, "Ye are all partakers of my grace" (verse 7). The way the sentence stands in the King James Version seems to imply that the believers at Philippi were participants in the grace that was given to Paul — God gives Paul grace to be an apostle, to preach the Gospel, to be able to present it clearly; and they share in it. Certainly Christians shared in the grace given to Paul by God, just as we all share in the graces given to one another. But that is not the teaching of this passage. The Greek says, literally, "all of you being participants with me of grace." It is not that Paul's grace is shared with them. It is rather that all alike, from the great apostle to the most humble believer, are participants in the grace of God. No truth will more quickly overcome divisions among Christians than the truth that we are all equally sinners and all equally recipients of grace.

At the World Congress of Evangelism held in Berlin, Germany, in the fall of 1966, many nationalities were represented, and all had their distinctive ways and appearances. But there was one pastor who was especially distinct. He was a native of central Africa and had obviously been converted out of stark paganism, for his face was marked by heavy cuts and had been colored in tattoo fashion by primitive dyes. He was a bit frightening even after his conversion and must have been terrifying before it. He spoke French and, of course, his tribal language. No one could mistake him. The testimony written in his face made him one of the most striking Christians at the Congress.

This man was present one night when two Auca Indians from Ecuador were giving their testimony. One of the Aucas had been among the troop that had killed the five missionaries. The other was a leader in the tribe. The Aucas spoke only their own dialect. They were culturally distinct from all the other delegates to the Congress. And they had come to Berlin from a home thousands of miles away. But they gave their testimony through a translator, and it was thrilling. They told how they had been held in superstition, how they had feared the gods of the jungle, how they had marked their lives by the great episodes of spearing brought on by warfare between the tribes. They told how men had come, how they had killed them in their ignorance, and how later they had heard the Gospel of salvation from sin through the death of Jesus Christ, and how they had believed. Now they said they wanted to tell that good news to other tribes scattered downriver. That was their story.

And as the Aucas spoke, the African believer jumped from his seat in the back of the 1200-seat auditorium, ran down the aisle, and threw his arm around them with tears streaming down his face. Why did he do it? He did it because he recognized in the experience of the Aucas that which had taken place in himself. He saw them, not as those of another culture, not as those who spoke another language, not as those who lived four thousand miles away. He saw them as sinners saved by grace. He knew that they were participants with him in the matchless grace of God.

Are there Christians whom you cannot stand and with whom you think you will never have anything in common? Is there a Christian from another race who does things differently from the way you do them and who thinks you are prejudiced against him? Is there a Christian from another denomination who seems obstinate in some peculiar doctrine and always seems to be getting at you over it? Is there another Christian in your church whom you cannot stand? When you see him coming in the front door do you slide down the side aisle and sit in the opposite corner of the building? If this is true of you, it is a fault that requires changing. God must change you. He wants to change you. And He will do it as you begin to pray, and in prayer to see that person as a participant together with you of God's grace.

Longing for One Another

The last thing that Paul says about all of the Christians is that he longs for them greatly. You see, it is not just enough to tolerate the other Christian. You must enjoy his company. You must learn from him. And you must miss him when he is gone. Furthermore, this fellowship must be one that is constantly expanding to include other Christians, even those whom you have never met but with whom you are forever united in the Lord.

There is a wonderful illustration of this expansion of Christian fellowship in the final chapter of Romans. Paul had probably been working at this great letter for weeks, and many of the Christians of Corinth must have gathered around to hear him as he dictated to his secretary. Now they were assembled to hear his final teaching. Gaius is there, a rich man but a believer, in whose house Paul was living. Gaius had provided Paul with a slave to transcribe his dictation. Erastus is also there. He is an elected official, the treasurer of the city. We have his name inscribed on a marble slab together with his office.

It was found in Corinth by archaeologists. Then there are Paul's fellow workers: Timothy, Lucien, Jason, and Sosipater. And there are slaves: Tertius, the slave who actually wrote the letter as Paul dictated it, and Quartus, a low ranking slave of the household.

Now look what happens as Paul draws his letter to a close. He has finished one set of greetings and has made some final remarks. He has added a benediction. But now he looks around on the group surrounding him, and he sees that they are all genuinely interested in these Christians at Rome whom they have never seen but to whom Paul is writing. And he begins to include greetings from the Christians at Corinth by name.

> Timothy, my workfellow, and Lucius, and Jason, and
> Sosipater, my kinsmen, greet you . . .

At this point Paul stops, and Tertius, the slave keeps on writing: as scribes sometimes did in antiquity: "I, Tertius, who wrote this epistle, greet you in the Lord." Then Paul picks up again with a reference to his host and the treasurer of Corinth:

> Gaius, mine host, and of the whole church, greeteth
> you.
> Erastus, the chamberlain of the city, greeteth you . . .

At this point Quartus, the least important slave, is afraid of being left out and timidly raises his hand. Paul adds quickly, ". . . and Quartus, a brother." All have been included. All have expressed their greetings in the Lord for a group of believers none of them had ever seen. And Paul goes on to end the epistle in four more verses.

Oh, what a revelation of true Christian fellowship is here! And what an example for us as Christians! You may not be an apostle like Paul, but you may be able like Gaius to open your house to Christians. You may not be rich like Erastus. You may be poor like Tertius and Quartus. You may have no house to open, but you can open your heart. And through you the love of Christ can go out to believers about you and to those whom you have never seen.

God is no respecter of men's wealth or of men's position. But He is pleased with the reality of Christian fellowship. "By this shall all men know that ye are my disciples, if ye have love one to another" (John 13:35).

7

The Secret of Spiritual Fruit
(Philippians 1:9-11)

ONE OF THE REASONS why God has saved us is that we might be fruitful Christians. He has not saved us merely that we might be free from judgment and go to heaven when we die, but that the character of Jesus Christ might be reproduced in us while here on earth. We are to live in the flesh but not of the flesh. We are to do good works that Christ might be glorified and that many might be brought to faith in Him.

This is stated in a wonderful way in Ephesians 2:10. Most Christians know the two verses that immediately precede verse ten: "For by grace are ye saved through faith; and that not of yourselves, it is the gift of God — not of works, lest any man should boast." But I wonder how many know the verse that follows: "For we are his workmanship, created in Christ Jesus unto good works, which God hath before ordained that we should walk in them." These verses say three things. They say that God has saved us by grace. They say that He has a plan for our lives. And they say that there are good works in that plan.

God is somewhat like a father who is raising a large family. He is pleased to have the family, and he is delighted that you are a member of it. But He is not satisfied only with that. He is also interested that you grow up to be a good citizen, spiritually speaking. He wants productive children. He wants your life to be fruitful with good works.

This is the message of Philippians 1:9-11. In praying for the Christians at Philippi, Paul asks for three things. He prays that their love might abound in all knowledge and discernment. He prays that their lives might be lived free of hypocrisy. And he prays, looking forward to the natural result of the first two requests, that they might be filled with "the fruits of righteousness."

There is an illustration of these relationships in the area of electrical science. Anyone who has any acquaintance at all with electrical theory knows the basic formula: Volts times Amperes equals Watts. Voltage is a measurement of pressure. Amperage is a measurement of flow. And Wattage is a measurement of power. It is the product of the pressure multiplied by the flow of electricity. Everything that Paul says can be expressed in this terminology. All good works depend on being filled with God's love. That is the pressure behind good works. Good works also depend on a channel where the amperage can be high. Our lives must not be filled with resistors (which impede the flow) or condensors (which store it up for private use). They must be open. The love of God, times a life free of resistance, equals good works.

Abounding Love

The first thing that Paul says the Christian needs is love, abounding love. "And this I pray, that your love may abound yet more and more in knowledge and in all judgment, that ye may prove things that are excellent" (verses 9, 10). The Christian must be filled with Christ's love.

This must be a love according to *knowledge*. The word used here is a special word *(epignosis)* that refers to advanced spiritual knowledge. In the New Testament the word is applied only to spiritual things — to the knowledge of God, to religious knowledge, spiritual knowledge, and doctrinal knowledge. It is a knowledge that comes to the Christian through a study of God's Word.

The love which is behind good works must also be *discerning*. This word has reference to the understanding given by the Holy Spirit. Just as the Word of God is a discerner of the thoughts and intents of the heart, so the Holy Spirit enables us to discern how love should operate.

Finally, the love with which the Christian should be filled must be *discriminating*. Paul says that we are to approve things that are excellent. The word translated "approve" is used in classical Greek to refer to testing something or someone. It is the technical word for testing money to determine whether or not it is counterfeit. It occurs in a political context for the testing of a candidate for office. Herodotus uses the word for the testing of oxen by Egyptian priests to see whether they are fit for sacrifice *(Histories, II, 38)*. And it is the word used by Paul when he says that Christians are to be renewed by the Holy Spirit so that they may "*prove* what is that good, and acceptable, and perfect, will of God" (Rom. 12:2).

The Christian life must be motivated and informed by love. Without love we are only clanging symbols. But this was never intended to be a namby-pamby, undefined, sentimental love. It is the love of Christ. And hence, it must be a love governed by biblical principles and exercised with judgment. It must be able to distinguish between false dollar bills and real ones.

WITHOUT OFFENSE

The second prerequisite of a fruitful life is that the life must be free of obstructions. This does not mean that we must be perfect, for none of us is. But it does mean that our lives must be open before God and before other men. There must be no hypocrisy.

Paul writes, "That we may be sincere and without offense till the day of Christ." What does that mean? What does it mean to be sincere? The answer comes from the literal meaning of the word in Latin and in Greek. The Latin words, *sine cera,* from which we get our word sincere, literally mean "without wax." And the Greek word it translates means "sun-tested." Both words point to an identical phenomenon of ancient life.

In ancient times the biggest industry in the world was the pottery industry. And pottery varied in quality just as cars vary today, or office supplies, or household goods. The cheapest pottery was thick and solid and did not require much skill to make. It is found everywhere at archaeological sites. The finest pottery was thin. It had a clear color, and it brought a high price. Fine pottery was very fragile both before and after firing. And it was often the case that this pottery would crack in the oven. Cracked pottery should have been thrown away. But dishonest dealers were in the habit of filling in the cracks with a hard pearly wax that would blend in with the color of the pottery. This made the cracks practically undetectable in the shops, especially when painted or glazed; but the wax was immediately detectable if the pottery was held up to light, especially to the sun. In that case the cracks would show up darker. It was said that the artificial element was detected by "sun-testing." Honest dealers marked their finer product by the caption *sine cera* — "without wax."

Paul is saying that the flaws in the lives of believers must not be covered up with wax. Our lives are not perfect. In this life we will always have flaws. But we must not disguise them artificially. We must be sincere. We must not give offense. God's love will not flow through a Christian whose life is a sham. Hypocrisy will stop the flow. Fortunately, however, we may also say that God's love will flow through an honest Christian, no matter how marred the vessel. Paul says, "We hold this treasure in earthen vessels, that the excellency of the power may be of God, and not of us" (II Cor. 4:7). Moreover, we look forward to the day when what is begun on earth, with all its imperfections, will be made perfect in heaven. There we will be sterling examples of God's fine workmanship.

FRUITS OF RIGHTEOUSNESS

All of this leads to the fact that we must be fruitful Christians. The verse reads, "Being filled with the fruits of righteousness, which are by Jesus Christ, unto the glory and praise of God" (verse 11). This does not refer to internal righteousness, love, joy, peace, and so on; these are the fruits of the Spirit. It refers to what is seen externally. The fruits of righteousness are the fruits which righteousness produces. And these are to be seen in the innumerable acts of kindness and service to which every believer in Jesus Christ is called.

We need to note also that the Christian is not only called to bear fruit. He is called to be fruitful, that is, to bring forth much good fruit. How is this to be done? In the first place, it must be done by depending on Christ. This is what Jesus Himself was talking about in the last moments He spent with His disciples before His crucifixion. Jesus said, "I am the true vine, and my Father is the vinedresser . . . Abide in me, and I in you. As the branch cannot bear fruit of itself, except it abide in the vine, no more can ye, except ye abide in me. I am the vine, ye are the branches. He that abideth in me, and I in him, the same bringeth forth much fruit; for without me ye can do nothing" (John 15:1, 4, 5). There will be no fruits of righteousness in any man's life apart from a dependence on Christ.

This means that the unsaved man can never do anything to satisfy God. He may go through the motions of good works, and men may call him fruitful. But God says that his works will be tarnished and that in His sight all of his righteousnesses will be as filthy rags. The unsaved man practicing good works is like a child just after he has fallen into a mud puddle. Worried that his mother may be upset, he comes in the front door and tracks through the living room to the piano and plays a bit. Then he goes into the bedroom and picks up his toys. After that he goes to the bathroom, and then he shows up in the kitchen. And everywhere he has been there is mud.

What does his mother do? Instead of praising him for his good deeds, she takes him to the bathtub and washes him. And then he is sent again to play the piano and to put away his toys. In the same way, the unsaved man must be washed of sin in Christ's blood before he can even begin to produce the good works that God the Father has ordained for every Christian.

Christ's parable about the vine and the branches also teaches that the power of Christ's life will flow through him. When Lawrence of Arabia was in Paris after World War I with some of his Arab friends, he took some time to show them the sights of the city: the Louvre, the Arch of Triumph, Napoleon's tomb, the Champs Elysees. But they found little of interest in these things. The thing that really interested them was the faucet in the bathtub of their hotel room. They spent much time there turning it on and off; they thought it was wonderful. All they had to do was turn the handle, and they could get all the water they wanted.

Sometime later, when they were ready to leave Paris and return to the East, Lawrence found them in the bathroom with wrenches trying to detach the faucet. "You see," they said, "it is very dry in Arabia. What we need are faucets. If we have them, we will have all the water we want." Lawrence had to explain that the effectiveness of the faucets did not lie in themselves but in the immense system of water works to which they were attached. And he had to point out that behind this lay the rain and the snowfall on the Alps.

Many people are living lives that are as dry as the deserts of Arabia. They have the faucets, but there is no connection to the pipeline. They must come to God through Christ. Other people are also parched, but they are parched for another reason. There are impurities that choke the lines. You are a Christian, but your life is unhappy and you need God's cleansing. You must come to Christ for cleansing. You must seek His way. And He will make you fruitful.

This will involve a more faithful study of the Bible, for it is through the Bible that we know Jesus. The first Psalm contrasts the way of the ungodly man with the way of the man whose life is fruitful. He is like "a tree planted by the rivers of water"; he brings forth "fruit in its season"; his leaf "shall not wither, and whatsoever he doeth shall prosper" (Ps. 1:3). And why is he like this? The answer is in verse two: "But his delight is in the law of the Lord; and in his law doth he meditate day and night." What a difference there could be in many lives if Christians would learn to let Christ flow through them as they seek Him in Scripture.

God's Pruning

Christ's parable about the vine and the vinedresser makes one more point about fruit-bearing. You not only need to be joined to Christ in order to be fruitful, you also need to be pruned. This is actually the way in which Jesus' parable begins. He says, "Every branch in me that beareth not fruit he taketh away; and every branch that beareth fruit, he purgeth it, that it may bring forth more fruit" (John 15:2).

Have you felt God doing this with you? He wants to, for your life has many things in it that are not bearing spiritual fruit. They may be hobbies, habits, acquaintances, aspects of your occupation. They may even be things that you consider so precious that you think you would die if they were removed. And yet they should be, and God will work to do it. It is true, of course, that not all hobbies, habits, or acquaintances require pruning. God may be using them in marvelous ways; He may be using them now. They are not all sinful. They may be what God wants you to do. Nevertheless, each of us holds to things that God would prefer to remove that we might serve Him better. And, of course, He will remove them. "He who hath begun a good work in you will keep on performing it until the day of Jesus Christ" (verse 6). The cutting may hurt. You may think that God is killing you. But the result will be good for you. For it will issue in good works, done by Jesus Christ in you, to the glory and praise of God.

8.

Suffering

(Philippians 1:12-14)

SOME PASSAGES OF THE BIBLE have to be understood by the emotions as well as by the mind. To understand them fully you must put yourself into the shoes of the Bible characters and try to feel as they felt. Can we really understand the chapter in Genesis where Abraham was asked to offer his son as a sacrifice at God's command unless we identify with the father in his struggles and understand something of what it means to a father to lose a son? It is impossible. Feeling is necessary. Moreover, it is only on that basis that we can go on to understand the story as a revelation of what it meant to God to give His Son on Calvary.

It requires an equal degree of sympathy with the apostle Paul to understand Philippians 1:12-14. Put yourself in the shoes of the Philippian Christians for a few minutes. It had been at least four years since they had seen Paul; they had heard rumors of the things that had happened to him, and they were worried. News had reached Philippi from Rome regarding their fellow church member, Epaphroditus, who had been sick. And those who bore the news certainly told all they knew of Paul's condition. But now some time had elapsed, and the Christians would be asking serious questions. Was Paul still in chains? Perhaps he was sick? Had he already come to trial? Perhaps he had already been martyred for his faith in Jesus Christ? The Philippians had no way of knowing the answer to these speculations. And so they waited.

At last news arrived from Rome and with that news a letter. The letter was written by Paul. At least he was alive. How eagerly they would have read it.

You can imagine them reading through the first eleven verses of the letter where the references are only to themselves. Perhaps they read these rather quickly the first time, hurrying on in the letter until they received news about Paul himself. But then they come to verses twelve through fourteen. Here they read, "But I would ye should understand, brethren, that the things which happened unto me have fallen out rather unto the furtherance of the gospel, so that my bonds in Christ are manifest in all the palace, and in all other places; and many of the brethren in the Lord, becoming confident by my bonds, are much more bold to speak the word without fear" (Phil. 1:12-14).

Here is some news. Many of the rumors they had heard were true, after all. Many unfortunate things had actually happened to Paul. He was still in chains. The future was still uncertain. Yet something else is true also. All of these things have really served to advance the Gospel, and for that Paul rejoices. In one deft sentence Paul shifts the legitimate interest of the Philippians from himself to the great undeterred purposes of God in history.

Paul has written that the things which happened to him have actually furthered the Gospel. What are those things? And how did they further the Gospel?

PAUL'S SUFFERINGS

We must remember, first, that the things which had happened to Paul were quite different from the things which Paul had planned for himself. Paul was the great missionary to the Gentiles, and for years he had carried the Gospel to various parts of the world. He had traveled through Syria and Crete, through most of what is now Turkey, and through Greece. Somewhere along the way he conceived the plan of taking the Gospel to the far west, to Spain, after returning once more to Jerusalem and stopping for a visit in Rome. These plans were not fulfilled. Instead of this he found himself a prisoner on trial for his life. At the time of writing Philippians he could have no real confidence that he would ever be free again.

The things that actually happened to Paul have been summarized in a stirring way by J. A. Motyer in a commendable study of this book. He writes:

> What . . . happened began in Acts 21:17 when the apostle set foot in Jerusalem, forewarned by the Holy Spirit that bonds and imprisonment awaited him . . . An entirely false accusation was leveled at him by his own people (21:28); he was near lynched by a religious mob, and ended up in the Roman prison, having escaped a flogging only by pleading citizenship (22:22 ff.). His whole case was beset by a mockery of justice, for, though all right was on his side, he could not secure a hearing. He was made the subject of unjust and unprovoked insult and shame (23:2), malicious misrepresentation (24:5; 25:6 f.), and deadly plot (23:12 ff.; 25:1 ff.). He was kept imprisoned owing to

official craving for popularity (24:27), or for money (24:26), or because of an over-punctilious facade of legalism (26:32) . . .

Even then his sufferings were not over. There came the prolonged trial of the storm at sea (Acts 27) where his life hung, as it seemed, by a thread, both because of the elements (verse 20) and because of petty officiousness (verse 42). Eventually, when he reached Rome it was far from the ambassadorial entry that he had doubtless looked for (19:21). He came in the company of the condemned, bound by a chain, and destined to drag out at least two years under arrest awaiting the uncertain decision of an earthly king. Nevertheless, still imprisoned, still chained, still unheard, still uncertain, he looks back and avers, "what . . . happened to me has really served to advance the gospel." *

Think of it! All of the frustration, all of the delay, all of the physical suffering. And yet, all this is overshadowed by the fact that it has served to spread the Gospel.

Have you experienced anything like that in your own Christian life? All suffering is not for this purpose. Suffering is of different kinds. And God has different purposes in permitting it to come upon us. Some suffering is corrective. It is intended to get us on the right path when we have gone astray. Solomon refers to such suffering when he says, "My son, despise not the chastening of the Lord, neither be weary of his correction; for whom the Lord loveth he correcteth, even as a father the son in whom he delighteth" (Prov. 3:11, 12).

Some suffering is intended to awaken us to the needs and the feelings of other people. Some of it is instructive. It is intended to mold us into the image of Jesus Christ, for we learn through the things that we suffer. Thus, Peter speaks of the Christian's confidence in God but adds that it may be true that "now for a season . . . ye are in heaviness through manifold trials, that the trial of your faith, being much more precious than of gold that perisheth, though it be tried with fire, might be found unto praise and honor and glory at the appearing of Jesus Christ" (I Pet. 1:6, 7).

Paul's suffering was not of this kind. It was not corrective. It was not instructive. It was simply a suffering permitted by God that the Gospel might be spread to others.

I do not think that many of us have experienced this, certainly not myself. But some of you have. Perhaps not as consistently as Paul but in ways equally bitter and equally filled with anguish. You must know that God has greatly honored you with this suffering. And you must take great joy even in the midst of it, as I know you do, as you see how your suffering has brought salvation to others. This is

° J. A. Motyer, *Philippian Studies* (Chicago: Inter-Varsity Press, 1966), pp. 32, 33.

a joy won through vales of tears, but it is one of the choicest prizes
of the Christian life.

THE PRAETORIAN GUARD

The second question that Paul's statement raises is this: How did
the things that happened to the great apostle result in the spread of
the Gospel? The first answer is that through them Paul was able to
bear a remarkable witness to the Praetorian Guard.

In the King James version of the Bible, the key verse is translated,
"So that my bonds in Christ are manifest in all the palace, and in all
other places" (1:13). Unfortunately, the King James translators did
not possess all of the information we have today, and as a result the
translation they made is in error. The word translated "palace" is
the word *praetorium*, which the ancient translators thought referred
to a building. Since the seventeenth century, however, many ancient
manuscripts have been uncovered which mention the Roman Praetorium, and in none of these manuscripts does the word ever refer to a
palace or to a building of any kind. In all of them it refers to people,
to the Praetorian Guard. This guard was the official bodyguard of the
emperor, which took charge of all imperial prisoners. Knowing this,
it is now necessary to translate the verse: "So that my bonds in Christ
are manifest to the whole Praetorian Guard and to all others."

We must visualize the scene at this point. Paul is imprisoned in
Rome, chained to a Roman guard. Ever since his arrest in Jerusalem
he had been chained to a guard, except for the moments on the ship
carrying him to Rome. He is now in care of the picked troops who
guard the emperor. Paul has some freedom of action. He may have
visitors. For a while at least he lived in a private home. But always
there was the guard.

What did Paul do in this situation? He might have complained:
"This is unjust; Roman law is slow; this soldier represents all that
Rome stands for, and I cannot bear the sight of him." But this was
never Paul's way. He himself was a soldier for Christ. And the man
at the end of the chain represented a person for whom Christ died.
Paul bore a witness. And he bore witness, not only to this soldier,
but to the one who replaced him for the second watch and the one
who replaced him for the third watch and so on throughout the days
and years. In this way in time Paul reached most of the imperial
guard.

Think how Paul must have lived to have this effect upon a corps
of tough Roman soldiers. One prisoner looks much like another. The
chain itself tells nothing, but the man himself does. Here was a man
who had every right to be thinking about himself, but instead his

talk was all of another. He spoke of Christ, even in prison. And even soldiers listened.

Some time ago I saw a cartoon that showed the effect of one man's ill temper upon others. It consisted of a series of five squares. In the first the boss of a company spoke harshly to one of his employees. This put the employee in a bad mood, and when he arrived home at night he had a nasty word for his wife. She in turn yelled at the son. He kicked the dog. And in the last square the dog was outside and bit the boss of the company. That is how ill temper spreads. In the same way the witness of a life lived for Christ even in the midst of suffering also spreads to others, only the results are opposite. Paul triumphed over his circumstances, and the result spread through Rome.

There is a special application here for those who do not have the freedom they would like to preach the Gospel. Paul was chained to a prison room. You may have chains of your own. You may be tied to a desk when you would like to be out in more direct Christian service. If you are a woman, you may be tied to a home, especially when the children are young and need constant care. You may be tied to a sick bed and may never see beyond your hospital room. Or you may be an invalid. This should not be a cause for discouragement. If you are in circumstances like these, this has been given you by God and can be used by Him. Dozens of people come by your desk, your kitchen sink, or your hospital bed. And you can bear a witness to them. If you do, God will bless your efforts. You will see spiritual fruit. And what is more, it will entirely change the way you look at your limitations, whatever their cause. You can learn to say with Paul, "But I would ye should understand, brethren, that the things which happened unto me have fallen out rather unto the furtherance of the gospel."

The Effect on Other Christians

There is a further way in which Paul's suffering for Christ served to advance the Gospel. It had an effect on other Christians. Paul says, "Many of the brethren in the Lord, becoming confident by my bonds, are much more bold to speak the word without fear" (verse 14). Christians moved from fear to boldness as a result of Paul's example. They learned to testify. Has your life ever had that effect on other Christians?

Someone is going to say to me that Christians should always be bold in their witness for Jesus Christ, that Christians should "be ready always" to give an answer to every man that asks a reason of the hope that is within them with meekness and fear. And that is true. But it is equally true that many Christians are shy. Many are afraid.

Many simply lack an example. It may be that God has placed you in a position where your witness can move one of God's shy ones to boldness.

JOB'S EXPERIENCE

Paul's words about the spread of the Gospel through suffering reveal the effect of his life upon non-Christians and upon believers. Non-Christians became Christians. And believers were emboldened to preach the Gospel. All of this is encouraging. But there is one more thing to be said. If these things are to be true in your life, you must let suffering draw you closer to the Lord. It can do the opposite; it can draw you away. It can embitter your heart and produce a complainer in you where there should be a victorious Christian. All too often Christians are like the man described by Epictetus, one of the pagan philosophers: "I am in sore straits, O Lord, and in misfortune; no one regards me, no one gives me anything, all blame me and speak ill of me." Epictetus asks, "Is this the witness that you are going to bear, and is this the way in which you are going to disgrace the summons which he gave you?" *(Discourses,* I, xxix).

It was entirely the opposite in the case of Job. Job trusted God even in the midst of great suffering, and suffering drew him closer to his Lord. All that Job had was taken away from him. His oxen and his asses were killed. His sheep were destroyed by lightning. Raiders made off with his camels. All of his children perished in a single moment. And Satan, who had asked God's permission to do it, stepped back waiting for Job to turn and curse God. Instead, Job received all of the evil with a quiet trust in God. Instead of cursing God he blessed Him and said, "Naked came I out of my mother's womb, and naked shall I return there. The Lord gave, and the Lord hath taken away; blessed be the name of the Lord" (Job 1:21).

Satan fought against Job even more intensely. God gave Satan permission to touch Job's body so long as he did not take his life. Satan inflicted Job with boils. And once again Job triumphed, blessing God even in the midst of his pain. Did suffering drive Job farther from God? Oh, no! It drew Job to Him. It deepened his faith. And Job bore a great testimony for God. In time God restored all that Job had lost. And Job became a great example of patience in suffering to God's people.

Has suffering ever done that to you? Has it ever brought you closer to God? If it has, you are well on the way to being a great blessing to God's people and to tasting the joy of seeing the Gospel spread through suffering.

9.

Christian Troublemakers

(Philippians 1:15-18)

Leo Tolstoy, who wrote the great classic, *War and Peace*, once complained about people who are always talking about the good old days. He said they are foolish and that in terms of all the important things of life — human aspirations, human feelings and failures, human nature — the good old days were no different from our own. Tolstoy was a humanist, of course, and he was thinking of human values. But the statement applies to Christianity, too. Every now and then we hear someone talking about the early Church as though it had been perfect. Wouldn't it be wonderful, they say, if the Church today could be as it was in the early centuries? And whole denominations are founded upon the idea that the prime duty of contemporary Christians is to be as much like those who lived in the age of the apostles as possible. But this is a false idealization. It is an attempt to make the early Church into something which it never was. And it is an attempt to escape the problems of our day by looking back to something that exists only in the Christian imagination.

There is hardly a problem in the Church of our day that did not exist in some form in the Church of the first Christian century. The church at Corinth was a church that the apostle Paul acknowledged to be a true church in every respect. In the first nine verses of I Corinthians Paul refers to the Christians at Corinth as "saints." They are "sanctified in Christ Jesus" (verse 2); they are recipients of "grace" (verse 4); they are "enriched" by Christ "in all utterance and in all knowledge" (verse 5); the testimony of Christ is "confirmed" in them (verse 6); they do not lack in spiritual "gifts" (verse 7).

Yet this was a church that was filled with problems. There were divisions. There were people who said they were of Paul's party. Others were of Peter. Still others were of Apollos. The pious ones said they were of Christ. Paul says that they pretended to be wise

65

but were actually foolish. We turn to chapter three and find that they were carnal, unable to digest the deep things of the faith. One of the Christians was living in fornication with his step-mother. There were law suits. Some were going to the pagan temples. Others were drunk when they came to the communion service. They had all of the problems that we have in our churches today and perhaps even more beside.

There were also problems at Rome. Paul had just written that the things that had happened to him had actually served to promote the Gospel. Some of the members of the Praetorian Guard had been converted, and those who were already Christians were encouraged (by Paul's courageous stand) to bear a witness for Christ. But there was a darker side to the situation also. Paul writes that some Christians preached the Gospel out of partisanship, hoping to make life more miserable for him. This is what he says: "Some, indeed, preach Christ even of envy and strife; and some also of good will: The one preach Christ of contention, not sincerely, supposing to add affliction to my bonds" (verses 15, 16). Think of it! Some preached Christ to add affliction to Paul's bonds. Such were the good old days in the Christian Church at Rome.

ENVY AND STRIFE

Now if we are to receive the full impact of Paul's experiences in Rome, we must recognize that it was Christians who were trying to get Paul into trouble by their preaching. Some commentators have found this truth difficult to accept and have sought to dodge it by arguing that the ones who preached Christ out of strife and envy were either non-believers or Judaizers, the kind of teachers that had tried to undermine Paul's work in Galatia. But this interpretation is impossible. Of the Christians in Rome, Paul said, "Notwithstanding, every way, whether in pretense or in truth, Christ is preached; and in that I do rejoice, yea, and will rejoice" (verse 18). But of the Judaizers in Galatia, Paul had written, "There are some that trouble you, and would pervert the gospel of Christ." And he added, "If any man preach any other gospel unto you than that ye have received, let him be accursed" (Gal. 1:7, 9). It will not do to call the trouble makers unbelievers. These people were Christians. They were not anti-Christ. They were anti-Paul. But they were anti-Paul with a vengeance.

The verses that we are studying tell us that these Christians preached Christ out of unworthy motives — jealousy, strife, and partisanship.

Jealousy refers to their jealousy of Paul. Beyond any doubt Paul's was the greatest mind of the early Christian Church. No one came near to matching his grasp of the Gospel until St. Augustine restated it for his age over four hundred years later. Then, too, Paul had a long string of triumphs to his credit. He had taken the Gospel to what is now modern Turkey. He was the first missionary to Greece. He had waged battles against the legalizers in the Church and had won them, both in Jerusalem and on the mission field. And now the Roman Christians were jealous of his success.

Moreover, their outlook was characterized by strife. They were pugnacious Christians, the kind who loved a good battle and were not particularly worried if they shot down their own soldiers while attacking the enemy. In fact, they even preferred shooting at Christians. This attitude led them into opposing camps, and their primary efforts were directed toward promoting the interests of their own party rather than the interests of the entire Church of Christ.

This was deplorable. The church was divided by jealousy, strife, and partisanship. But what does Paul say? Strangely enough, he points to the fact that even in the midst of such conditions Jesus Christ was preached. The Gospel was spread. And in that, he says, he rejoices.

THE CHURCH TODAY

All of this finds a direct parallel in the Church of Christ today. And it is not difficult to find contemporary examples of the problems that troubled the early congregations at Rome. In the first place, the Church today is torn by jealousy. There is jealousy within churches. And there is jealousy of nationally known evangelical leaders.

There are also examples of strife. There are men whose whole approach to Christian work is pugnacious and who cannot believe that they are doing God's work unless they are fighting someone over it, especially other Christians.

Examples of partisanship are seen every day in denominations that will not cooperate with other denominations (or even with evangelicals within those denominations) for the spread of the Gospel and the advancement of common goals. About the only thing that most evangelicals can get together for is an evangelistic crusade. And even then there are some who will not lend support. With the Church as divided as this, none of us dare sing the third verse of "Onward Christian Soldiers" without a heartfelt prayer for forgiveness. We sing:

> We are not divided, all one body we,
> One in hope and doctrine, one in charity . . .

But we are divided. And if we are honest, we must admit that all of the envy, strife and partisanship present in the church at Rome is present in our churches also.

What should our attitude be toward those who are responsible for it? It is easy to speak up against it. It is easy to dismiss all those who are unpleasant in their preaching of the Gospel. But this was not Paul's way. If Paul's example is to count for anything, it must teach us that we are to rejoice if Christ is proclaimed, even by those who do it out of less than worthy motives and who seem, from our point of view, to dishonor the Gospel by their methods. You should say, "Notwithstanding, every way, whether in pretense or in truth, Christ is preached; and in that I do rejoice."

THE RESULTS OF ENVY

None of this is meant to imply that envy and strife and partisanship will not yield bitter fruit to the one who sows them. They are not of the Spirit, and God will not bless them. In fact, they will often hurt the witness of the Church and other Christians.

Let me illustrate this from Paul's day. Did you know that Paul very likely lost his life as the result of the trouble caused by the troublemaking Christians at Rome? It seems that he did. There is very little information from the early Church age about the death of Paul and the things that led up to it, but such information as exists points to this conclusion: envy led some Christians to denounce Paul and, as a result of their denunciation, Paul and perhaps others also were presumably executed under Nero.

The first strand of evidence for this view lies in the New Testament itself. We have already seen that Paul was not very well received in Rome. For a while he was forgotten. When Onesiphorus arrived in Rome no one seemed able to tell him where Paul was, and it was only after considerable searching that this faithful Christian found him (II Tim. 1:16, 17). Then Paul began to make converts through the Praetorian Guard. His views spread through Rome. And those who thought they were the leaders of the Roman congregations became jealous and preached against him. Paul alludes to this situation in Philippians and in the second letter to Timothy.

The second strand of evidence is from Roman historians who knew of unrest within the Christian-Jewish community under the emperor Claudius and later under Nero. Suetonius, a Roman historian who wrote the lives of the Caesars, tells us that "since the Jews constantly made disturbances at the instigation of Chrestus," Claudius expelled them from Rome. The word *Chrestus,* is the word "Christ." Hence, it seems that Suetonius was actually alluding to friction in Rome brought about by those who preached Christ's name; apparently he thought that Christ was the ringleader. The New Testament also knows of this expulsion of Christians and Jews, for it speaks of the edict of Claudius under which Aquila and Priscilla left Rome (Acts 18:2).

The third strand of evidence comes from a letter written about A.D. 90 to the believers at Corinth from a Roman Christian named Clement. In chapters three through six Clement warns the Corinthians about the bad effects of jealousy which, he says, has always resulted in suffering and death among God's people. This was true in Old Testament times, according to Clement, and he includes seven examples to prove it. Among them are Cain's jealousy of Abel, Esau's jealousy of Jacob, the friction between Joseph and his brothers, and similar examples of envy from the lives of Moses, David, and Saul. Clement also gives seven examples from what were to him more recent times. Among these he speaks of Paul. He says, "By reason of jealousy and strife Paul by his example pointed out the prize of patient endurance . . . and when he had borne his testimony before the rulers . . . he departed from the world and went to heaven" (I Clement 5). The point is that jealousy among Christians in some way caused Paul's execution.

Now, of course, some of these statements may only be tradition and may be unreliable. Suetonius and I Clement are not infallible, and they may be wrong. But all of the lines of evidence seem to present a remarkably consistent picture. They seem to suggest that after Paul had written Philippians the strife and jealousy already present in the church at Rome degenerated into open attacks upon him. These may have led some of the Christians to denounce Paul to the authorities. In this case Christ's statement that his disciples would betray one another (Matt. 24:10) would have an early and literal fulfillment. What is certain is that Clement believed Paul perished as a result of the jealousy and strife that existed among Roman Christians.

Envy and strife caused trouble in those days. So do they cause trouble today. Not necessarily in death, but in the declining impact of the Gospel of Christ upon our society and upon the world. Never in the history of the world have the opportunities been greater for the proclamation of the Gospel. Yet never has the believing Church been more irrelevant or more divided. We have money. We have talent. There are opportunities for spreading the Gospel through all of the modern means of mass communication. Yet the evangelical churches seem unable to take advantage of them.

I have often thought that there are great opportunities in television, but it would take a united evangelical witness to make them effective. Billy Graham has demonstrated that a Christian program can be successful on television. It can be sustained financially, and stations will compete for the opportunity to show it. But Billy Graham cannot sustain it alone, either financially, or in terms of talent. He is on only for a few nights several times a year. But if all evangelicals were working together, there could be a more elaborate program, and it could be fascinating. It could present the work of evangelical missions or of inner city work such as that conducted in New York city by Jim Vaus and David Wilkerson. Programs could feature great evangelical artists: Jerome Hines, Robert Elmore and others. There could be programs along the line of Moody science films. The lack of such a witness is one of the bitter fruits of the strife and envy that divide today's believers.

God's Remedy

Paul gives the solution to this situation in the next chapter. First, he says that we are to develop a low opinion of ourselves. This is often hard to do, but it should be easy. We are merely to see ourselves as God sees us, and this will happen as we study His Word. Dr. Donald Grey Barnhouse often illustrated this process by the story of a man walking along the street at night toward a street light. He is on his way to a party. It has been raining, and he has just been splashed with mud by a passing car. He thinks it is not too bad. He will be able to brush it off. But as he gets closer to the light he begins to see that it is much worse than he imagined. And when he finally stands underneath the light he realizes that he will simply have to go home and change his clothes. In the same way, as we draw near to Christ by reading the Scriptures, Christ's light will fall on us and we will begin to see ourselves as He sees us. When we do, we will look to Him for cleansing.

Second, we are to have a better opinion of others, especially those who are troublemakers. Paul says, "Let each esteem others better than themselves." This will come about as God makes us sensitive to the work of His Holy Spirit within other believers. It does not mean that we shall say, "Oh, so-and-so has such a sweet temper, much sweeter than I," if that is not so. But it does mean that we shall become sensitive to the fact that God has been curbing his temper from what it was and is constantly curbing it more. It will not mean that we shall consider another Christian honest if he is not. But we shall see that he is more honest as a Christian than he was before becoming one. And we will look into our own hearts for those areas where God wishes to be at work in us.

Third, Paul says that we are to possess the mind of Christ. He challenges the Philippians, "Let this mind be in you, which was also in Christ Jesus" (Phil. 2:5). How does this come about? It comes about by fellowship with Him as He works in us, gradually molding us into His own image.

Now I know that someone is going to object, "Oh, but that is hard. First you say that we are to rejoice when people preach the Gospel, even if they do it in a nasty way and try to hurt other Christians. You say that we are to think highly of them for the sake of God's work within them. Then you say that we are not to be like that ourselves. That is unreasonable. Are we to go against all that is most natural within us?"

The answer to that question is "Yes." Yes, you are. That is God's way, and God will give you strength to do it. You are to see His hand at work in the lives of other Christians, even those who are obnoxious to you. And you are to think highly of God's work in them. Moreover, you are to work with them, as far as possible. For in this way the Gospel is spread, believers are taught and strengthened, and Jesus Christ is honored.

10.

No Disappointments

(Philippians 1:19, 20)

THERE IS A GREAT DEAL of disappointment in this life. And everyone has experienced it. People know disappointment as children when they do not receive something they want very much. Young people know disappointment when they are shunned and left out by their friends. Businessmen, struggling to be successful, are often disappointed; only a few make it to the top. Some are disappointed in love. We all face disappointments with other people. Looking at these things, the poet Dryden wrote:

> When I consider life, 'tis all a cheat,
> Yet, fooled with hope, men favor the deceit;
> Trust on, and think tomorrow will repay.
> Tomorrow's falser than the former day.

Perhaps Dryden wrote those words in a fit of melancholy, but melancholy or not, they aptly describe much of our existence. Everything human is stained with disappointment.

And yet, there is no disappointment with God.

The verse in the epistle to the Philippians to which we now come is a great expression of this truth. Paul had carried the Gospel of Jesus Christ through much of the Roman empire, and now he was imprisoned in Rome itself. He wanted to preach the Gospel in the western part of the Roman empire, to the area we now call Spain, but instead it seemed that he must soon be executed for his faith. From a human point of view, everything seemed to be going against him. But despite this, Paul remained confident that God's purpose for his life would not be shaken. He writes, "For I know that this shall turn to my salvation . . . according to my earnest expectation and my hope, that in nothing I shall be ashamed, but that with all boldness, as always, so now also Christ shall be magnified in my body, whether it be by life or by death" (Phil. 1:19, 20).

To understand this verse, we have to understand that the word "ashamed" did not always have the meaning for the biblical writers that it has for us today. The primary biblical meaning is not even in most of our dictionaries. *Webster's New Collegiate Dictionary* defines "ashamed" as being "affected by shame"; and shame is defined as a "painful emotion excited by a consciousness of guilt," "disgrace," or "dishonor." When you are at a party and are humiliated, you are ashamed. If you make a fool of yourself publicly in the sight of your friends, you are ashamed.

But this is not the biblical understanding of "shame." The biblical understanding has to do with disappointment. According to Scripture, the person who is not ashamed is the person whose trust is not misplaced and who, therefore, is never disillusioned.

This meaning is unmistakable at several important places in the Bible. In the fifth chapter of Romans Paul writes about the Christian hope, noting that "hope maketh not ashamed" (Rom. 5:5). At this point the Roman Catholic Confraternity version correctly says, "Hope does not disappoint." And Phillips correctly paraphrases, "A steady hope that will never disappoint us." Another verse that requires this translation is Isaiah 49:23. It is quoted twice in Romans. Here God says, "Thou shalt know that I am the Lord; for they shall not be ashamed who wait for me." The verse means that no one who trusts God will ever be disappointed.

Have you ever thought of the ways in which God does not disappoint the Christian? There are three verses in the Bible that more than others tell of the great ways in which God does not disappoint us. All contain the word "ashamed," and all teach that there is no shame for Christians.

The Power of God

The first verse is Romans 1:16: "For I am not ashamed of the gospel of Christ; for it is the power of God unto salvation to everyone that believeth; to the Jew first, and also to the Greek." Paul says that he has never been disappointed in the Gospel, for whenever and wherever it is preached the power of God accompanies it and produces supernatural results. What is the Gospel? It is the message of God's grace revealed in Jesus Christ, and it is centered on His death, burial, and resurrection. Paul summarizes it in these words, "For I delivered unto you first of all that which I also received, that Christ died for our sins according to the scriptures; and that he was buried, and that he rose again the third day according to the scriptures" (I Cor. 15: 3, 4).

It is very interesting that Paul speaks of the power of the Gospel when writing to the church at Rome. Paul was entirely at home in three conflicting cultures, just like a man might be at home today in the United States, in Germany, and in the Middle East. Paul was at home in Jewish culture, Greek culture, and Roman culture, and he preached the Gospel to each of these diverse groups of people. Each had its particular difficulty in accepting the Gospel. The Jew came with centuries of religious training and tradition. He lived within a fixed spiritual system, and Jesus Christ had no place within that system. Hence, for the Jew, Jesus was a stone of stumbling. It was necessary for Paul to show that Jesus, far from being a stone of stumbling, was actually God's foundation for the entire structure of revealed religion.

The Greek did not pride himself on his religious traditions. There was little to be proud of in that quarter. But he was proud of his wisdom. The Greek traced his intellectual ancestry to Homer, Plato, Aristotle, the Cynics, the Epicurians, the Neo-Platonists — all of the competing systems of knowledge that preceded Paul's day. Most of these systems spoke of an unbridgeable gap between the infinite and the finite, between God and man. Hence, to the Greek, the preaching of the birth, death, and resurrection of God's Son was foolishness. Paul found it necessary to show that the cross of Christ was actually the wisdom of God. It was a wisdom that exposes the foolishness of human understanding.

The Roman took pride in his power. The power of the Roman legions had conquered the civilized world, pushing the long phalanxes of the empire deep into the deserts of Africa, northward through the British Isles, and east to the frontiers of Persia. It was the strong arm of Rome that guaranteed Roman justice throughout the conquered dominions. To the Roman this was power; the Gospel of Jesus Christ was weakness. Paul found it necessary to show that it was actually the power of God. The Gospel possesses a power that does not disappoint the Christian.

There are several words for power in the Greek language, and each moves within a different sphere of thought. There is the word *exousia*. This word refers to the power that comes from authority. It is the word that occurs in John 1:12: "But as many as received him, to them gave he *power* [authority] to become the children of God, even to them that believe on his name." There is also the word *kratos* from which we get the words democrat, autocrat, and plutocrat. It refers to the naked power of rule, a power which one may exercise whether or not one has legitimate authority to do so. Then there is the word *dynamis,* from which we get the explosive words dynamite, dynamo, and dynamic. This is the word that occurs in Romans 1:16, the word by which Paul commends the Gospel of Christ to the power-conscious Romans. Paul says that it is the effective, explosive power of God. He knew that the Gospel always accomplished the purposes for which God sent it forth.

It still does today. It takes the savage from the jungles of Ecuador, frees him from a slavery to superstition and fear, and makes him a missionary of Jesus Christ to other primitive tribes. It takes the immoral hedonist and gives him a purpose in life by which he contributes to his society instead of tearing it down. It changes the alcoholic into a man of whom his family can be proud. It turns the pious, hypocritical American churchgoer into God's man for this hour and makes him a prophet and a witness for Christ. Moreover, the Gospel can change you. It can transform your life and satisfy your deepest spiritual longing.

A Sure Deposit

The second verse that tells of a way in which God will not disappoint us is II Timothy 1:12. There Paul writes, "Nevertheless, I am not ashamed; for I know whom I have believed and am persuaded that he is able to keep that which I have committed unto him against that day." The French translation of this verse says, "*Il a la puissance de garder mon depot.*" The metaphor is that of banking; and the translation actually means, "God has the power to keep that which I have deposited with Him."

Every now and then we read in the papers of some financial tycoon who has engaged in dishonest practices and whose financial empire has collapsed overnight when the dishonesty has been discovered. A man like this has often sold stock to unsuspecting people while pushing the price of the stock to unrealistic heights through dishonest dealings. The value is there on paper, but not in reality. And the tycoon has no power to preserve what has been committed to him. The warehouses turn out to be vacant lots. The storage tanks turn out to be empty. The fleet of tankers turns out to be a handful of antiquated cargo ships. And all that the stockholders have invested is lost beyond recovery.

It is not this way with God. Men and women insist on placing their deposit with those who cannot guard it — with cult religions, with schemes for world government, with dreams of human betterment. But all of these devices fail the investor. Only God is able to guarantee our deposits.

Have you trusted in God through faith in Jesus Christ? If so, think of the capital investments that you have placed on deposit with Him.

You have placed your faith for salvation in the life to come. Can God keep that? Of course He can, for we read, "My sheep hear my voice, and I know them, and they follow me. And I give unto them eternal life; and they shall never perish, neither shall any man pluck them out of my hand" (John 10:27, 28). And again, "For I am persuaded that neither death, nor life, nor angels, nor principalities, nor powers, nor things present, nor things to come, nor height, nor depth, nor any other creation, shall be able to separate us from the love of God, which is in Christ Jesus, our Lord" (Rom. 8:38, 39). You have also placed your faith in the fact that God can accomplish His purposes in you for this life. Can God keep that? Of course He can, for He tells us that "we are his workmanship, created in Christ Jesus unto good works, which God hath before ordained that we should walk in them" (Eph. 2:10). We have committed to Him our faith that He can see us through temptation. Can God keep that? Yes, that too. For we read, "There hath no temptation taken you but such as is common to man; but God is faithful, who will not permit you to be tempted above that ye are able, but will, with the temptation, also make the way to escape, that ye may be able to bear it" (I Cor. 10:13). Certainly God is able to keep our capital assets.

And think what marvelous dividends He pays on the investment. It is not only that we are secure for the future and for this life also, but also that we partake so richly of God's present blessings. There is a partaking of His love. There is joy. There is the peace that passes understanding. And there are a thousand other things besides.

I have often noticed in my own life how God delights in paying dividends. There have been times when I have spent my time working for something that I judged worthwhile. I did not succeed in any outstanding way, but I knew that I had tried to do what I believed God wanted me to do and I had tried to do it in the best way possible. And then God gave a dividend. Sometimes it was small, sometimes large, but always something entirely unexpected. And my face brightened, and I lifted my heart in gratitude to such a loving and painstaking heavenly Father.

In one of his interesting books J. B. Phillips has a chapter in which he speaks of "serendipities." Serendipities are "happy and unexpected discoveries," and the serendipities that Phillips has in mind are those spiritual discoveries that came to him quite by accident (as it seemed) during his work of translating the New Testament into contemporary English. In a similar way I believe that there should be serendipities in the life of every Christian. They are God's dividends, additional evidence that He is guarding our spiritual deposits.

CHRIST MAGNIFIED

The third verse which tells how God will not disappoint us is our text in Philippians. Paul is on trial for his life. But only on a human level is he uncertain of the outcome. On the spiritual level Paul knows that whatever happens will work to his salvation. He will not be ashamed, for "Christ shall be magnified in my body whether it be by life or by death."

Think of the scope of this statement. In the first place, Paul knew that Christ would be magnified. Paul lived in an environment in which the pagan gods were worshiped and in which all power seemed to be on the side of pagan Rome. But he knew that Christ would ultimately be exalted and would rule in power until He had crushed all enemies beneath His feet. This was the basis of Paul's confidence.

Secondly, Paul knew that God's determination to exalt His Son also extends to those who are united to Him by faith. Paul did not merely say that Christ would be magnified. He said that Christ would be magnified in him. If you are a Christian, do you know that God the Father is determined to exalt His Son in you? You may not want Him to. You may resist His attempts as best you are able. But He will do it anyway. For "he who hath begun a good work in you will keep on performing it until the day of Jesus Christ" (Phil. 1:6). This is one more thing in which the Christian will not be disappointed.

Thirdly, Paul recognized that Christ would be magnified in him whether he lived or died. Do you see what this means? It means that Paul was so confident that God's will for him was perfect — that it was the best possible thing for him — that he was able to accept it willingly even if it meant death at the hands of a Roman executioner.

I wonder if you have such confidence in God. When life is smooth it is easy to say, as we often do, "all things work together for good to them that love God." It is easy when you have everything you want, when God blesses you materially and blesses your family. But it is not so easy at the grave. It is not so easy in the face of bitter disappointment and pain. If you are to have confidence in God in such moments, you must learn to trust Him in the small disappointments of life.

I know a couple who are extremely fond of children and who early in their courtship planned to have a large family. They were married, and not long afterward there came sickness and an operation that left the woman unable to bear children. I have never met a couple for whom this was a greater disappointment and consequently a greater opportunity for bitterness. But they did not allow it to become this in their lives. They accepted it from God as His perfect will for them, and asked instead that they might act as spiritual parents for those who needed them. God blessed them in this way. They befriended many lonely people. Many became Christians. And when I last saw them God had used them to found three different Christian congregations. In a very real sense they became a father and a mother to many dozens of young Christians. They testify that even in this great crisis they have not been disappointed in God.

So it will be with us. You may not see it now. You may resist God's will and drown yourself in pity, even in legitimate sorrow. But the day is coming when you will see it as you stand before your loving heavenly Father. You will look back from a vantage point in eternity in what we could call millions of years from now and will confess that God knew what He was doing in your life. You will see that Christ was certainly exalted. And you will not be disappointed.

11.

Christ Magnified — Through You!

(Philippians 1:20)

MANY CHRISTIANS DIVIDE their lives into two compartments. One compartment they label "sacred," and the other compartment they label "secular." The sacred part of life consists of what they do on Sundays and the other days of the week when they are praying, witnessing, or reading their Bible. The secular part of life involves nearly everything else — work, recreation, family life, sports, and so on. There is almost no connection between the two. Their lives are organized in the way *Time* magazine divides the news. Politics and business are in front. Books come last. And along the way they fit in modern living, entertainment, and religion.

It is easy to understand how this happens. To a large extent Christians live in two worlds and divide their time accordingly. We labor in one world. And it is necessary to put much time into what is often mundane work just to make a living. At the same time we are citizens of heaven. We who were no people have become God's people. And there is Christian work to do. Consequently, we begin to think that the Christian work is important and the other work is not. Many Christian people cherish the notion that God is honored only by their devotional life or by what they do on Sundays.

I do not believe that this was true of any of the biblical writers. David was a deeply spiritual person and wrote beautiful Psalms. But there is not a line of the Old Testament to suggest that he served God more as a poet than as the king of Israel, the one who fought the Lord's battles. He honored God in that which God gave him to do. Jesus Christ knew no division of His life, for everything He did pleased His heavenly Father. Jesus said, "I do always those things that please him" (John 8:29).

So it was with Paul. Paul knew that the child of God is called to live all of life under the eye of his heavenly Father and to do all things to His glory. In I Corinthians Paul even says that Christians are

79

to feed themselves to God's glory: "Whether, therefore, ye eat, or drink, or whatever ye do, do all to the glory of God" (I Cor. 10:31). Because of these truths Paul knew that Christians are to present their bodies "a living sacrifice, holy, acceptable unto God" which is their reasonable service. In Philippians 1:20 Paul applies this thought to his own experience, noting that Christ will be magnified in his body whether by his life or his death.

We have already seen in a previous study how this statement is an expression of Paul's confidence in God. We must now go on to see what this means practically for the living of the normal Christian life.

God's Temples

The first truth we must establish on the basis of this text is that in this life Christ must be magnified in the bodies of those who believe in Him, or He will not be magnified at all. The reason for this is that God dwells only within His children. And if He is to be seen at all in this life, He must be seen in the lives of those who know Him.

Throughout the history of the Christian Church this truth has been perverted over and over again. Men have often made the mistake of identifying the hand of God with the development of the Reformation churches, the cause of democracy, the movement for prohibition, pacifism, or even civil rights. But God is not magnified in these. There is no doubt that many of these movements have been based on Christian principles, at least in part, and that God has often blessed them and blessed people through them. But God's hand is never seen in the movement itself. It is seen in the lives of those who guided it. Where men honor God in their bodies God prospers their work. When they cease to honor Him the institution ceases to be a vehicle in which His glory is seen, even though its beneficent effects may last for generations.

Some people have sought to limit God to the Bible. But this is wrong also. The Bible is free of error. God has chosen to honor it as He will honor no words of men. But God does not dwell in the Bible. God is only magnified as He enters into the life of believers through the Bible and forms their lives in accordance with its principles.

Some people have sought to glorify God by building great churches, but Christ is not magnified in buildings. I have a friend of a sentimental nature who is certain that God is to be found in great churches more than in other places. On many occasions she has returned from a trip to tell me that she was certain that God was specially present in some church she visited, sometimes even when it was empty. It is a fine thought, but it is wrong. And I have answered by telling her about the three greatest churches I have visited. The first is the Church of the Holy Sepulchre in Jerusalem. This church is built over the site that Constantine selected as the original location of the cross and tomb of Christ about A.D. 325. You would think that such a site would be holy. But if you have ever been there, you will know that the church is divided into areas in which the various church orders compete for prominence and seek to entice tourists to their particular attraction. Imagine God dwelling in a place like that!

The second church is Chartres Cathedral, the highest flowering of the genius of Gothic architecture in Europe. I have visited it many times. Its three rose windows are probably the most beautiful manmade creations I have ever seen. But one must remember that this church was constructed in the Middle Ages when the common people who built the cathedral were held in spiritual bondage through their fear of God. The famous east portal contains the stern terrors of Christ presiding over the final judgment, and the entire period of the construction of the cathedral was marked by fits of self-chastisement as people tried to ward off evils which they believed God was visiting upon them. Imagine God dwelling in a building constructed out of such distorted conceptions of God's nature and of the Christian message!

The third church is the great basilica of St. Peter's in Rome. Here is the pinnacle of Renaissance architecture embellished with the highest achievement of Renaissance art. Michaelangelo worked here. And so did Raphael. But I always remind visitors to Rome that these men were paid with the indulgence money squeezed from the peasants of Germany and that it was in protest against such injustices that Luther started on the path that gave birth to the Protestant Reformation. Is it any wonder that Paul stood upon Mars Hill in Athens and reminded the Greeks of his day that "God, who made the world and all things in it, seeing that he is Lord of heaven and earth, dwelleth not in temples made with hands" (Acts 17:24)?

THE TEMPLE OF SOLOMON

Someone is going to object that God did dwell in the Jewish temple, first in the wilderness and later in Jerusalem, and that this was dramatized by the presence of the cloud or Shekinah. But there are two things wrong with this objection. In the first place, the presence of God in the temple (symbolized by the cloud) was only a figurative way of teaching certain lessons. Hence, even Solomon in his great prayer of dedication of the magnificent first temple acknowledged that heaven and earth could not contain God, much less a building that he had constructed. The second error is this. Even granting that in a certain sense Jehovah was present in the temple, all of that is now past from the perspective of God's ongoing revelation in history. When Jesus came to earth He claimed that His body was God's temple (John 2:18-21). And when He departed into heaven He promised that God would come to dwell within those who believe on Him (John 14:16, 17). It is on this basis that Paul later claims, "What? Know ye not that your body is the temple of the Holy Spirit who is in you, whom ye have of God, and ye are not your own?" (I Cor. 6:19). And Paul adds, "Therefore, glorify God in your body" (verse 20).

In this life Christ must be magnified in the bodies of those who believe in Him, or He will not be magnified at all.

THE EYES

The second truth arising out of Philippians 1:20 is this: if Christ is to be magnified in our bodies, He must be magnified in each of its constituent parts.

This means, first of all, that Jesus must be magnified in our eyes. I have been impressed in a study of the Sermon on the Mount (Matt. 5-7) by the fact that the eyes are mentioned twice in these chapters, once in a passage warning against sexual sins and once in a passage warning against materialism. How closely each of these errors is connected with the eyes! In Matthew 5:29 Jesus speaks of the eyes, saying, "If thy right eye offend thee, pluck it out, and cast it from thee; for it is profitable for thee that one of thy members should perish, and not that thy whole body should be cast into hell." It is quite evident that this is a warning against the snares of improper sexual desires; for the verses that come just before refer to adultery, and the verses which immediately follow deal with the problems of divorce. Similarly, Matthew 6:22 deals with the role of the eyes in materialism. Jesus begins with a reference to human greed; He finishes with the truth that a man cannot serve God and money. In the middle He says, "The lamp of the body is the eye; if, therefore, thine eye be healthy, thy whole body shall be full of light. But if thine eye be evil, thy whole body shall be full of darkness." Jesus recognized that the eyes are the primary means by which one is tempted to sexual sins and greed.

It is particularly true in our American culture. Radio, television, billboards, and newspapers bombard us with stimulants to covet the abundant life. Movies and magazines encourage adultery and invite the Christian's participation in sexual sins. America is pre-occupied with sex and committed to materialism. But this is not to be the rule for Christians. Christians are to serve the Lord, and they must use their eyes for that purpose. They must look at all that is wholesome and must direct their desires accordingly. One young woman told me that one of her first great steps forward in the Christian life took place when she realized clearly for the first time that advertising generally appeals to non-Christian elements in our character, and she determined to shift her life accordingly.

THE TONGUE AND THE MIND

The Bible also teaches that Christ must be magnified in the way we use our tongues. In fact, a whole chapter of the book of James is given over to that teaching. James comments on the power of the tongue for good and evil, and he notes the difficulty men have in taming it. It is a difficulty even for Christians. He concludes, that with the tongue "bless we God, even the Father; and therewith curse we men, who are made after the similitude of God. Out of the same mouth proceed blessing and cursing. My brethren, these things ought not so to be" (James 3:9, 10).

Dr. Frank E. Gaebelein, one of the editors of the New Scofield Bible, has written of these verses: "James is right; so far as man goes, the tongue *is* incorrigible. Yet as James' divine brother declared: 'The things which are impossible with men are possible with God' (Luke 18:27). The fact is that many Christians through the ages have been given the grace to control their tongues and use them constructively to God's glory. They have not retreated into monasteries, but in the temptations and difficulties of daily living they have been given victory over the unruly member. They have done it, not in their own strength, but through submission of mind and heart to the indwelling Christ." *

How are men to gain control of their tongues? Only by submitting their minds to Christ. We speak what we think. Hence, if Jesus is to be magnified in the way we use our tongue, He must be magnified in the way we use our mind also. Paul writes of Christians "casting down imaginations, and every high thing that exalteth itself against the knowledge of God, and bringing into captivity every thought to the obedience of Christ" (II Cor. 10:5). Paul knew that there can be no purity of speech apart from a genuine purification of our minds. Jesus also taught this truth when He said, "Out of the abundance of the heart the mouth speaketh" (Matt. 12:34). Righteous words come from a righteous heart. And such a heart is one which has been surrendered

---

* Frank E. Gaebelein, *The Practical Epistle of James* (New York: Channel Press, 1955), p. 80.

to Christ, has been cleansed by Him, and has been filled with the thoughts He strives to place there.

If Jesus Christ is to be honored in your thoughts and in your speech, as He desires to be, there must be no preoccupation with idle thoughts, even less with anger and cursing. There must be spiritual thoughts. You must fill your mind with God. Moreover, you must participate in a constant and sympathetic encouragement of other believers, as spiritual truths and spiritual lessons are shared between you.

SURRENDERED LIVES

A final truth arising out of our text in Philippians is that if the Lord Jesus Christ is to be magnified in our bodies, our bodies must be surrendered to Him. Romans 12:1 says, "I beseech you therefore, brethren, by the mercies of God, that ye present your bodies a living sacrifice, holy, acceptable unto God, which is your reasonable service." Two things are involved here: our inmost selves who do the presenting and our bodies that are presented. Clearly we must first belong to God ourselves before anything can be offered to Him.

This means that the kind of life the Bible advocates is impossible for the non-Christian; it is impossible for the one who has failed to come to God solely on the merits of Christ and His atoning death on Calvary. Nothing in the unsaved man can satisfy God in the slightest degree. All acts of human sacrifice apart from Christ, all acts of self denial apart from Christ, all acts of penance apart from Christ — all these are acts of human righteousness. And God calls such acts filthy rags when measured by the standards of His holiness. It is only after a man has come to Christ, accepted Him as Savior, and committed himself to Christ irrevocably, that God moves him to make that sacrifice of his body through which Jesus Christ is magnified. Have you done this? Have you made this first and great commitment? If not, you need to. For all other steps in the Christian life flow from it.

Then, too, we must surrender our bodies to the Lord to use as He determines. Merely to see this truth is not sufficient; it must also be practiced. You must practice yielding your body to Christ. You must practice living to His glory as He gives you grace to do so. You must wake with the name of Jesus on your lips and commit the day to Him. You must surrender your thoughts to Him at breakfast. You must yield yourself to Him for guiding what you say when you enter the office or the factory, or when you begin to go about your household chores. You must ask Him to take control of your eyes that they might be given to His service. You must give Him your tongue. Moreover, you must do so each moment as each is yielded to His direction.

In such a way Jesus Christ will be truly magnified in you, and you will be able more and more to say: It is "my earnest expectation and my hope, that in nothing I shall be ashamed, but that with all boldness, as always, so now also Christ shall be magnified in my body."

12.

What Is Christianity?

(Philippians 1:21)

PHILIPPIANS 1:21 IS A TEXT which cuts like a surgeon's scalpel to the heart of Christianity. What is Christianity? This question rises to the lips of many people. It is a puzzle to non-Christian historians, sociologists, psychologists, and others. It also puzzles the man on the street, the housewife, the college student.

What is Christianity? The answer to that question is not unknown to the believing child of God. Christianity is a person, the Lord Jesus Christ. And all that is rightly associated with Christianity finds its center of gravity in Him. John R. W. Stott, the minister of All Souls Church in London, has written correctly, "The person and work of Christ are the foundation rock upon which the Christian religion is built . . . Take Christ from Christianity, and you disembowel it; there is practically nothing left. Christ is the centre of Christianity; all else is circumference." *

STOPPING SHORT

Many people do not realize this. They see only the paraphernalia of Christianity. Consequently, they form false conclusions about its essence and reject it on these grounds. In October of 1967, the Soviet Union launched a space probe designed to crash upon the surface of Venus and send back vital statistics about its surface temperature and atmospheric pressure. When the space probe ceased transmitting 3,774 miles from the center of the planet, presumably because it had struck the surface, the temperature reading was 520 degrees Fahrenheit and the atmosphere twelve to twenty times greater than the atmosphere on earth. This information seemed unquestionable (in spite of several reasons for thinking differently) and it suggested that there might be life on Venus. Now, however, scientists have determined that the

* John R. W. Stott, *Basic Christianity* (Grand Rapids: Wm. B. Eerdmans Publishing Co., 1958), p. 20.

radius of Venus is only 3,759 miles, meaning that the Russian ship ceased transmitting when it was still fifteen miles above the planet's surface. Consequently, all of its figures were misleading. It gave the temperature fifteen miles above the planet's surface, but it did not provide the information that the scientists most wanted to know. Actually, the surface temperature of Venus may be close to 900 degrees Fahrenheit and the pressure may be 75 to 100 times that on the surface of the earth. At that temperature and at that pressure life as we know it is impossible.

In the same way thousands of well-meaning people stop receiving data when they are miles from the heart of Christianity. For many people a knowledge of Christianity stops at contact with those who claim to be Christians. They identify Christianity with so-called Christian character, and since many believers are far from what God intends them to be, this data gives a false impression. Other people actually get into the atmosphere, perhaps as far as the organization, and then conclude that Christianity is the visible church. This is like identifying life with a test tube full of chemicals, and this impression is misleading also. Other people get as far as the ceremonies of the church and often pass for Christians because they participate properly. The fact that so many congregations are filled with people who have gone no further than this is certainly one reason for the weakness of the Christian Church today. Some people actually come as close as the creeds, and they can recite them with much volume: "I believe in God the Father Almighty, Maker of heaven and earth; And in Jesus Christ His only Son, our Lord." Unfortunately, this too is less than Christianity, important as the creeds may be.

Christianity is a person, the Lord Jesus Christ. And nothing about Christianity will be rightly understood until there is faith in Christ and a personal relationship with Him.

CHRIST AND PAUL

This truth was well known to the apostle Paul, and our text is a great expression of it. Paul writes: "For me to live is Christ, and to die is gain" (verse 21). This verse should be taken together with Galatians 2:20 which is Paul's definitive commentary on it: "I am crucified with Christ: nevertheless I live; yet not I, but Christ liveth in me; and the life which I now live in the flesh I live by the faith of the Son of God, who loved me and gave himself for me."

These two verses, one from the early days of Paul's ministry and the other from the end, summarize the living essence of Paul's faith. Put the two together, and you have a great expression of what was undoubtedly the heartthrob of Paul's life and Christian ministry. "For

to me to live is Christ, and to die is gain . . . I am crucified with
Christ: nevertheless I live; yet not I, but Christ liveth in me; and the
life which I now live in the flesh I live by the faith of the Son of God,
who loved me an gave himself for me."

One Christmas when I was a child I was given a kaleidoscope. I
shall never forget how amazed I was to pick it up for the first time
and look into the small opening at one end of the tube and to see
the brilliant arrangement of colors as the bits of tinted glass were refracted many times by mirrors. I was even more amazed to find that
the beauty increased infinitely as the kaleidoscope was turned. Our
text from Philippians is like that. It is beautiful in itself. But it is
even more beautiful as it is turned about and seen from new perspec-
tives. What does it mean to say that Christianity is Christ or that the
Christian life is Christ? As we turn the text about we can see that
Christianity is faith in Christ; it is fellowship with Christ; and it is
following after Christ. These are various aspects of the heart of Christianity.

Faith in Christ

When you say that Christianity is Christ, you say, in the first place,
that Christianity is faith in Christ. It is the acknowledgment that you
can do nothing to save yourself, that you deserve hell from God rather
than heaven, and that Christ has provided salvation for you by dying
in your place. Moreover, it is a receiving of Jesus Christ as your
Savior and as the Lord of your life. This is certainly the message of
the book of Galatians, and it is the central thrust of Paul's words in
Galatians 2:20.

To understand this verse properly, we must look at the historical
background to the letter to the Galatians. The churches of Galatia
were among the first that Paul had founded, and they were particularly
close to his heart. As Paul traveled through the Roman province of
Galatia in what is now central Turkey — through the cities of Antioch
in Pisidia, Iconium, Lystra, and Derbe — he endured real hardships
as a result of preaching the Gospel. We read in Galatians 4:13 that
Paul had first preached in an "infirmity of the flesh," and we are told
in Acts that he had been stoned at Lystra. Such labors were hard.
But they bore fruit, and everywhere Paul went he established congregations of believers. How Paul loved these people. He visited them
on his second missionary journey and again on the third. He had put
forth much energy on their behalf. He had lived with them and prayed
with them. They were grounded in the Gospel. They had trusted
Christ and Christ alone for their salvation.

Then Paul went on to found churches elsewhere. And in his wake, like crows following behind a farmer as he plows a field, non-believers came trying to profit from Paul's ministry. These came with a great show of authority and much human wisdom, teaching that salvation depended, at least in part, on human goodness. They reminded the Galatian Christians of the Jewish traditions and claimed a special relationship to the Jerusalem apostles. They even cast doubt on the validity of Paul's apostleship. It is not enough, they said, to have faith in Christ to have salvation. It is also necessary to do good deeds. It is necessary to become a Jew first. There must be circumcision. Then there must be a keeping of the Jewish holy days, and many other things. To these legalizers salvation was not by faith alone.

The news reached Paul, and he was filled with righteous anger. These men were threatening to undo everything that he had accomplished among the Galatian people. Paul writes back, "I marvel that ye are so soon removed from him that called you into the grace of Christ unto another gospel, which is not another; but there are some that trouble you, and would pervert the gospel of Christ. But though we, or an angel from heaven, preach any other gospel unto you than that which we have preached unto you, let him be accursed. As we said before, so say I now again, If any man preach any other gospel unto you than that ye have received, let him be accursed'" (Gal. 1:6-9). For Paul, salvation was by faith in Christ alone. And he expressed this conviction vividly.

Are you trusting in Christ for your salvation? Mention was made above of those who reject Christianity, stopping short at human character, the creeds, or Christian ceremonies. Unfortunately, many of these persons also trust these things to save them. Do you do that? Do you have faith in relics, or in proper phrases, or in the sacraments of your church, or in things you can do to improve your human character? These things will not save you. They have no value in reconciling you to God. You must let God strip them away like worn out clothing so that you may fling yourself on Christ. This is Christianity. It is faith in Christ, and in Christ alone.

FELLOWSHIP WITH CHRIST

Another aspect of the truth that Christianity is Christ is the fact that Christianity is fellowship with Christ. This fact is a necessary complement to the truth that Christianity is faith in Christ, for Christians often tend to think of faith impersonally. Christianity is belief in Christ, but it is also communion with Him. It is fellowship with Christ. And fellowship must be cultivated. The great evangelist and Bible teacher, A. W. Tozer, has written, "The modern scientist has lost God amid the wonders of His world; we Christians are in real danger of losing God amid the wonders of His Word. We have almost forgotten that God is a Person and, as such, can be cultivated as any person can." *

The fact that Christianity is a life to be cultivated is quite apparent in the early verses of I John. The writer of these verses is interested in the facts concerning the life of Jesus Christ. In fact, he emphasizes that his testimony is of that which he has heard and seen and handled. But the testimony does not stop with facts, nor is it given only to lead his readers to have orthodox opinions. John writes, "That which we have seen and heard declare we unto you, that ye also may have fellowship with us; and truly our fellowship is with the Father, and with his Son, Jesus Christ" (I John 1:3). Doctrine must lead to fellowship and fellowship to the riches of the Christian life. The next verse adds, "And these things write we unto you, that your joy may be full" (verse 4).

How unfortunate it is that many Christians go through life with somber faces! They know the facts of Christian faith. They trust Christ for their salvation. But there is no joy; there is nothing that gives evidence of God's presence in the midst of life or in its tribulations. This should not be so. The presence of our Lord brings joy. And if there is no joy (or peace, or longsuffering, or patience, or any other Christian virtue for that matter), the cause may well be a lack of fellowship with Jesus.

If you lack Christian joy, it may be that things are keeping you from Him. If so, you need to set them aside awhile and spend time in Christ's presence. You must remember that the tribe of Levi had no share of the land. But they had God, which was far better.

It may be that activities are keeping you from Him. In that case it is far better that these be set aside. Mary and Martha were both friends of Jesus, and both were quite orthodox. In fact, it was Martha who ran to meet Jesus when He returned to Bethany following the death of Lazarus. It was she who expressed faith in the final resurrection (John 11:24) and revealed her personal faith in Jesus: "Lord, if thou hadst been here, my brother had not died" (John 11:21). But when Jesus was in the home of Mary and Martha, it was Mary who sat at His feet while Martha served. And Jesus said, "Martha, Martha, thou art anxious and troubled about many things. But one thing is needful, and Mary hath chosen that good part" (Luke 10:41, 42). One thing is needful! How often we reverse the two. We think our service

---

* A. W. Tozer, *The Pursuit of God* (Harrisburg: Christian Publications, 1948), p. 13.

is needful and fellowship dispensable. We need to learn that nothing can be a substitute for the cultivation of the presence of God.

FOLLOWING AFTER CHRIST

To these truths we must also add that Christianity means following Christ. The Christ in whom we believe is a Christ on the move, and the fellowship we enjoy is not so much the fellowship of the living-room as it is the fellowship of the soldier marching under the eye of his commander. In its simplest form Christ's call was always the call to "Follow me." It was the call to Matthew. It was the call to the rich young ruler. It was the call to the multitudes who came to hear Him. Jesus always invited men to follow Him and to unite their efforts with His cause. He invites them to follow Him today.

Now it is evident that you cannot follow Christ unless you have previously forsaken all that keeps you from Him. Peter and Andrew left their nets. James and John left Zebedee. Matthew left his money tables. And you must leave your sin, your personal sinful aspirations, and your own conception of yourself. Moreover, you must continue to do so throughout the years of your Christian life.

For this to be possible Paul says that there must be a crucifixion. It is true that he says, "For to me to live is Christ, and to die is gain." He says again, "The life which I now live in the flesh I live by the faith of the Son of God, who loved me and gave himself for me." This is victory in the Christian life. But before he can say any of these things, Paul must be able to say that he is crucified with Christ. "I am crucified with Christ: nevertheless I live." There must be the tearing of the flesh, the breaking of the bones, the shedding of blood before the spirit of the disciple is set free. Christianity is no easy thing. It is the walk of the disciple who must bear his own cross.

In Judea in the first Christian century there were certain customs that surrounded the relationship between a rabbi and those whom he chose to be disciples. One of these was the fact that when the master moved from place to place the disciples literally followed behind him. He led; they followed, just as women did in ancient times and as they still do in many places of the world today. We must imagine this being true many times of Christ and His disciples. He led them literally, as well as figuratively, and they followed where He led. During the days of Christ's ministry there were hours spent in pleasant places — at a wedding or by the Sea of Galilee. At other times there were steps through angry crowds and steps before the faces of Christ's enemies. But all the time they followed. At last the steps of Christ led up the steep ascent to Jerusalem and stopped at the foot of the cross. The disciples were stunned. The work of three years appeared to have been undertaken in vain. But then the work was finished. Atonement was made. The veil was rent in two. And Christ provided access for all believers into God's presence.

In the same way our following of Christ must lead to crucifixion and beyond the cross to glory. Neither you nor I must linger in the pleasant places. We must cast these behind and follow Jesus. Have you followed Him through hostile crowds and dangers? Have you yielded yourself to crucifixion?

In one of our hymns we sing:

> Jesus, keep me near the cross;
> There a precious fountain,
> Free to all — a healing stream —
> Flows from Calvary's mountain.

The hymn embodies a great truth, but the truth we have been studying should be taken with it. We could also sing:

> Jesus, keep me *on* the cross;
> Let me wander never;
> Then a twice-born child of God,
> I'll rise and live forever.

No man can crucify himself. But God will crucify the Christian. He will place you on the cross, knowing that through death to self lies resurrection power and the removing of the veil.

13.

The Christian's 'Death Benefits'

(Philippians 1:21-26)

THE SECOND HALF OF Philippians 1:21 moves from the subject of life in Christ to death in Him and teaches that there are great benefits in death for Christians. Paul says, "For to me to live is Christ, and to die is gain." Two verses farther on he adds, "For I am in a strait between two, having a desire to depart and to be with Christ, which is far better" (verse 23). Death a "gain"! And death "far better"! How vividly these words express the triumphant outlook of a Christian as he looks toward eternity.

DEATH FOR UNBELIEVERS

Unfortunately, it is necessary to say that although death holds benefits for Christians, it certainly does not hold benefits for unbelievers. A Christian may experience much of hell on earth — although in God's grace it is always mingled with a taste of heaven. But beyond that is the bliss of heaven and unbroken fellowship with God. On the other hand, all that the unbeliever will know of heaven is the heaven he makes for himself on earth. After that, his future is condemnation and suffering.

Subconsciously the non-Christian knows this. Hence, death looms large as a dreadful enemy. Philosophers have pictured death in abstract language, attempting to lessen its terror in that way, and poets have romanticized it. But the fear of death lies deep in the mind of the unbeliever. The poet James Russell Lowell called death as "beautiful as the feet of a friend, coming to welcome us at our journey's end." But Francis Bacon was closer to reality when he said that "men fear death as children fear the dark." Men sense that in that sleep of death bad dreams come. And they flee from it. They know that in death a man must meet his Maker; they sense that apart from Christ no man is prepared for this encounter. Dr. Samuel Johnson told of his horror at the death of a friend: "At the sight of this last conflict I felt a sensation never known to me before: a confusion of passions, an awful stillness of sorrow, a gloomy terror without a name" *(The Rambler,* No. 54).

How grateful the Christian can be that Christ came to free him from such terrors! The Bible says of Jesus, "Forasmuch, then, as the children are partakers of flesh and blood, he also himself likewise took part of the same, that through death he might destroy him that had the power of death, that is, the devil, and deliver them, who through *fear of death,* were all their lifetime subject to bondage" (Heb. 2:14, 15).

THE BEST IN LIFE

Some people have imagined that, if a man suffers enough in life, death comes necessarily as a blessed release from suffering; some have speculated that it is only in this sense that death can be a gain for Christians. Christians have often been tortured for their faith; many have suffered great natural calamities. To the imagination of the unsaved man few things could be worse than the things some Christians have suffered. From this perspective death has sometimes been called a greater blessing.

But this is a distortion of the biblical picture. Death for the Christian is never pictured in the Bible as a gain over the worst in this life. *It is portrayed as an improvement on the best.* Certainly it is in this sense that Paul intends his words to the Philippians. We might imagine that Paul was suffering in prison and was anxious for a speedy release, even by the portal of death. But this is just the opposite of what Paul experienced. Paul's life was full. He had been enriched by fellowship with Christ. He writes, "For to me to live is Christ" (verse 21). He was confident that Christ would be magnified in the way he led his life. He speaks of his "earnest expectation and . . . hope, that . . . as always, so now also Christ shall be magnified in my body" (verse 20). He was filled with delight that his work at Philippi had prospered; he even saw evidence of the spread of the Gospel of Jesus Christ at Rome. These facts fulfilled his deepest desires. Consequently, all of the statements that surround his circumstances at Rome are optimistic.

It is against this background that the great apostle terms his death "far better." One of the most useful commentators on this book has written, "Life and death look to us like two evils of which we know not which is the less. As for the Apostle, they look to him like two immense blessings, of which he knows not which is the better . . . On either side of the veil, Jesus Christ is all things to him . . . Only, the conditions of the other side are such that the longed-for companionship of his Master will be more perfectly realized there." *

What are the benefits of death to those who trust in Jesus? They are at least these: freedom from the evil of this world, conformity to the image of Christ, and fellowship with Jesus Christ forever. These truths may be put in three sentences: We shall be free from evil. We shall be like Jesus. We shall be with Jesus.

Freedom From Evil

The first great benefit of death for Christians is that death brings a permanent freedom from evil. The unsaved man may not desire this, preferring to wallow in his sin, but the Christian who has tasted the delight of God's righteousness longs for a purity that he will never have on earth. He longs to be free of sin, pain, care, and anxiety. And he knows that death brings freedom.

There is an interesting image in these verses which conveys this thought. In verse twenty-three Paul says that his desire is to "depart" and be with Jesus. The Greek word translated by the English word "depart" is a word from which we get our word "analysis": *analuo.* It had various uses in ancient times, sometimes referring to the freeing of a slave, sometimes to the sailing of a ship, sometimes to solving a problem, and often to the breaking of camp by one of the Roman legions. In every instance it conveyed the idea of leaving something permanently behind.

We can see this most clearly in the military operations of the Roman army. Whenever a party of Roman soldiers reached the end of a long day's march they first of all made camp. This was no ordinary camp constructed out of a few tents and several fires. A Roman camp, even when the legion was under pressed marches, was always an elaborate affair. First a rectangle was paced off, large enough to hold the contingent of soldiers. Within the rectangle roads were marked out, a main road leading from the mid-point on one of the long sides of the rectangle to the mid-point on the other long side, and a second main road leading from the mid-point on one of the short sides of the rectangle to the mid-point on the other short side. Where these roads crossed the commander erected his headquarters. All of the troops occupied assigned places within the encampment. After the rectangle was paced out the entire encampment was secured by moat and rampart, often to a combined height of ten or twelve feet. The top was reinforced. The corners were strengthened. After this the soldiers

* H. C. G. Moule, *Philippian Studies* (Glasgow: Pickering & Inglis, n.d.), pp. 71, 78.

settled down for rest and for their evening meal. In the morning camp was struck, and the soldiers moved on. With them went their arms and baggage. Behind lay the camp with all its fortifications like a discarded chrysalis, mute testimony to the fact that they had been there.

Paul suggests that in a similar way Christians break camp to be with Jesus. All that is not useful lies behind — all of the sin, all of the pain, all of the care and anguish of this world. In death there is great freedom.

It is to convey such peaceful freedom that the Bible also speaks of death as sleep. Stephen is said to have fallen asleep when his earthly life was brought to an end by stoning (Acts 7:60). Christ spoke of Lazarus as having fallen asleep (John 11:11). And Paul wrote many times of the sleep of believers. "We who are alive and remain unto the coming of the Lord shall not precede them who are asleep" (I Thess. 4:15). "Behold, I show you a mystery: We shall not all sleep, but we shall all be changed" (I Cor. 15:51).

What does this mean? Some people have taken the references to sleep literally, and hence have invented the strange doctrine of soul-sleep, teaching that the believer sleeps in an unconscious state between the moment of his death and the resurrection of the body at Jesus Christ's return. But this is not right. Jesus taught that His reference to sleep was figurative. And there are other verses in Scripture that teach an immediate passage of the Christian into the presence of God at death. We cannot say, "For to me to live is Christ, and soul-sleep is gain." Or "to be absent from the body is soul-sleep." The image is not used to teach that. It is used to teach that in death, as to a lesser degree in physical sleep, the individual is free of the cares that trouble life and is partaker of the peace that has a heavenly origin.

To Be Like Jesus

The second great benefit of death to the believer is that he will be like Jesus. John writes, "Beloved, now are we the children of God, and it doth not yet appear what we shall be, but we know that, when he shall appear, we shall be like him; for we shall see him as he is" (I John 3:2). It is not enough to say that death brings freedom from evil. It is true, but it is a negative thing. Annihilation would be just as effective and death is better than that. The Bible teaches that death brings a final perfection of that sanctification of the believer which has begun on earth.

We shall be like Him. That means that we shall be like Him in *righteousness,* for Paul speaks of "a crown of righteousness, which the

Lord, the righteous judge, shall give me at that day; and not to me only, but unto all them also that love his appearing (II Tim. 4:8). The thought is almost breathtaking. Crowned with righteousness! We do not know that righteousness now; we have only tasted it slightly. But the day is coming when we shall be what we should be. And "things that are not now, nor could be, then shall be our own."

We also shall be like Him in *knowledge*. Now we see things imperfectly. We know in part, and our knowledge (even of spiritual things) is always mixed with error. In that day we shall know as God knows us, and all that has puzzled us in this life will become clear.

There is an illustration of this in the realm of photography. Have you ever held a colored slide up to some weak light to see the picture that is etched there in the various emulsions? I have done that many times and have learned that, while it is possible to see the general outlines of the picture and to have a sense of its colors, it is really only possible to see the whole scene in all its colors when the slide is projected large by the strong light of a projector. In the same way you and I have a sense of things now as we study their general outlines in the Bible. But the day is coming when God's light will shine upon its pages, and we shall see all of history and all of reality as God sees them. If Paul had been living in our day, he might have used this image instead of an imperfect mirror in I Corinthians 13. But the teaching is the same. "For now we see in a mirror, darkly; but then, face to face; now I know in part, but then shall I know even as also I am known" (I Cor. 13:12).

We shall also be like Christ in *love*. What a joy to be like Him in this. There is always so much of self in everything we do, but Christ's love was selfless and self-sacrificing. It was a love that reached to us when we were sinners and saved us for this life and for eternity. We sing with great truthfulness:

> The love of God is greater far
> Than tongue or pen can ever tell;
> It goes beyond the highest star
> And reaches to the lowest Hell.

How wonderful that God's love stooped low enough to reach us and that it will yet carry us beyond the highest star into His presence.

There is a beautiful picture of this truth in Revelation. I did not understand this as a child but it means a great deal to me now as I think of the perfection that will be ours as we are made like Jesus. It is the picture of the new Jerusalem descending out of heaven. The city is portrayed as a cube surrounded by a wall, and in each of the four sides pointing north, east, south, and west are three gates named after the twelve tribes of Israel. The city is filled with precious jewels. The streets are paved with gold. The whole is lighted by the radiance of God and of the Lamb who dwell within it. When I was young I took this vision literally, although not without some puzzlement. The picture of a large golden cube descending from heaven was always a bit ludicrous and even, it seemed to me then, pointless. But I reasoned that if man can shoot a satellite up into heaven, God can float a city down. And I left it at that. Subsequently I came to see that the new Jerusalem is actually a picture of the Church, Christ's bride, as she will be in all her God-given perfection; and this conception was far more wonderful. Of course, this is exactly what John says. John writes, "And there came unto me one of the seven angels . . . and talked with me saying, Come here, I will show thee the bride, the Lamb's wife. And he carried me away in the Spirit to a great and high mountain, and showed me that great city, the holy Jerusalem, descending out of heaven from God" (Rev. 21:9, 10).

What a splendid picture that is! The dimensions of the city are meant to symbolize perfection. Gold symbolizes purity. The jewels symbolize the fact that she is precious. And the most glorious truth is that you and I will help to constitute that city in the day of our death, when we are made like Jesus.

We Shall Be With Him

The illustration of the heavenly Jerusalem has already anticipated the third benefit that comes to believers at their death, for it has spoken of Christ as dwelling in it and has spoken in another image of the union of the bride with the bridegroom. Certainly the greatest benefit of the believer's death is that he will be with Jesus. Now we know Him. It is correct to say that He is with us in this life. We may trust in the fact that He will be particularly close to us in death. For we are told that "God is our refuge and strength, a very present help in trouble" (Ps. 46:1). And again, "Precious in the sight of the Lord is the death of his saints" (Ps. 116:15). But the day is coming when, in a special sense, we shall be with Him as never before, as the bride is with her husband on the evening of their marriage. In that day there will be no tears, no unfulfilled longings or disappointments, and no separation.

Death is always a separation, even for the Christian. For the unbeliever, death is the separation of the soul and the spirit from God. For the Christian, death is the separation of the soul and the spirit from the body. But there is one respect in which death is no separation at all for those who trust in Jesus. There is no separation from Him. Even for Paul the dilemma in which he stood was not a dilemma between Christ and not Christ. It was a dilemma "between Christ and Christ, Christ much and Christ more, Christ by faith and Christ by sight." * And it was resolved ultimately only by a permanent union with Him. How wonderful that you and I also can look forward to that union.

Do you? Then you must live for others now. It is true that death holds benefits for believers — freedom from evil, likeness to Christ, the union with Him. But this was never intended to make Christians flee from the duties of this life, as some have claimed. Have you ever noticed that practical considerations always follow upon the mention of this subject in Scripture? John argues that "every man that hath this hope in him purifieth himself even as he is pure" (I John 3:3). The great chapter on the resurrection, I Corinthians 15, closes with these words: "Therefore, my beloved brethren, be ye steadfast, unmovable, always abounding in the work of the Lord, forasmuch as ye know that your labor is not in vain in the Lord" (I Cor. 15:58). It is the same in the opening chapter of Philippians. No sooner has Paul said that death is gain than he turns back once more to those who are still in his charge. In a few brief words he acknowledges that if in God's wisdom he remains in this life, then that is more needful for others. "And having this confidence, I know that I shall abide and continue with you all for your furtherance and joy of faith, that your rejoicing may be more abundant in Jesus Christ for me by my coming to you again" (verses 25, 26).

So it must be with us. We must lift our minds to contemplate the joys of heaven, but if we see them aright we will turn back once more to those for whom our life in Christ and our witness to Him are needful.

---

* H. C. G. Moule, *Philippian Studies* (Glasgow: Pickering & Inglis, n.d.), p. 257.

14.

Christian Conduct

(Philippians 1:27)

EVERY CHRISTIAN MUST LEARN the principle that privilege implies responsibility. Let me illustrate this from the lives of the English kings. In Shakespeare's history play *Richard II*, an unfortunate king brings great trouble on himself by failing to live up to his responsibilities. He is a legitimate king; but he is impetuous, passionate, and arbitrary in the administration of justice. Such behavior is unfit for one who wears a crown, and Shakespeare tells how eventually he lost it. Privilege brought responsibility, but Richard II did not fulfill it.

The three plays involving King Henry V—*Henry IV* (Parts I and II) and *Henry V* — show just the opposite character. In his early youth Henry is irresponsible and profligate. He spends much time carousing with old John Falstaff and enjoys it. Then the old king dies, and Prince Henry begins to live as befits his kingly status. He does not hold the crown through any virtue in himself. At one point he confesses to the dying king, his father: "You won it, wore it, kept it, gave it me." But having the crown he vows to live worthy of the possession:

> . . . . The tide of blood in me
> Hath proudly flowed in vanity till now.
> Now doth it turn and ebb back to the sea,
> Where it shall mingle with the state of floods,
> And flow henceforth in formal majesty.

Becoming king produces a change in Henry. And from this point on Henry V lives as one of the noblest kings of England.

In a similar way Christians are to live worthy of their spiritual possessions. If you are a Christian, you do not hold your possessions in Christ through any virtue of your own. What you have you only have from Him who is the King of kings — who won it, wore it, kept it, gave it to you. But having it you must live worthy of your calling. Old things are to be put away; all things are to be new.

This is the point of the section to which we now come in our study of Philippians. Paul has spoken of the privileges that the Christians have in Christ. He now speaks of their obligations. Are they fulfilling their duties as Christians? Do they stand together against increasing opposition? Are they faithful in prayer? Do they draw together increasingly in love, having their fellowship enriched by the Holy Spirit? Are they one in mind and purpose? If these things are so, then Paul will have great cause for rejoicing. They will be mature Christians, for their conduct will be worthy of their calling.

How much all of us need this emphasis on Christian conduct! Perhaps there has never been a period in history when true Christians have lived more like those who are in the world and have demonstrated so little of the high standards of the Christian faith. This is inexcusable. It must be resisted. Moreover, it must be resisted in the only way that it will ever be possible to resist it — in the way you live your life and in the way I live mine. Privilege implies responsibilities. If you and I have been called by Christ, we must now live worthy of that calling.

Citizens of Heaven

Paul teaches these truths in verse 27 by means of a word hard to translate properly into English. It is the Greek word *politeuo*, and it is based on the noun meaning city: *polis*. In the classical age the *polis* was the largest political unit, and the Greek belonged to it as we belong to a country. Consequently, the noun actually refers to citizenship, and the verb means "to conduct oneself worthily as a citizen of the city-state."

The translation "city-state" is not really a very good one, however, for in Greek eyes the *polis* was not much like a city as we understand it and yet much more than a state. In our day it is possible for a person to live in a city and yet feel no attachment to it. And he can be a citizen of a country, such as the United States, without participating in its government or in public life. This was not possible for a citizen of a Greek *polis*. The polis was his life. Its laws were part of his being. Its customs were something of which he was proud. He knew all about it, and he knew practically all of its inhabitants. The *polis* demanded his complete loyalty, and he gave it willingly. To him it was the best thing in life.

We may see something of this complex character of the Greek city-state in one of the Greek plays in which its nature is discussed. The play is Sophocles' *Antigone*. Early in the drama Creon, the king, comes forward with a public pronouncement. He says, "Sirs, our *polis* has been like a ship tossed by stormy waves; but thanks to the gods, it sails once more upon a steady keel." It is hard to miss the point that in this statement the *polis* resembles the state; we too apply the image of the "ship of state" to governments. Later on in the play Creon remarks that a law has been clearly proclaimed to the *polis*. Here the word refers to "people." Finally, further on in the play, Creon quarrels with his son Haemon. "Tell me," he says, "am I not to rule by my own judgment?" Haemon answers, "That is no *polis* which belongs to one man." In this case the major concept is that of a "community," and Haemon's point is that the affairs of one member are the affairs of all. It was this conception of the city-state that led to the uproar against Paul at Ephesus and to the united action taken against him in other cities of the empire.

All of this is directly applicable to the responsibility of Christians. When Paul writes that the Christians at Philippi are to conduct themselves worthily as citizens, he is not thinking of a literal city to which his readers belong. He is thinking of the Church. And in this context his admonition points to their mutual duties as members of a local Christian commonwealth. Is the *polis* a state? So is the Church. Consequently, Christians are to work within the organization. Is the *polis* people? So is the Church. Consequently, we are to preserve individual interests and respect individual contributions. Is the *polis* a living community? The Church is also. Consequently, Christians are to share a common life and contribute to each other's well-being as ilving members of Christ's body.

There are always problems when Christians forget any of these aspects. When Christians forget that they are members of a Christian state, however loosely it may be conceived, then the right of the individual conscience reigns supreme and each does what is right in his own eyes. When the organization dominates, the individual is suppressed, and it takes a Martin Luther or a Calvin to re-establish the direct relationship between a Christian and God. When the matter of community is obscured, believers lose concern for one another and neglect the insights that the other Christians provide. Paul did not want the Christians at Philippi to omit any of these elements. And neither should we. Knowing ourselves to be members of a living community of which Jesus Christ is head and being conscious of our common life together, you and I are to live lives worthy of our calling. We are to live as Christians. We are to live as members of Christ's body.

Further light is shed upon this verb by the fact that Philippi enjoyed a privileged relationship to Rome. Prior to the great civil war in which Octavian finally defeated Anthony, Philippi was like any other city in the empire. After the battle a number of soldiers who had been favorable to Anthony were settled there. Because of this the city was given special prominence, and from this time on the town of Philippi became a Roman colony. This meant that as far as the courts were concerned Philippi became a part of Rome, even though it was nearly 800 miles away. The ground at Philippi became Italian soil. Citizens of the city became Romans. Roman law was practiced by the local civil administration. As far as possible the frontier city on the outer bounds of the empire adopted Roman customs. To be a colony was something of which any city in the empire was proud. Consequently, the Philippians took great delight in identifying themselves as Romans. We read, for instance, that when Paul had first preached the Gospel in Philippi a number of the citizens accused him before the magistrates saying, "These men, being Jews, do exceedingly trouble our city, and teach customs which are not lawful for us to receive, neither to observe, *being Romans*" (Acts 16:20, 21).

All of this explains why Paul's phrase "to conduct oneself worthy of citizenship" is so significant. Paul knew how proud the Philippians were of their earthly citizenship. He knew that they allowed it to affect not only the laws of their city but also their social customs and the daily conduct of their lives. How much more then were they to be proud of their citizenship in heaven! This was the greater citizenship. They were to cherish it. They were to live by its laws and its customs. Moreover, they were to extend the influence of this commonwealth in the midst of a pagan and spiritually hostile environment.

So must we. Neither you nor I have ever been a member of a Greek city-state, or anything like it. We have not known Roman citizenship. But we have a citizenship in heaven "from where also we look for the Savior, the Lord Jesus Christ" (Phil. 3:20). You were like Abraham, a foreigner in a distant land. But God called you to be a citizen of heaven. Now you sojourn in a "land of promise, as in a foreign country, dwelling in tents." But you are a citizen of heaven, "a city which hath foundations, whose builder and maker is God" (Heb. 11:9, 10). Being a citizen of heaven, you are to live by the laws of that citizenship.

UNITY OF SPIRIT

At this point Paul turns to two practical expressions of proper Christian conduct, expressions that follow logically upon his reference to citizenship. How do you live as a citizen of heaven? First, Paul says that we are to *stand fast in one spirit,* and, second, with one mind we are to *strive together* for the advancement of the Gospel.

The first distinguishing mark of Christian conduct is that we stand together. We are "to keep the unity of the Spirit in the bond of peace"

(Eph. 4:3). Christians are not to divide along doctrinal or sociological lines. They are to be one. And this is to be a mark of their conduct.

Unfortunately, evangelical churches are not known for "standing together." In fact, the opposite is true. Instead of an honest attempt to join hands across denominational, racial, and cultural barriers for the furtherance of common goals, Christians have all too often sought to tear down those who are not in perfect agreement with them even on the most insignificant of matters. This is a scandal, and it is dishonoring to Christ. Moreover, it is a scandal that hinders the preaching of the Gospel. These things ought not to be. In place of these divisions Christians should know a unity that is visible and has practical results.

AGGRESSIVE CHRISTIANITY

The second practical expression of true Christian conduct follows naturally from the first. If believers will conduct themselves in a manner that leads to Christian unity, then they will find that this also leads them to strive together to advance the Christian Gospel. And the result will be an aggressive Christianity. The Christians at Philippi knew what it meant to stand fast as Romans at the frontiers of the Roman world. They knew the obligation that was theirs to advance Roman rule in the face of barbarism. In the same way, Paul would have them united for an aggressive advancement of the faith.

How we need to recover an aggressive faith today! For the most part Christianity in our day has retreated into spiritual ghettos, and believers seem content to have it that way so long as they are safe and their children never wander beyond the barricades. Some Christians publicly wash their hands of all involvement in community and national life. And I have actually heard other Christians rejoice in the face of rising wars, inflation, riots, lawlessness, and immorality — all on the basis that these things must happen before the Lord's return. Remember that no one looked more earnestly for the Lord's quick return than Paul, but it was preeminently Paul who set out with all the enthusiasm he could muster to claim the world for Christ. So must we. And we must do so more and more as we see the hour of His return coming. We must carry the battle for men's souls beyond the confines of the churches into the universities, the law courts, the world of business, and the marketplace. And we must present the claims of Him who came to save men from their sin and whose life lived within the Christian will transform even his environment.

E. Stanley Jones recently wrote: "The early Christians did not say in dismay: 'Look what the world has come to,' but in delight, 'Look what has come to the world.' They saw not merely the ruin, but the resources for the reconstruction of that ruin. They saw not merely that sin did abound, but that grace did much more abound. On that assurance the pivot of history swung from blank despair, loss of moral nerve, and fatalism, to faith and confidence that at last sin had met its match, that something new had come ino the world, that not only here and there, but on a wide scale, men could attain to that hitherto impossible thing — goodness." *

Do you believe that this spirit is possible today and that our contemporaries in the Church can be equally aggressive? Another contemporary has written about Jones' words, "I am convinced that this offer of abundant life . . . has a scriptural ability to fascinate the sallow spirit of modern man and to coax him anew to a hearing of the claims of Christ upon his life" (Carl F. H. Henry in *Christianity Today*, Sept. 13, 1968, p. 15). Every Christian should be equally convinced of that. And we should unite to effect it, joining hearts and minds in an aggressive proclamation of the Gospel. We should realize that this too is an aspect of our Christian conduct.

---

* E. Stanley Jones, *Abundant Living* (Nashville: Abingdon Press, 1942), p. 183.

15.

Stand Up and Be Counted

(Philippians 1:28-30)

CERTAIN THINGS IN LIFE happen in such an unalterable sequence that we can hardly think of one without at once thinking of the other. Take a boy and a girl as an example. They meet sometime in their teens and begin going together. They find out that they have mutual interests and that they enjoy one another's company. Love begins to blossom. And no sooner is love in the heart and on the lips than the couple begins to think about marriage. Love and marriage go together. And the sequence is so normal that the parents and friends of the couple are often thinking about it before the young people do.

In the same way there are sequences that apply to spiritual things, and again the order is largely unalterable. Sin brings death. Blessing follows obedience. Faithfulness in small things leads to faithfulness in many things, and so on. Another important sequence is in the verses that close the first chapter of Philippians. Paul has been emphasizing the need for Christian conduct. A Christian must be like Christ. No sooner has he mentioned this, however, than a sequence comes into his mind. And this prompts him to talk about a side subject; we might call it a parenthesis involving verses 28 to 30. Paul does not get back to the theme of Christian conduct until chapter 2.

What is this sequence? The sequence is this: wherever Christians will live as they ought to live in this world, where they will live righteous lives and aggressively seek to spread the Gospel, in that place there will be persecution. This is true for all Christians. If you bear a proper witness for Jesus Christ, as God intends you to do, there will be persecution for you. It will not always be physical persecution as it was in Paul's day, although that still happens. Watchman Nee is in prison in China because of his witness, and there are others like him. But you will suffer persecution of some sort nevertheless. It will be the natural result of your confession.

SCORN BY THE CROWD

Sometimes it will be ridicule by the crowd. Once as Dr. Donald Grey Barnhouse was parked on the street of a large city on the west coast, he witnessed an accident a few yards away. A car wove through the traffic and collided head on with another car that was coming in the opposite direction. The driver was apparently drunk. Another man in the car pushed the drunk aside and got behind the wheel himself. When the policeman came the sober man began to berate the driver of the other car, saying he was at fault. At this point Dr. Barnhouse came forward and gave his testimony to the policeman. He said, "I saw what happened. This drunk was the man who was driving; the accident was his fault, and after the crash this man exchanged places with him." As Dr. Barnhouse said this the crowd that had gathered around the scene of the accident began to growl: "What business do you have interfering?" "Let them argue it out!" "Leave it to the police!" Dr. Barnhouse replied that it was not a matter of intrusion, but of right and wrong: "If this man perjures himself in court by saying that it was the innocent driver's fault, I will fly to the west coast from Philadelphia and will testify against him. And I'll identify this drunk by the scar on his cheek." Then he gave his name and address to the driver of the other car and to the policeman and walked away. As he did so the crowd yelled out after him and cursed. Dr. Barnhouse believed that a Christian must stand up and be counted whenever there is a clear-cut moral issue. And he knew that this must be true even though the crowd would hate him for it.

Sometimes our conduct will lead to persecution in business. I know of a banker who was in charge of an influential branch of a large bank. A policy grew up in the bank over a period of time that vice-presidents in charge of the various branches were to encourage business by entertaining lavishly at the bank's expense. Important customers were to be given a round of nightclubs, shows, and so on. The Christian banker did not think that this was proper conduct for a Christian, nor did he think that this was the right way to do business. He felt that banking was best done in a sober mood during banking hours, and by operating on this principle his section of the bank flourished. This branch had the largest accounts in spite of official disapproval. Yet his convictions stuck in the throat of the management. There came a time when they would not take it any longer. They sent him home for two months, put someone else in his place, and two months later rehired him for another position where he could not cause them trouble. This was persecution.

DARKNESS AND LIGHT

The greatest example of persecution suffered for the sake of right-eousness is in the life of Jesus Christ. Jesus came into the world as the Light of the world. But the world was in darkness. Where there is darkness, men do the works of darkness, and they do not want their deeds to be brought to light because their deeds are evil. When Jesus appeared, His life cut like a knife into the human conscience. Men could get along with hypocrisy between one another, for men are alike in their hypocrisy; but when Christ stood in their midst He exposed the hypocrisy, and they hated Him for it. Men could get away with pride, dishonesty, sexual perversion, and legalism among themselves. But they could not do it in Christ's presence. Consequently, those who rejected His standards eventually crucified Him.

It is often the same with Christ's followers even today. Christ is the Light of the world, and there is a sense in which those who follow Him should also be lights in the world. Jesus said, "He that followeth me shall not walk in darkness, but shall have the light of life" (John 8: 12). If you believe in Christ, if you have committed your life to Him, then that light and life should be manifested in you. The world should see it. And where it shines forth, there will be persecution.

Have you experienced ridicule or prejudice for Christ's sake? If so, you must realize that God knows it and permits the persecution. Besides that, you are to receive it as a gift from God and recognize that in it God is accomplishing His purpose. That is one aspect of God's sovereignty.

PROOF OF SALVATION

Now I know that at this point the reader may be asking: Why does God allow persecution? What is its purpose? Paul gives two good reasons. One is that it is a token of salvation for the Christian. The other is that it is a token of destruction to the one who fails to believe.

The word that is translated "token" in the New Scofield Bible is rendered in different ways in other translations. The Revised Standard Version translates it "omen"; Phillips calls it a "proof"; the New English Bible speaks of a "sign." In every case the idea is of an undeniable manifestation of reality. It is not possible for a Christian to stand firm under persecution and for the world to dismiss it as nothing. It is evidence of a supernatural power. Consequently, it is a token of salvation to the Christian and of destruction to those who will not believe.

Have you ever visited a practical joke store and seen those little cubes of sugar that are actually styrofoam plastic? They look like sugar, and presumably they have often been used as if they were sugar by the unwary. But they will not dissolve. If you put them in your coffee and look back five minutes later, they will still be there. The humor, if there is any, lies in their indestructibility. In some respects Christians are to be like that. Human character by itself can dissolve under the persecution of life. Life can beat it down. And that is why many people are disheartened and even ruined by life. But the Christian is to be made of "sterner stuff." He is to endure in the face of temptation and persecution. Moreover, the very fact that he endures is evidence that God has done a supernatural work in his heart. And it is evidence to the Christian as well as to the unbeliever.

AHAB AND MICAIAH

The second reason why God permits Christians to be persecuted is that persecution is a token of damnation to the one who fails to believe. How? Let me illustrate by a story from the Old Testament, found in I Kings 22.

During the days of the divided monarchy, while Ahab was King of Israel and Jehoshaphat was King of Judah, the two kingdoms were relatively strong compared to the kingdoms around them. And at one point Jehoshaphat went north to visit Ahab. Ahab said to Jehoshaphat, "Look, why are we sitting here idle when Ramoth-gilead is in the hands of the Assyrians and we are strong enough to take it from them?" And Jehoshaphat replied, "I'm with you." Actually the Bible reports him as saying, "I am as thou art, my people as thy people, my horses as thy horses." So they embarked upon their aggression.

Ahab was a wicked king and represented all that was wrong with Israel. But the kings of Judah were always a bit more sensitive to spiritual things. So before they went out to battle Jehoshaphat said, "Let's ask the Lord what we should do." He was like many Christians in our day who have already decided what they are going to do, but who after they have decided stop to see if they cannot get the Lord's approval. This was no way to find the Lord's blessing, but at any rate Jehoshaphat did it. And Ahab responded by collecting four hundred of the court prophets of Samaria. Like many politicians Ahab knew the value of religious opinion. He said, "Shall I go against Ramoth-gilead to battle, or shall I forbear?" And the false prophets answered, "Go up; for the Lord shall deliver it into the hand of the king." These men were good prophets from Ahab's point of view.

Jehoshaphat looked at the four hundred prophets and reacted like a back-sliding Christian. That was the answer he wanted, but he was made just a little bit uneasy by the thought that it was probably not really an answer from the Lord. So he said to Ahab, "Now look, it is very nice that we have these four hundred prophets, and that is the

answer I wanted. But can't we find a prophet of the Lord somewhere
that we could enquire of him?" Ahab said, "Yes, there is yet one man,
Micaiah, the son of Imlah, but I hate him because he never says anything good about me." And Jehoshaphat said, "Is that any way for
a king to talk? It doesn't befit your dignity." So Ahab called for
Micaiah.

While they were waiting Ahab staged a great reception for this one
unpopular prophet. He set up two thrones in the marketplace of
Samaria — one for himself and one for Jehoshaphat. Here sat the
kings. And all around them were the armies collected for the war.
They were on the outside of the square, Ahab and Jehoshaphat were
in the middle and around them at the base of the thrones were the
four hundred false prophets who had said, "Go out, and the Lord will
deliver Ramoth-gilead into your hand." There they sat waiting for
Micaiah to come and bear his testimony.

In the meantime the messenger had found Micaiah and had tried
to warn him before his meeting with Ahab. He said, "The king wants
to see you, and he wants your prediction on the battle. I'll just tell
you this beforehand: everybody has said that it is going to be all right,
and you had better do the same. If you give the same prediction as
the false prophets and you are wrong, well, Ahab will be dead, and
nobody will care what you said. But if you say that the kings will lose
the battle, Ahab will dispose of you. And that will happen regardless
of the outcome. So why don't you just go along with what the four
hundred prophets have forecast, and nothing will happen to you." Micaiah answered, "What the Lord has told me, that will I speak."

Samaria sits high on a great out-cropping of rock in the midst of
a plain. And from the top of Samaria Ahab and Jehoshaphat and the
four hundred prophets and all of the armies looked down to see Micaiah coming with the messenger. It would have taken at least thirty
minutes for Micaiah to ascend the hill of Samaria, and all the while
tension was building. Everyone was wondering what Micaiah was
going to say. At last Micaiah came to the gate of the city, the soldiers
and the false prophets parted, and Micaiah stood before the kings.
"All right," said Ahab, "let's hear it."

Now Micaiah was one of those rare men who are always in great
possession of themselves. And in the midst of all of this pressure he
actually made fun of the kings. Micaiah said to Ahab, "Go, and
prosper; for the Lord shall deliver it into the hand of the king." This
was mockery, for Micaiah was using the exact words of the false
prophets. And everyone knew that this was not really the word of
Jehovah. Ahab said, "I adjure thee that thou tell me nothing but that
which is true in the name of the Lord." Micaiah said, "All right then.

I saw all Israel scattered upon the hills, as sheep that have not a shepherd. And the Lord said, These have no master; let them return every man to his house in peace." Ahab turned to Jehoshaphat at that point and said, "See, what did I tell you? Did I not tell you that he would prophesy no good concerning me, but evil?"

Micaiah then went on to give the rest of the prophecy, "I saw the Lord sitting on his throne, and all the host of heaven standing by him on his right hand and on his left. And the Lord said, Who shall persuade Ahab, that he may go up and fall at Ramoth-gilead? And one said on this manner, and another said on that manner. And there came forth a spirit, and stood before the Lord, and said, I will persuade him. And the Lord said unto him, By what means? And he said, I will go forth, and I will be a lying spirit in the mouth of all his prophets. . . . Now, therefore, behold the Lord hath put a lying spirit in the mouth of all these thy prophets, and the Lord hath spoken evil concerning thee."

How unpopular the testimony of Micaiah was! Yet the story ends by showing that events did fall out the way Micaiah had predicted. Ahab was killed. Israel was scattered. And Micaiah is never heard of again. He appears in the Old Testament only in this one brief moment of history. But in that moment he bore his testimony to what was true. And his testimony stood, not only for what we might call a token of his own salvation, but as a token of the destruction that was closing in on Ahab.

God's Gift

It may be that God will call you to bear a testimony like that. It may not be in as dramatic a way as with Micaiah, but it may result in persecution. You may do it in a quiet way, and no one may ever hear of your witness. No one will know of your courage. But God knows. And your witness will go down in the books of eternity as evidence that here was a Christian who lived as God called him to live and who bore the testimony God called him to bear. History will bear out that the things spoken by you were true and that your conduct is vindicated.

If you will see persecution in this light, then you will see it for what it really is, a gift from the hand of God. Paul refers to persecution as a gift twice in the last verses of the first chapter of Philippians. He says that it is a token of salvation, "and that of God." And he says, "For unto you it is given in the behalf of Christ . . . to suffer for his sake." Given by God! Given as a token of His grace! How wonderful that persecution can be received in that way by Christians.

16.

The Mark of Christ

(Philippians 2:1, 2)

DURING THE YEARS that I spent in Switzerland doing graduate study, my wife and I had the opportunity of getting to know an old Swiss gentleman named Speiser who had helped to patrol the borders of Switzerland in World War II. He had many stories to tell about the war, but the story he seemed to enjoy the most was about his wartime relationship with Karl Barth, the well-known Swiss theologian. Professors are set on a very high pedestal in Europe, and Barth was on one of the highest. So Speiser was greatly honored to have known him. During the war Barth and Speiser served together in a military unit assigned to guard one of the Rhine bridges. Our friend told how the common danger brought them together, and for a time at least they shared stories about their lives and spoke to each other with the familiar, intimate form of address of the German language: *Du,* Barth, and *Du,* Speiser. After the war each returned to his own work, and the familiarity of the wartime years ended.

Another story also concerns Karl Barth and a person's familiarity with him. Toward the end of my stay in Switzerland Dr. Barth celebrated his eightieth birthday, and I was asked by *Christianity Today* to try for an interview with him and to write it for subsequent publication in that journal. I called Barth's home and was told that the professor would see me one Saturday afternoon at two o'clock. The Saturday came, and at two I arrived on the doorstep and was greeted by Barth's wife. "I am a student at the University," I said, "and I have an appointment with Dr. Barth." She invited me in and a moment later turned to call up the stairs to her husband, using the same pronoun that our friend Speiser had used with Barth during the war twenty years before: "*Du,* Karl, du hast ein Gast." We would say, "Karl, you have a visitor." Later, in the course of our conversation, Barth called for a notebook that his secretary was carrying, and he used the familiar form with her. She too was a member of his immediate circle. It was evident that the close relationship that existed within the home was one that had grown up over a lifetime and would continue until death.

These stories illustrate a truth that underlies the verses to which we now come in our study. In the last four verses of the first chapter of Philippians and in the opening verses of chapter two, Paul speaks of a need for a close intimate relationship among believers. It is a matter of unity, and there are two reasons why it is necessary. The first, which we have already studied, is that it is necessary in time of war. Christians are often besieged by the forces of this world, and they must draw together like Barth and Speiser if they are to defend the Gospel successfully and to advance the claims of Christ in the midst of their environment. That is a practical reason. It is what Paul means when he says that we are to "stand fast in one spirit, with one mind striving together for the faith of the gospel" (1:27).

A Family Relationship

However, the danger of warfare is at best a secondary ground for unity. For what if the opposition should let up for a moment? What if the victories of the Church bring a temporary peace? Or what if Satan should fool the Church with an apparent end to hostilities? Are Christians then to fly apart? Are they to forget their mutual citizenship? Of course not! For we know that, although unity is made terribly necessary by the dangers we face, the real reason for Christian unity lies rather in our mutual relationship to Christ and in what we know of Him. This relationship is lasting, like that between Barth and his immediate family.

Paul says that there are four solid legs for Christian unity: 1) because there is a "consolation in Christ," 2) because there is a "comfort of love," 3) because there is a "fellowship of the Spirit," and 4) because there is an experience of the "tender mercies and compassions" of God. Because of these four things you and I are to be "like-minded, having the same love, being of one accord, of one mind" (2:1, 2). It is because you and I are members of God's family, and have learned from Him, that we must live in peace and unity with one another.

Let us be very honest with each other at this point. You and I will always be tempted to divisiveness in ways that will injure our witness. But in such situations our natural reactions must constantly be overcome. How? Let me illustrate how by this story. At one time, a new road was being constructed underneath the Mall, in Washington, D.C., to carry cars from the Virginia side of the District of Columbia under the busiest part of the city to northeast Washington. When the engineers first began the project they observed that it would be made difficult by the fact that the ground level lies within ten feet of the water level in the Tidal Basin. "If you dig down here to construct a road," they said, "the water will enter and flood the site of the construction, and the result will be a lake midway between the Capitol and the Washington monument." The actual construction proved them right. Consequently, it was necessary to install extra thick walls in the tunnels and to place pumps in operation that run constantly to offset the pressure of the water. If the pumps should stop, the tunnel would soon be flooded and the roadway made useless.

In the same way, there are constant pressures from sin within Christians. These will eventually destroy Christian unity and render our witness useless unless they are offset by the supernatural realities of Christian comfort, fellowship, love, mercy, and compassion. Have you found these things real in your relationship to God? Of course you have, if you are a believer in the Lord Jesus Christ. In that case you are also to allow them to become realities in your relationships with other Christians.

CONSOLATION IN CHRIST

The first reality to which Paul points is consolation, consolation in Christ. In our day "console" means largely to comfort, and consolation is what we seek to give to someone in a state of grief or shock. In the time of the King James translators, however, the word "consolation" meant more than this. It meant encouragement or support. Consequently, the word came to be used in architecture for a bracket used to support a cornice or part of an arch. And it was used in music for the cabinet of an organ, the part that supports the stops. Paul was speaking of the encouragement to unity that Christians find in Christ. Hence, the Revised Standard Version renders this phrase, "So if there is any encouragement in Christ." And Phillips paraphrases, "Now if your experience of Christ's encouragement and love means anything to you . . . live together in harmony, live together in love."

What is this encouragement in Christ? It is the support Jesus Christ gave to His followers to live together in love. Jesus taught that the disciples were to covet the lowest places at the table, giving honor to the other person. He taught that love was to be their highest virtue. He prayed for all who should believe on Him through the word of the disciples, "that they all may be one, as thou, Father, art in me, and I in thee, that they also may be one in us; that the world may believe that thou hast sent me" (John 17:21). I know that some teachers take this to refer only to a so-called spiritual unity which all believers possess, regardless of their actual deeds and feelings. And I know that there is such a unity. There is a sense in which all who confess

Christ's name are actually one in Him. But I do not believe that this is what John is describing. This is a visible unity. It is not an organizational unity, of course. For Christ did not come to establish an organization. But it is still a visible unity, for it is a unity that the world can see and on the basis of which people can come to believe in Jesus. This unity must be expressed in deeds, gestures, and speech — in short, in the way you think about, talk to, and act with other Christians.

Can you accept the fact that this type of unity is what Jesus desires for you? Can you accept the fact that He actually encourages you to achieve it and offers to support you in the attempt? If you have difficulty with this, it may be because you are more interested in your own desires than in His wishes. And you must ask Him to correct that fault in you.

THE INCENTIVE OF LOVE

The second reality of the Christian life bearing on unity is the incentive of love. Paul knew that Christians are hard to get along with. They were probably as hard to get along with in his day as they are in ours. But Paul also knew that the Christian had a duty to see more than the other Christian's faults. The Christian must also see the person, and he must love him with a love patterned on the love with which God the Father loves us. The person who really loves the other Christian in this way will not seek to separate from him because he is cantankerous or because he sees some minor doctrine differently. He will seek to know him, to learn from him, and to help him on spiritually as both together advance in the Christian life.

As you seek to do this, always remember that your love is to be patterned on God's love. In fact, your love is actually to be an outpouring of His love through you as you are transformed by the indwelling presence of His Spirit. Jesus Christ taught this to His disciples just before His crucifixion. He said, "A new commandment I give unto you, that ye love one another; as I have loved you, that ye also love one another" (John 13:34). This statement leaves no room for qualification. It is sanforized against all shrinkage to human proportions. Your love must be as pure for other Christians as Christ's love is for you.

Have you experienced this love? If you are a believer, you have understood something of its meaning. Does God cast away the one who offends Him? or makes a doctrinal mistake? or sins? Not at all! On the contrary, His love reaches out even farther as He seeks to draw the sinner to Himself. That love must flow through you, and it must be your pattern. It must be your incentive as you live with other Christians.

CHRISTIAN FELLOWSHIP

The third thing Paul mentions is Christian fellowship. In an earlier chapter ("A Great Fellowship," Phil. 1:3-5) we saw that this is not merely a human fellowship, like the fellowship between friends who have a number of things in common. It is not man-centered. The fellowship which exists between Christians is a fellowship created by God. And it exists, not because we may have much in common, but because by grace we have been made mutually dependent members of Christ's body.

This dimension of the Christians' fellowship is taught clearly in the opening verses of I John. After beginning his letter with an exalted confession of the deity of the Lord Jesus Christ, John goes on to speak of Christian fellowship. He says, "That which we have seen and heard declare we unto you, that ye also may have fellowship with us [that is, a horizontal fellowship between ourselves and other Christians]; and truly our fellowship is with the Father, and with his Son, Jesus Christ [that is, a vertical fellowship between the individual Christian and God]" (I John 1:3). What does this mean? It means that because you have been brought into a vertical fellowship with God by grace there must also be a horizontal fellowship that extends outward to embrace other Christians.

Moreover, you cannot even claim one aspect of that fellowship unless you have the other, for John goes on to say, still speaking about fellowship, that if we walk in darkness where our Christian brother is concerned we do not have fellowship with the Father. "If we say that we have fellowship with him, and walk in darkness, we lie, and do not the truth; but if we walk in the light, as he is in the light, we have fellowship one with another, and the blood of Jesus Christ, his Son, cleanseth us from all sin" (I John 1:6, 7).

Do you have a Christian brother with whom you are not speaking or a member of your household who is a Christian but with whom you are on very bad terms? Are there Christians of another denomination who are anathema to you and with whom you will not have fellowship? If that is so, then I tell you on the authority of these verses that there is something lacking in your own relationship to God. Your lack of fellowship with the other Christian is not of God's doing. It is your doing, and it indicates a lack of fellowship with Him. His Spirit seeks to draw you together. Participation in the Spirit is one of the strongest incentives for true harmony.

MERCIES AND COMPASSIONS

The fourth element in Paul's appeal for unity is the Christian's knowledge of God's mercy and compassion. Compassion is a word that is used both of men and of God, but this is not true of the Greek word translated mercy. This word is always related to God. It is the word that occurs in Romans 12:1: "I beseech you therefore, brethren, by the mercies of God. . . ." It occurs in II Corinthians 1:3: "Blessed be God, even the Father of our Lord Jesus Christ, the Father of mercies, and the God of all comfort." And both "mercy" and "compassion" are used in James 5:11: "The Lord is compassionate and of tender mercy."

In the light of these verses it is clear that Paul is appealing to the believer's experience of mercy from God. Are you a believer in the Lord Jesus Christ? If so, then you have experienced God's mercy. You deserved hell. Yet He loved you and died for you; He leads you in this life and will yet lead you to heaven. You have known great mercy. How, then, can you fail to show mercy to those who also confess Christ's name, even though they might have offended you or disagreed with your interpretation of Scripture?

How does the matter of Christian unity stand with you? Are there divisions that ought not to exist? Are there hard feelings? Are there rationalizations for divisive, non-Christian conduct? The Bible says, "If there be, therefore, any consolation in Christ, if any comfort of love, if any fellowship of the Spirit, if any tender mercies and compassions, fulfill ye my joy, that ye be like-minded, having the same love, being of one accord, of one mind." Jesus said, "By this shall all men know that ye are my disciples, if ye have love one to another."

17.

Living for Others

(Philippians 2:3, 4)

SEVERAL YEARS AGO there was a well-known advertisement for a brand of underwear called BVDs — from the initial letters in the name of the firm that manufactured it. The advertisement read: "Next to myself I like BVDs best." Naturally the advertisement was based on the fact that underwear is worn next to the skin. But the humor came from the equally well-known fact that no one is better liked by anyone than the individual himself. All men look out for Number One. And most people are really only happy when they can look about them and sing:

> Oh, what a beautiful morning!
> Oh, what a beautiful day!
> I've got a beautiful feeling,
> Everything's going my way.

The concern of each man for himself is so well ingrained in human nature that almost no one contests it. And the policies of governments as well as the conduct of millions of individuals flows from it.

Our text is the Christian refutation of this principle, for it says that the one who has believed in Christ is first of all to look out for someone else. Paul writes, "Let nothing be done through strife or vainglory, but in lowliness of mind let each esteem others better than themselves. Look not every man on his own things, but every man also on the things of others" (2:3, 4). The New English Bible says, "There must be no room for rivalry and personal vanity among you, but you must humbly reckon others better than yourselves. Look to each other's interest and not merely to your own."

Paul has been speaking to the Christians at Philippi about proper Christian conduct. He has told them that they are citizens of heaven and that they should be united in an aggressive proclamation of the Gospel. He now applies these themes to the conduct of the individual believer. One commentator has written, "Paul does not leave the

118

question of the worthy life which produces the steadfast stand until he brings it to rest on the worthy life as it is found in the individual, a man not of self-seeking conceitedness, but with a correctly humble estimate of himself, seeking the welfare of others and putting them first. Steadfastness depends on unity, and unity depends on me." *

A Christian Principle

The principle that Paul is stating here is one that is found throughout the New Testament. The unbeliever naturally puts himself first, others second, and God last. And he may think that he merits the order. The Bible teaches that we should reverse the series. God is to be first; others must be second; and we must come last. The Bible says, "Bear ye one another's burdens, and so fulfill the law of Christ" (Gal. 6:2). "For though I am free from all men, yet have I made myself servant unto all, that I might gain the more. . . . I am made all things to all men, that I might by all means save some" (I Cor. 9: 19, 22). "Be kindly affectioned one to another with brotherly love, in honor preferring one another" (Rom. 12:10). "We, then, that are strong ought to bear the infirmities of the weak, and not to please ourselves. Let every one of us please his neighbor for his good to edification" (Rom. 15:1, 2).

This is the heart of Christian conduct. Jesus gave Himself for others. The follower of Christ is also to give himself for others. Jesus said that His own would feed the hungry, clothe the naked, visit the prisoner, make welcome the one who is lonely (Matt. 25:31-46). And he added, "Inasmuch as ye have done it unto one of the least of these my brethren, ye have done it unto me" (verse 40).

The Fall of Satan

I imagine that you may be tempted to dismiss the force of these verses by attempting to put them aside, as if they were only one of a very great number of things a Christian is expected to do and are therefore not very important. If you are doing this mentally, let me warn you that you cannot get away with it at all. In the first place, a command is not any less important just because it is one of a large number of commands, just as telling the truth on Monday is not unimportant because you are also expected to tell the truth on Tuesday, Wednesday, Thursday, Friday, Saturday, and Sunday. Secondly, the commands to care for others are not really on an equal footing with many incidental matters. Care for another person is at the heart of a

* J. A. Motyer, *Philippian Studies* (Chicago: Inter-Varsity Press, 1966), pp. 71, 72.

right relationship to God. And all rebellion against God is inevitably linked to a corresponding disregard for others.

This is seen beyond any doubt in the story of the fall of Lucifer by which the "star of the morning" became Satan. The story itself is recorded in the twenty-eighth chapter of Ezekiel. This is a difficult passage, but several things are clear. First, Ezekiel does speak of Satan. For although the first half of the chapter (verses 1-10) is spoken (no doubt quite literally) to the earthly prince of Tyre, the second half of the chapter (verses 11-19) deals with a figure who has supernatural attributes and who apparently stands behind the earthly ruler as the power behind his throne. Paul warns against such principalities and powers when he warns the Christian that our warfare is not against flesh and blood (Eph. 6:12). In this context the devil is called the King of Tyre, not the Prince of Tyre. And the passage teaches that this figure was originally the highest of all created beings.

The second thing that is clear from Ezekiel twenty-eight is that Lucifer (or Satan) was entrusted with the worship of God by the creation. The passage speaks of sanctuaries. It says that the figure described here was the anointed Cherub. Only kings and priests were anointed in the Old Testament period. And it says that it was Lucifer's task to handle certain merchandise for God. We must not be misled at this point by our use of the term merchandise to describe only material items, for the word correctly refers to anything that passes through one's hands. Apparently Satan passed the commands of God down to the lower orders of creation and at the same time passed the worship of the creation back to God. In this he exercised the offices of a king of the creation and of a priest before the Lord.

The third clear point in the passage is that Lucifer mishandled the merchandise of the creation through pride. This was sin, and it brought instant judgment. Instead of passing the worship of the creation on to God, as he was created to do, Lucifer began to retain that worship for himself. Ezekiel says, "Thou wast perfect in all thy ways from the day thou wast created, till iniquity was found in thee. By the multitude of thy merchandise they have filled the midst of thee with violence" (verses 15, 16). Isaiah adds in a similar passage, "O Lucifer, son of the morning! How art thou cut down to the ground, who didst weaken the nations! For thou hast said in thine heart, I will ascend into heaven, I will exalt my throne above the stars of God . . . I will be like the Most High" (Isa. 14:12-14).

Why "the Most High"? In one of his last books, *The Invisible War*, Dr. Donald Grey Barnhouse asks why from all the possible names of God — and there are almost four hundred of them in the Bible — did

Satan choose the name "the Most High"? "Why did he not say, I will be like the Creator? Why did he not aspire to be like God in His names of Savior, Redeemer, Comforter? Why did he not desire to be like the Eternal Word, the Shepherd, the I AM, the Light, the Way, the Life, the Truth, or any of the other names by which we may know our God?" The answer may be found by pointing to the meaning of the name "the Most High" where it first occurs in Scripture.

"Back in the story of Abram we have the record of an incident revealing the inwardness of the name 'the Most High.' Abram was returning home after the battle with the kings and the deliverance of Lot. We read that 'Melchizedek, king of Salem, brought forth bread and wine . . . and he blessed him, and said, Blessed be Abram of the most high God, possessor of heaven and earth . . .' (Gen. 14:18, 19). Here is the key to the pride of Satan. God is revealed as *El Elyon,* the Most High God, and in this character He is 'the Possessor of heaven and earth.' This is what Lucifer wanted to be. His rebellion was not a request for God to move over so that he might share God's throne. It was a thrust at God Himself. It was an attempt to put God out so that Satan might take his place as possessor of the heavens and the earth." *

How terrible this is! We know from the Word of God that the plan did not succeed. We learn too that Satan and all his hosts will one day suffer a total and permanent defeat. But the plan succeeded well enough — although only by the forbearance of God — that it brought misery to millions of men and angels and still continues to do so. The chief good of the creation lies in communion with God. In opposition to this truth Lucifer exalted himself and brought misery to those who followed him.

THE GREAT ALTERNATIVE

What a contrast we have when we look at Jesus Christ. Instead of exalting Himself, which He had every right to do, Jesus emptied Himself of all outward aspects of His glory and became man for man's salvation. We read a few verses farther on in Philippians, "But [he] made himself of no reputation, and took upon him the form of a servant, and was made in the likeness of men; and, being found in fashion as a man, he humbled himself and became obedient unto death, even the death of the cross" (2:7, 8). Jesus Christ humbled Himself for others.

Think what the self-denial of Jesus meant to the spotless Lamb of

---

* Donald Grey Barnhouse, *The Invisible War* (Grand Rapids: Zondervan Publishing House, 1965), p. 50.

God. In the first place, it meant living in a world of impurity and, to His mind, of the most revolting sin. Imagine yourself stepping for an hour into the lowest moral environment you can imagine, into the company of men promoting the sale of debilitating drugs, into the company of prostitutes, homosexuals, or of hardened criminals awaiting execution. That would only be a suggestion of what the incarnation meant to Christ.

Then, too, His coming meant death upon the cross. A great deal of sentimental emotion has grown up around the cross in the last twenty centuries, but we must not think of it that way. The cross was a symbol of the most severe suffering known in Christ's day. The victims died from exposure and from a slow suffocation caused by the muscular fatigue of the diaphragm. Yet Jesus, knowing all of this and understanding that this was to be the climax of His ministry, faced it without flinching. Mark describes the moment in which this inflexibility first impressed itself on the disciples. "And they were on the way going up to Jerusalem, and Jesus went before them; and they were amazed and, as they followed, they were afraid. And he took again the twelve, and began to tell them what things should happen unto him, saying, Behold, we go up to Jerusalem; and the Son of man shall be delivered unto the chief priests, and unto the scribes; and they shall condemn him to death, and shall deliver him to the Gentiles. And they shall mock him, and shall scourge him, and shall spit upon him, and shall kill him; and the third day he shall rise again" (Mark 10:32-34).

Did Jesus relish these things? Of course not! They were as dreadful to Him as they would have been to you. Yet He endured them, denying Himself for our sakes. How glad we should be that Jesus did not look first upon His own things, but on the things of others!

Spiritual Warfare

It should be evident from all of this that when Paul admonished the Philippians to "esteem others better than themselves" and to "look first on the things of others" he was actually carrying them to the frontier of that great war being waged between the powers of light and darkness.

Perhaps you have heard ministers speak of the Christian's warfare for souls, that great battle which is being waged for the hearts and minds of men. That is a great battle, but there is another that is equally important. It is an internal battle, and the point is not whether you will preach or witness but whether you are becoming the kind of man or woman who will love people and will give yourself for them in the sense that Jesus Christ gave Himself for us. God deals in quality, not quantity. And He wants men to reproduce the qualities of Christ.

Will you do that? Well, you might say, I'd like to, but I don't think I can. Of course, you can't — not in yourself. But God will do it in you as you yield to Him and seek the outworking of His own nature in your life.

How to Live for Others

How may a person live for others? If this is to be true of you, at least three things must happen.

First, you must admit that in yourself you do not care for others and that, left to yourself, your choice will always be Satan's choice rather than the choice of Jesus Christ. Your way will be the way of self-aggrandizement and pride. And it will always be harmful to others. In one of the chapters of *Mere Christianity* C. S. Lewis discusses this problem, asking at the end how it is possible to acquire a character that will truly deny itself for others. He calls it humility. "If anyone would like to acquire humility, I can, I think, tell him the first step. The first step is to realize that one is proud." He adds that it is "a biggish step, too. At least, nothing whatever can be done before it" (p. 99).

The second step is to humble oneself before God. Peter writes, "All of you be subject one to another, and be clothed with humility; for God resisteth the proud, and giveth grace to the humble. Humble yourselves, therefore, under the mighty hand of God" (I Peter 5:5, 6). Maybe you will think that such a relationship is odd. You imagine that if you humble yourself before God, admitting His worth, you have every right to expect that others should be humbled before you. But it does not work this way at all. To see God aright is to admit your total unworthiness. If you will say with Peter, "Depart from me; for I am a sinful man, O Lord" (Luke 5:8), or with Isaiah, "Woe is me! For I am undone, because I am a man of unclean lips, and I dwell in the midst of a people of unclean lips" (Isa. 6:5), you will have little cause for setting yourself and your own interests above others.

The final step involves a daily fellowship with Christ. He is the source of our life, and we must stay close to the source if we are to realize the self-giving life He advocates. Without Him we can do nothing. On the other hand, says Paul, "I can do all things through Christ, who strengtheneth me.'"

Watchman Nee, the Chinese evangelist, tells of a Christian he once knew in China. He was a poor rice farmer, and his fields lay high on a mountain. Every day he pumped water into the paddies of new rice. And every morning he returned to find that an unbelieving neighbor who lived down the hill had opened the dikes surrounding the Christian's field to let the water fill his own. For a while the

Christian ignored the injustice, but at last he became desperate. What should he do? His own rice would die if this continued. How long could it go on? The Christians met, prayed, and came up with this solution. The next day the Christian farmer rose early in the morning and first filled his neighbor's fields; then he attended to his own. Watchman Nee tells how the neighbor subsequently became a Christian, his unbelief overcome by a genuine demonstration of a Christian's love for others.

Can you live for others? At work? At home? With friends, enemies, or relatives? If you are a believer in the Lord Jesus Christ, it is not only possible, it is also an important aspect of your calling.

18.

The Great Parabola

(Philippians 2:5-11)

IN THE FOURTEENTH CHAPTER of Isaiah there are two verses that tell of the thoughts that entered Lucifer's head at the moment when he first rebelled against God. Isaiah writes, "For thou hast said in thine heart, I will ascend into heaven, I will exalt my throne above the stars of God; I will sit also upon the mount of the congregation, in the sides of the north, I will ascend above the heights of the clouds, I will be like the Most High" (Isa. 14:13, 14). Every verb in this passage, every image, points to Satan's desire to rise to the apogee of God's universe. I will ascend above the clouds, above the stars, above the heavens. I will sit on the mount of the congregation. I will be like the Most High. Satan boasted that he would go up. But the words that follow speak of his actual destiny: "Yet thou shalt be brought down to sheol, to the sides of the pit."

The second chapter of Philippians contains the New Testament counterpart to Satan's words in Isaiah. "Let this mind be in you, which was also in Christ Jesus, who, being in the form of God, thought it not robbery to be equal with God, but made himself of no reputation, and took upon him the form of a servant, and was made in the likeness of men; and, being found in fashion as a man, he humbled himself and became obedient unto death, even the death of the cross. Wherefore, God also hath highly exalted him, and given him a name which is above every name, that at the name of Jesus every knee should bow, of things in heaven, and things in earth, and things under the earth, and that every tongue should confess that Jesus Christ is Lord, to the glory of God the Father" (2:5-11).

These verses have been called the great parabola of Scripture, for they picture the descent of the Lord Jesus Christ from the highest position in the universe down . . . down . . . down to His death on the cross, and then they carry the mind of the reader up again to see Him seated once more on the throne of His glory before which every knee shall bow. "I will go up . . . up . . . up," said Satan. "You will be cast down to hell," God answered. "I will go down to the cross," said Jesus. "You will be given a name that is above every name," said God our heavenly Father.

This passage is among the most glorious sections of the New Testament. In these few verses we see the great sweep of Christ's life from eternity past to eternity future. And we are admitted to the breathtaking purposes of God in man's salvation.

EARLY CHRISTIANITY

These verses are also remarkable even from the point of view of early Church history. And they must be considered briefly in this context. The apostle Paul is talking about a man, Jesus of Nazareth, who had lived only a generation earlier in Jerusalem. He is stating tremendous things about Him. And yet he says these things in such a way that we know he is neither inventing doctrines, nor arguing for a hotly contested position, but merely presenting in a general way what he knew to be the accepted teaching of all the Christian churches. Suppose someone said this about a man who had lived in 1940. It would be preposterous, unbelievable. And yet Paul says these things as if everyone — certainly all Christians — knew them to be true beyond question.

One of the great English commentators on this book has written, "We have here a chain of assertions about our Lord Jesus Christ, made within some thirty years of His death at Jerusalem; made in the open day of public Christian intercourse, and made (every reader must feel this) not in the least in the manner of controversy, of assertion against difficulties and denials, but in the tone of a settled, common, and most living certainty. These assertions give us on the one hand the fullest possible assurance that he is man, man in nature, in circumstances and experience, and particularly in the sphere of relation to God the Father. But they also assure us, in precisely the same tone, and in a way which is equally vital to the argument in hand, that he is as genuinely divine as he is genuinely human." * These verses bring us near to the bedrock of the early Christian faith and preaching.

What do these verses contain? The answer is that they contain most of the distinctive articles of the Christian creed. They teach the divinity of Christ, His pre-existence, His equality with God the Father, His incarnation and true humanity, His voluntary death on the cross, the certainty of His ultimate triumph over evil, and the permanence of His ultimate reign. How foolish in the light of these statements

---

* H. C. G. Moule, *Philippian Studies* (Glasgow: Pickering & Inglis, n.d.), p. 97.

are the views of scholars who attempt to dismiss the distinct doctrines of Christianity as late developments in the history of an historically conditioned and slowly evolving Church. There was no evolution of these doctrines. There were repeated attempts to clarify them. The history of theology is full of examples. There were often advances in the direction of a fuller understanding of their significance. Many teachers have brought additional insights. But the doctrines themselves were always known. Christianity is Christ — this Christ. And these things were believed about Him from the beginning.

In the following studies we shall be taking a close look at the statements made in this passage about the Lord Jesus. At this point it would be valuable to take a broader view of the passage. Only after we have seen it in this way, like a mountain climber gazing across the valley at the peak he is going to climb, shall we begin the step-by-step ascent.

The Pre-eminence of Jesus

The first view we have of Jesus is in reference to His pre-incarnate state. Here He is pre-eminent. Paul says that before the incarnation Jesus was in the form of God and was God's equal. These words do not mean that God has a material form, but only that Jesus Christ possesses all of God's attributes. They mean that He is God. Is God omniscient? So is Jesus. Is God all-powerful? So is Jesus. Is God the creator, the redeemer, the truth, the way, the life, the past, the present, the future? So is Jesus. Paul's phrase, "being originally in the form of God," is a deliberate claim of His divinity.

Here Paul's words soar to the same height to which John soars in the magnificent prologue to his gospel. "In the beginning was the Word, and the Word was with God, and the Word was God. The same was in the beginning with God. All things were made by him; and without him was not anything made that was made. In him was life; and the life was the light of men" (John 1:1-4). The same pre-eminence was taught by Jesus Himself when He referred in prayer to "the glory which I had with thee before the world was" (John 17:5). This is Christ's past glory. It is this great pre-eminence that gives all value to the citation of Christ's life as the ultimate pattern of humility and self-sacrifice.

His Condescension

The second view of Jesus is in His condescension. Christ had been above all men, above all angels, and yet He became lower than both in love for men and in obedience to His heavenly Father. Even Paul, who himself had suffered beatings, and shipwrecks, torture and stoning, would never have had to go to the extremes which Jesus suffered. Paul was a Roman citizen and was exempt from crucifixion. There was no depth to which Jesus did not go.

We can imagine the scene that must have taken place in heaven on the eve of Christ's birth in Bethlehem. God is omniscient, but the angels are not. And the Bible tells us that there are aspects of salvation which the angels do not understand but "desire to look into" (I Peter 1:12). We must imagine, therefore, that something like rumors of Christ's descent to earth had been circulating around heaven and that for weeks the angels had been contemplating the form in which Christ would enter human history. Would He appear in a blaze of light bursting into the night of the Palestinian countryside, dazzling all who beheld Him? Perhaps He would appear as a mighty general marching into pagan Rome as Caesar did when he crossed the Rubicon. Perhaps He would come as the wisest of the Greek philosophers putting the wisdom of Plato and Socrates to foolishness by a supernatural display of intellect. But what is this? There is no display of glory, no pomp, no marching of the feet of the heavenly legions! Instead Christ lays His robes aside, the glory which was His from all eternity. He steps down from the heavenly throne and becomes a baby in the arms of a mother in a far eastern colony of the Roman empire. At this display of divine condescension the angels are amazed; and they burst into such a crescendo of song that even the shepherds hear them on the hills of Bethlehem.

CHRIST IN GLORY

The final picture we have is of Jesus again on the throne of heaven. Four times in His ministry Jesus spoke on the text: "Whosoever shall exalt himself shall be abased; and he that shall humble himself shall be exalted" (Matt. 18:4; 23:12, Luke 14:11; 18:14). And He lived the text. His own life is the greatest example of that principle.

The first half of each clause in the sentence — "Whosoever shall exalt himself shall be abased; and he that shall humble himself shall be exalted"— has an active verb. The individual must humble himself, rather than exalt himself. The second half of each clause has a passive verb: "shall be abased" and "shall be exalted." The individual is exalted by God. We find the same thing in the book of Philippians. Everything that is said in the first four verses of Philippians 2:5-11 has Jesus Himself as the subject. *He* thought it not robbery to be equal with God. *He* made Himself of no reputation. *He* became obedient. The second half of the passage has God as the subject, and Jesus is passive: "Wherefore, God also hath highly exalted him, and given him a name which is above every name, that at the name of Jesus every knee should bow."

Isn't that wonderful? Jesus shall reign, and God the Father will see to it. How glorious! But the thought is solemn also, for it embraces all of mankind. You will see Him. You will bow before Him. Will it be in love and adoration as you fall gratefully before the one who loved you and died for you? Or will it be by compulsion as you are forced to your knees by the angels moments before you are removed from His presence forever? Jesus said, "Come unto me all ye that labor and are heavy laden, and I will give you rest." He is your Savior. He loves you. He gave Himself for you. Today is still the day of His mercy and grace. Won't you come to Him today?

LOOKING UNTO JESUS

A final item of importance is the way in which this splendid passage is introduced into the letter to the Philippians. It is not an abstract statement of a difficult doctrine. It is not at all a controversial section. It is simply a part of Paul's argument to the hearts of his readers on behalf of Christian conduct.

Bishop Handley Moule, whose work was briefly quoted earlier, has an excellent passage on this theme. He writes:

> St. Paul is not here, as elsewhere in his epistles, combating an error of faith; he is pleading for a life of love. He has full in view the temptations which threatened to mar the happy harmony of Christian fellowship at Philippi. His longing is that they should be "of one accord, of one mind"; and that in order to that blessed end they should each forget himself and remember others. He appeals to them by many motives; by their common share in Christ, and in the Spirit, and by the simple plea of their affection for himself. But then — there is one plea more; it is "the mind that was in Christ Jesus," when "for us men and for our salvation He came down from heaven, and was made man, and suffered for us." Here was at once model and motive for the Philippian saints; for Euodia, and Syntyche, and every individual, and every group. Nothing short of the "mind" of the Head must be the "mind" of the member; and then the glory of the Head (so it is implied) shall be shed hereafter upon the member too: "I will grant to him to sit with Me in My throne, even as I also overcame, and am set down with My Father in His throne."
>
> What a comment is this upon that fallacy of religious thought which would dismiss Christian doctrine to the region of theorists and dreamers, in favor of Christian "life"! Christian doctrine, rightly so called, is simply the articulate statement, according to the Scriptures, of eternal and vital facts, that we may live by them. The passage before us is charged to the brim with the doctrine of the person and the natures of Christ. And

why? It is in order that the Christian, tempted to a self-asserting life, may "look upon the things of others," for the reason that this supreme fact, his Savior, is in fact thus and thus, and did in fact think and act thus and thus for His people. Without the facts, which are the doctrine, we might have had abundant rhetoric in St. Paul's appeal for unselfishness and harmony; but where would have been the mighty lever for the affections and the will?

Oh reason of reasons, argument of arguments — the Lord Jesus Christ! Nothing in Christianity lies really outside of Him. His person and His work embody all its dogmatic teaching. His example, "His love which passeth knowledge," is the sum and life of all its morality. Well has it been said that the whole gospel message is conveyed to us sinners in those three words, "Looking unto Jesus." Is it pardon we need, is it acceptance, free as the love of God, holy as His law? We find it, we possess it, "looking unto Jesus" crucified. Is it power we need, victory and triumph over sin, capacity and willingness to witness and to suffer in a world which loves Him not at all? We find it, we possess it, it possesses us, as we "look unto Jesus" risen and reigning, for us on the throne, with us in the soul. Is it rule and model that we want, not written on the stones of Horeb only, but "on the fleshy tables of the heart"? We find it, we receive it, we yield ourselves up to it, as we "look unto Jesus" in His path of love, from the throne to the cross, from the cross to the throne, till the Spirit inscribes that law upon our inmost wills. *

How true that is! How much we all need constantly to look to Jesus! Have you done that? Will you do it? To look to Him is to look to one who is altogether lovely and who is able to satisfy the deep longings of your heart.

* H. C. G. Moule, *Philippian Studies* (Glasgow: Pickering & Inglis, n.d.), pp. 102-104.

19.

The Truth About Jesus Christ

(Philippians 2:6)

HAVING TAKEN A SURVEY of the great Christological passage of the book of Philippians (2:5-11), we settle down now to a verse-by-verse study of the text. In verse 6 Paul writes that before His incarnation Jesus Christ was in the form of God and was God. Phillips paraphrases the verse, "Let Christ Jesus be your example as to what your attitude should be. For he, who had always been God by nature, did not cling to his prerogatives as God's equal." Who is Jesus Christ? The only adequate answer to that question is one that carries the mind back to Christ's equality with God before creation and which projects it forward to see Him reigning with God and as God forever.

ETERNITY PAST

One summer, a friend and I took a trip around the Mediterranean Sea that carried us in time to Luxor, the city in upper Egypt from which tourists may visit the remains of ancient Thebes. Thebes was once the capital of Egypt, and there are extensive ruins there. We had traveled overnight by train from Cairo and had arrived early in the morning to begin our sightseeing in the company of an old guide who had once worked with the Egyptian Department of Antiquities. The first thing we saw was the great temple of Luxor erected by Amenophis III. The columns of this temple are over six feet in diameter and reach high in the air. On top of one column near the edge of the excavated area there was a small house. We were curious about how it got there, and we asked the guide about it.

He said that during the last century, before the excavations at Luxor were begun, the area on which we were standing was covered with sand. It was mostly the outlying area of the modern city and there were a number of small houses scattered about. One local farmer tried to find a solid foundation for his home and scratched about in the sand to find some bedrock on which to build. In time he came

131

upon a smooth stone surface, and he erected his home there. In the desert where the wind is constantly blowing and where the sand shifts according to the air currents, anything permanent will cause the sand to shift away from it. In time this happened to the home of the Egyptian farmer. As the sand drifted away from his cottage the farmer discovered that his house was actually built on a piece of handcarved stone, presumably from an ancient temple. At first he thought it was merely lying in the sand. In time he realized that it was part of a column. It was only after the excavations had begun that the farmer realized that it was a standing column, and after the excavations were completed he found that his home was nearly eighty feet above ground level.

There is a parallel here to some people's understanding of the Lord Jesus Christ. Many people claim that their lives are built on Jesus Christ, but they may know as little about Jesus Christ as that Egyptian farmer knew about the foundation of his home. Many men in our day will admit Christ's existence. Many will acknowledge His example and speak of Him as a great religious teacher. These things are true. And yet by themselves they are as misleading as the belief of the Egyptian farmer that he was building his house on bedrock. Jesus Christ did exist. He was a teacher. But if you can say no more about Him than this, then you have an inadequate understanding of His person. To see Him in proper perspective you must push aside all of the years of human history and must catch a glimpse of Him coexisting with God the Father from eternity.

The New Testament writers do this quite frequently. John writes, "In the beginning was the Word, and the Word was with God" (John 1:1). John later says that the Word became flesh. But the one who became flesh was no other than the one who existed with God and was God from the beginning. In Colossians Paul speaks of Christ, "who is the image of the invisible God" (Col. 1:15). The author of Hebrews writes in a passage that parallels the one in the second chapter of Philippians: "God, who at sundry times and in diverse manners spoke in time past unto the fathers by the prophets, hath in these last days spoken unto us by his Son, whom he hath appointed heir of all things, by whom also he made the worlds; who, being the brightness of his glory, and the express image of his person, and upholding all things by the word of his power, when he had by himself purged our sins, sat down on the right hand of the Majesty on high" (Heb. 1:1-3).

All of these passages teach that Jesus Christ cannot be understood on the basis of His earthly life alone. Jesus Christ is a man. But He is also God. And we must first say that about Him.

THE FORM OF GOD

The same truths are taught in Philippians 2:6 by means of two words that deserve closer study. The first is the Greek word *morphe*. It occurs in the phrase, "being in the form of God." In English the word "form" is generally associated with the outward shape of an object, and it has that meaning in the Bible. Even in English, however, we also give another meaning to the word. We can ask a person, "Are you in good form today?" In this case the word points inward and asks about things that cannot be detected on the surface. Both of these meanings are present in the Greek word, and consequently both apply when the word is used of Jesus. He is "in the form of God." And this means, as one commentator has said, that He "possessed inwardly and displayed outwardly the very nature of God" Himself (J. A. Motyer, *Philippian Studies,* p. 74).

The second word that occurs in Philippians 2:6 of Jesus Christ is *isos,* meaning "equal." We have this word in the scientific terms *isomer, isomorph, isometric,* and in the phrase an *isosceles* triangle. An isomer is a chemical molecule having a slightly different structure from another molecule but being identical with it in terms of its chemical elements and weight. Isomorph means "having the same form." Isometric means "in equal measure." And an isosceles triangle is one with two equal sides. In Philippians 2:6 the word *isos* teaches that Jesus is God's equal.

How quickly these two phrases cut across the lesser confessions of Christ's deity. Many men will admit that Jesus Christ was divine in the sense, so they say, that all men are divine. Men will call Him the Son of God in the sense that we are all sons of God. The late theologian Paul Tillich can speak of Christ's "permanent unity with God" in the sense that we all should attain such unity. But this is not the teaching of Scripture. When Christians speak of the person of the Lord Jesus Christ they are not speaking about any such divinity. They are speaking of the eternal and unique Godhead of the Lord Jesus Christ. And they maintain that He existed eternally as the second person of the Godhead, and as such was equal with God the Father.

Everything that God Almighty is to me, so also is the Lord Jesus Christ. Is that true for you? It should be, for that is the teaching of the Bible. There is no real knowledge of the Father apart from a knowledge of the Son.

THE GLORY OF GOD

The teaching of Philippians 2:6 is also conveyed by a phrase used elsewhere that points emphatically to the divine nature, and consequently is also used of Jesus. The phrase is "the glory of God." Jesus speaks of this glory when He prays: "I have glorified thee on the earth; I have finished the work which thou gavest me to do. And now, O Father, glorify thou me with thine own self with the glory which I had with thee before the world was" (John 17:4, 5). These verses say four things about glory. First, Jesus possessed a glory before the incarnation. Second, this glory was God's glory. Third, He did not have it after the incarnation. And fourth, there is a sense in which He did possess it while on earth, for He revealed it by finishing the work that God gave Him to do.

How can this be? How can Christ possess God's glory, renounce it, and yet have it? And what does the phrase "the glory of God" mean anyhow? When we have understood the real meaning of glory we shall understand these things. And we shall also understand, not only the relationship of Jesus to God before the incarnation, but also what it is He laid aside in the incarnation in order to become man.

In the early years of the Greek language when Homer and Herodotus were writing, there was a Greek verb *(dokeo)* from which the Greek noun *doxa* (meaning "glory") sprang. The Greek verb meant at first "to appear" or "to seem," and the noun that came from it then meant an "opinion." From this meaning we get the English words *orthodox, heterodox,* and *paradox* for "straight opinion," "other opinion," and "contrary opinion." The great theological Greek dictionary edited by Gerhard Kittel gives several pages to document this early history of the words. In time the verb was used only for having a good opinion about some person. And the noun, which kept pace with the verb in this development, came to mean the "praise" or "honor" due to one of whom a good opinion was held. Kings possessed glory because they merited the praise of their subjects. It is in this sense that Psalm 24 speaks of God as the King of glory. "Who is this King of glory? The Lord strong and mighty, the Lord mighty in battle. . . . The Lord of hosts, he is the King of glory" (Ps. 24:8, 10).

At this point, of course, we can see the effect of taking the word over into the Bible and applying it to God. For if a man had a right opinion about God, this meant that he was able to form a correct opinion of God's attributes. The orthodox Jew (the one with correct opinions) knew God as all-powerfull, all-knowing, ever-present, merciful, faithful to His children, holy, just, loving, and so on with all His other perfections. When he acknowledged this he was said to give God glory. God's glory consisted of His intrinsic worth embedded in His character, and all that could be known of God was merely an expression of it.

This understanding of God's glory is reinforced in the English language by a word that means almost the same thing as glory and that might have been used for it had not the French word *gloire* superseded it in everyday speech. This is the Anglo-Saxon word "worth." It too refers to intrinsic character. The worth of a man is his character. The worth of God is God's glory. Consequently, when men are engaged in praising God they are acknowledging His worth-ship. Since these last two syllables are difficult to say together in English, a number of the consonants have been dropped, and our present word "worship" is the result. Philologically the worship of God, the praise of God, and the giving of glory to God are identical.

It is this glory — a glory that embodies the idea of God's intrinsic worth and character — that Jesus claimed to share and to have made known to His disciples. What does it mean when Jesus claims to have glorified the Father on earth or when the disciples are said to have beheld Christ's glory at the wedding feast in Cana? It means that the disciples beheld His character and that this was the character of God. If you have seen Jesus in this way, you have seen the Father.

Shekinah Glory

Alongside this conception there is another and entirely different meaning of the word glory that has nothing to do with the original meaning in Greek and which entered the Greek language at a later time only through its contact with Hebrew religion and culture. It is the idea of "light" or "splendor," and it is found in the Greek language only after the translation of the Old Testament into Greek. The Hebrew historian Josephus (37 — ca. 95 A.D.) is the first non-biblical Greek writer to use it.

In Hebrew thought any outward manifestation of God's presence involved a display of light so brilliant that a man could not approach it. This brilliant outward manifestation of God's presence was described by the word *shekinah,* and in the Greek Old Testament the word *doxa* is often used to translate it. This glory was the radiance that was transferred to the face of Moses during the days he spent upon Mount Sinai with God "so that the children of Israel could not steadfastly behold the face of Moses for the glory of his countenance" (II Cor. 3:7). It was embodied in the cloud that overshadowed the wilderness tabernacle during the years of Israel's wandering and which later filled Solomon's temple in Jerusalem until it was withdrawn to heaven as a result of Israel's sin. Glory accompanied the angels as they appeared to the shepherds to announce the birth of Jesus. It was the glory of Jesus, Moses, and Elijah that the disciples saw on the mount of transfiguration. Glory filled the sky when Jesus appeared to Paul on the road to Damascus, and it left him blinded. It is this glory with which Jesus will be clothed when He returns one day for those who believe on Him and who await His coming.

Put these two meanings of the word "glory" together and you have a clear picture of Christ's oneness with God and of the humbling of Himself that went with the incarnation. Before His incarnation Jesus Christ existed with God and was identical with God both inwardly and outwardly. He shared to the full the divine nature, and He was clothed with the splendor that had always surrounded God's person. During the incarnation Jesus laid aside the outward glory (which would have made it impossible for human beings to approach Him) and took the form of a servant. What remained was God's glory in the inward sense, for even in the flesh Jesus Christ was God and retained all of the divine nature. Finally, in the garden just before His crucifixion, Jesus prayed that He might once more receive the visible glory that He had enjoyed with God before He became man. And He received this when He ascended again into heaven and took His rightful place with God the Father.

If you love the Lord Jesus, the idea of Christ's glory should evoke praise in your heart. But there is something even more personal than this. If you are a child of God, God is conforming you to the image of Jesus Christ. And this means that since Jesus Christ perfectly manifests God's glory, you also are to share that same glory — as amazing and as unbelievable as that may seem. Paul writes, "But we all, with unveiled face beholding as in a mirror the glory of the Lord, are changed into the same image from glory to glory, even as by the Spirit of the Lord" (II Cor. 3:18).

In the preceding verses Paul had been speaking of the veil worn by Moses so that the people might not be blinded by his glory. But now, he says, it is different; now there is no veil between the believer and his Lord. You see Him in Scripture. And in Him you see God's glory. You see God's character in Jesus. And, as you see it, you are changed into the same likeness by the presence of His Spirit in you.

And that is not all. One day you will participate even in the visible glory. For the work begun by Christ's atonement and applied to each believer individually in the moment of his belief in Jesus Christ does not remain unfinished but continues through daily victory over sin in this life to the moment when the entire company of the redeemed stands spotless in the glorious presence of the Father. In that day the glorified body of believers will appear as a brilliant jewel, refracting in a million ways the bright radiance of Him who is the Father of lights and of His Son in whom is no darkness at all. And you and I will not only point to that radiance, we shall also participate in it — to the glory of God.

20.

The Real Tin Soldier

(Philippians 2:7, 8)

In one of the chapters of *Mere Christianity* C. S. Lewis has a winsome illustration of Jesus' incarnation. He says in that chapter, "Did you ever think, when you were a child, what fun it would be if your toys could come to life? Well suppose you could really have brought them to life. Imagine turning a tin soldier into a real little man. It would involve turning the tin into flesh. And suppose the tin soldier did not like it. He is not interested in flesh; all he sees is that the tin is being spoilt. He thinks you are killing him. He will do everything he can to prevent you. He will not be made into a man if he can help it.

"What you would have done about that tin soldier I do not know. But what God did about us was this. The second person in God, the Son, became human himself: was born into the world as an actual man — a real man of a particular height, with hair of a particular color, speaking a particular language, weighing so many stone. . . . The result of this was that you now had one man who really was what all men were intended to be. . . . One tin soldier — real tin, just like the rest — had come fully and splendidly alive." [*] At this point Lewis goes on to show how the other tin soldiers could become real also by what he terms a "good infection" caught by a close association with the real man — Jesus Christ.

The illustration used by Lewis must not be pressed beyond bounds, but it does teach the most essential truths about the incarnation. What is the meaning of the incarnation of Jesus Christ? It is this: Jesus Christ became like us in order that we might become like Him. The incarnation was not an end in itself. It was God's way of coming to man that man might be redeemed from the penalty of sin and then be transformed from within into the image of His Son. The Bible says, "For ye know the grace of our Lord Jesus Christ, that,

---

[*] C. S. Lewis, *Mere Christianity* (New York: Macmillan, 1958), pp. 139, 140.

though he was rich, yet for your sakes he became poor, that ye through his poverty might be rich" (II Cor. 8:9). In the verses which are our text Paul states the first part of the doctrine like this: "But [Christ] made himself of no reputation, and took upon him the form of a servant, and was made in the likeness of men; and, being found in fashion as a man, he humbled himself and became obedient unto death, even the death of the cross" (Phil. 2:7, 8).

He Became Like Us

The second person of the Godhead, the Son, became like us, or rather like each of us should be. The thought is breathtaking. Can God become like man, to feel as we feel and suffer as we suffer? The Bible answers, "Yes." And it does so on many of its pages. Isaiah, for instance, writes, "For unto us a child is *born,* unto us a son is *given*" (9:6). Notice the two verbs in this sentence. Jesus was always God's Son; consequently, as a son He was *given.* In the incarnation Jesus Christ became a man and before that a child. Hence, as a child He is *born,* not given. The divine nature is without beginning. The human nature dates from the moment of His birth in Bethlehem.

There is a similar contrast in two more passages of Scripture. Writing to the Romans, Paul says that Christ "was *made* of the seed of David according to the flesh, and *declared* to be the Son of God with power, according to the spirit of holiness, by the resurrection from the dead" (Rom. 1:3, 4). Jesus Christ was declared to be the Son of God, because He was eternally God's Son. But He was *made* man in the line of His earthly ancestor, David. In exactly the same way, Galatians 4:4 says that "God *sent* forth his Son, *made* of a woman, *made* under the law." As the Son He was sent. But He became man.

In Philippians, the meaning is identical. Paul writes that the one who was in the form of God and was God's equal from all eternity took the form of a man at a particular moment in history. He took upon Himself the form of a servant; He was made in man's likeness.

In these verses Paul uses three different words to describe what it meant for the eternal Son of God to become a man. The first word is the one translated by the English word "form" in the phrase "the form of a servant." The Greek word is *morphe,* and it is precisely the word used earlier when it said that Christ was in "the form of God." First in "the form of God," now in "the form of man." We noted in an earlier study that the Greek word *morphe* has different senses in Greek; it refers both to the inward character of a thing and also to the outward form that expresses its inward character. Hence, when Paul says that Christ took upon Him the form of a servant he means that Christ became man both inwardly and outwardly. We have already seen that Jesus possessed inwardly and displayed outwardly the very nature of God Himself. In the same way He also took upon Himself the very nature of man both inwardly and outwardly. With the exception of being sinful, everything that can be said about a man can be said about the Lord Jesus Christ.

The second word that Paul uses to describe the incarnation is the one translated "likeness." Paul says that Christ was made in the "likeness of man." The word *morphe* refers to man's nature; the second word *homoioma* refers to the outward appearance of humanity. Jesus Christ did not just have a man's feelings, or intellect, or outlook on life, but He looked like a man also. He was born a Jewish baby, and as He grew He looked like others of His race. From a physical standpoint also He was perfectly man.

The third word Paul uses is *schema,* and it occurs in verse eight. Paul writes that Jesus was found "in fashion as a man." Here the thought is of conformity to human experience. Paul says that Christ was not only man inwardly in all His feelings and emotions, that He was not only man outwardly in the sense of physical likeness, but He was also man in the sense that He endured all that we endure in this world — its pressures, its longings, its circumstances, its influences for good and for evil. Jesus knew all this. Consequently, there is nothing about being a man that was not also part of Jesus' experience.

How comforting this should be to every Christian. Christ was like you, and He experienced all that you have experienced. He knows your problems. And because of that He can help you in the midst of them. He can provide salvation, not only for the life to come, but also for this life as you triumph over the things that constantly try to force you into the image of this world.

VICTORY IN TEMPTATION

Think of the ways in which Jesus Christ became like us. In the first place He became like us in temptation, for Hebrews 4:15 says that He was "in all points tempted like as we are, yet without sin." We have a summary account of that in Matthew 4. After His baptism Jesus was driven into the wilderness by God's Spirit, and He then spent forty days in fasting. At the end of this period Satan came to Him, and the temptations began. The first temptation was *physical.* Satan said, "If thou be the Son of God, command that these stones be made bread." We learn the significance of this temptation by the answer which follows. Jesus said, "Man shall not live by bread alone, but by every word that proceedeth out of the mouth of God." The first temptation was to put physical needs above spiritual ones, and Jesus rejected it on biblical principles.

I am sure that you have been tempted like this many times, so let me add this. There is nothing wrong with material things in themselves. God gives them to us, often abundantly, and we may be thankful when they come from His hands. But there is always a temptation to put things in place of God, to seek material objects in place of His work in our lives. Has God called you to a spiritual work — perhaps on the mission field, perhaps with your neighbors — and do you feel unable to do it because you have a house to take care of, children to put through school, or friends you are afraid to leave or alienate? If God has called you to a particular work, He will take care of these other things. Do not allow physical things to keep you from His best for your life.

The second temptation was a *spiritual* one. The devil took Jesus up to Jerusalem and sat Him upon a pinnacle of the temple. He said, "If thou be the Son of God, cast thyself down; for it is written, He shall give his angels charge concerning thee, and in their hands they shall bear thee up, lest at any time thou dash thy foot against a stone." Satan was tempting Christ to presume upon God, to place Himself in a situation that was not of God's leading and then to expect a supernatural deliverance. Jesus answered that a man must not put God to the test.

I think that you have probably been tempted in this way too. God gives you a job to do, and at once you begin to think of something else that would be more spectacular. Perhaps you act in your own way, get into trouble, and then expect God to move in and bring blessing in a situation that was not His will for you originally. This is not venturing out on faith. Faith is believing God's Word and acting on it. This is presumption, and Christ said that you should not tempt God in that way. Instead, you are to go forward under His direction knowing that then He will take care of you and bless your life and testimony.

The third temptation was *vocational*. The devil knew that Christ was to receive the kingdoms of this world, for the fact was told beforehand in the second Psalm: "Ask of me, and I shall give thee the nations for thine inheritance, and the uttermost parts of the earth for thy possession" (verse 8). But he argued that Jesus could have the prize without working for it. Satan said, "Look, the way you are choosing for yourself is the way of the cross. I will give you all of these things myself if only you will fall down and worship me." Again Jesus set His face to go in the way that God had chosen for Him.

There is no temptation that comes to you or me that falls outside the scope of these temptations. There is physical temptation, vocational temptation, and spiritual temptation. And Christ shows the path to victory in them all. Do you stand in similar circumstances? Christ knows it. He has experienced it all. He offers help to you if you will come to Him. As He became like us in temptation, so He would have us become like Him in our ability to withstand it and triumph over sin.

A Pattern in Suffering

Jesus not only became like us in temptation, He also became like us in suffering. He became like us in suffering that our suffering might become like His. This truth runs throughout Scripture, and it does so more and more as we come to the later books of the Bible. In the early days of the Christian Church there was not a great deal of persecution for believers. But as the group of Christians grew, as the force of Christianity became something to reckon with in the social structure of the Roman world, suffering increased for Christians. In these times the sufferings of Jesus took on a new significance for His followers.

A great example is found in I Peter. Peter was writing to Christians who were living in what is now modern Turkey and who were suffering there for the stand they had taken for Jesus. He writes to encourage them, and as he writes he thinks almost inevitably of the sufferings of Jesus Christ. Their suffering was to be like His. They were to suffer patiently — without back-biting, without anger, without bitterness — committing themselves into the hands of God. "For even hereunto were ye called, because Christ also suffered for us, leaving us an example, that ye should follow his steps" (I Pet. 2:21).

The word "example" in this verse is most interesting. It refers to a copybook prepared by a teacher for pupils to copy. It is perfect. The letters are perfect. And it is to be the model as the child tries to scratch the letters out in imitation of the teacher's script. Peter says that Jesus became our "copybook" so that we might pattern our reaction to suffering on His. I wonder if you have noticed how poignant this is as it comes from the pen of Peter. Peter had been the first to say, "Lord, I will follow you anywhere, even to death." And then the cross came, and he denied his Lord. Here, writing to those who were in similar circumstances, Peter encourages Christians to follow after Christ in suffering even as he was now trying to do also.

Like Him in Disappointments

Finally, Jesus Christ not only became like us in temptation, not only like us in suffering, He also became like us in disappointment. Christ wept real tears over Jerusalem: "O Jerusalem, Jerusalem, thou that killest the prophets, and stonest them who are sent unto thee, how often would I have gathered thy children together, even as a hen gathereth

her chickens under her wings, and ye would not!" (Matt. 23:37).
Christ knew disappointments.

And you have disappointments also. You may have disappointments
with your family, with your wife, husband, or children. You may have
disappointments in your work. You may be disappointed in love; the
affection that you have for another may not be returned. You may
think yourself a failure. You may lack purpose in life. But Christ
knows about it. He became like you in all your disappointments, and
as a result He is able to understand your sorrow. Will you let Him
make you like Himself in disappointments? He cast Himself upon God.
He threw Himself upon God's love and upon His 'purposes in human
history. He found God able to help. If you will do that, God will
soothe your disappointments. He will give you a new purpose in this
life. And He will point you with confidence toward the day when all
things will come to perfection in Christ. In that day the tin soldiers
will have become live ones. And you will recognize that God has used
temptation and suffering and disappointment to make you more like
Jesus.

21.

Why the Cross?

(Philippians 2:8)

PHILIPPIANS 2:5-11 HAS BEEN CALLED the great parabola of Scripture. It pictures the descent of Jesus Christ from the highest position in the universe down to His death on the cross, and it carries the mind of the reader back up to see Him seated once again at the right hand of the Father. Philippians 2:8 deals with the lowest point on that curve, for it deals with Christ's death. "And being found in fashion as a man, he humbled himself and became obedient unto death, even the death of the cross."

CENTRALITY OF THE CROSS

The meaning of this verse is of great importance in understanding Christianity. For if it is to the Bible that you must go for an understanding of the meaning of salvation, it is to the cross of Christ that you must turn for an understanding of the Bible. The cross is the central feature of the New Testament. All of the gospels devote an unusually large proportion of their narratives to Christ's final week in Jerusalem culminating in His death and resurrection, and it is no exaggeration to say that the cross overshadows the life of Christ even before this point. Two-fifths of Matthew's gospel is concerned with the final week in Jerusalem. And the events of the same week take up three-fifths of Mark, one-third of Luke, and nearly one-half of John. The very name "Jesus" looks forward to an act of saving significance; for the angel that announced Christ's birth to Joseph said, "Thou shalt call his name Jesus, for he shall save his people from their sins" (Matt. 1:21). Jesus Himself spoke of the suffering which was to come (Mark 8:31; 9:31), linking the success of His mission to the crucifixion: "And I, if I be lifted up from the earth, will draw all men unto me" (John 12:32). John speaks of the crucifixion as that vital "hour" for which Christ came and to which His ministry proceeded (John 2:4; 7:30; 8:20; 12:23, 27; 13:1; 17:1).

Besides that, the cross of Christ is in a real sense the central theme of the Old Testament. The Old Testament sacrifices prefigure Christ's suffering, and the prophets explicitly foretell it. Jesus taught the downcast Emmaus disciples that the Old Testament foretold His death and resurrection: "O foolish ones, and slow of heart to believe all that the prophets have spoken! Ought not Christ to have suffered these things, and to enter into his glory? And beginning at Moses and all the prophets, he expounded unto them, in all the scriptures, the things concerning himself" (Luke 24:25-27). It is not surprising that the centrality of Christ's cross has been recognized by Christians in all ages, even before Constantine made it the universal badge of Christendom. The cross stands as the focal point of the Christian faith. Without the cross the Bible is an enigma, and the Gospel of salvation is an empty hope.

Our Example

This is not to say, of course, that Christians have always agreed on the meaning of Christ's suffering or that some of the explanations of it given by Christians are not inadequate. Some speak of Jesus' death primarily as an example, but this is misleading unless the description is also coupled with a recognition that Jesus died for others as their sinbearer, and that He is their example only because He is first their Savior and Lord. A man who is drowning in the ocean may wish that he had taken better swimming lessons, and he may take them some day. But before he takes them, before he gets his example, he first needs a lifeguard. In the same way Christ must be our Savior before He can be our example.

It is true, of course, that the sufferings of Christ do have value as an example. In fact the verses we are studying in Philippians refer to the sufferings of Jesus as an example of humility and of obedience to the will of God for Christians. In I Peter, too, the patient endurance of Jesus is brought forward as an example to those who were suffering under the strictures of an unyielding Roman rule. Peter writes that they were called to suffer patiently, adding that "Christ also suffered for us, leaving us an example" (I Pet. 2:21).

All this is true, yet the New Testament never forgets the unbridgeable gulf that exists between the suffering of Christ and all other suffering endured by men and women. Christ suffered innocently. And this cannot be said in the same way even of the most innocent men. Moreover, at best men suffer by and for themselves. Of Christ it is said, even by Peter at the very moment when he is appealing to Him as an example, "Christ also suffered for us" (I Pet. 2:21; cf. Gal. 2: 20). And he immediately adds, by way of explanation, "He . . . bore our sins in his own body on the tree, that we, being dead to sins, should live unto righteousness; by whose stripes ye were healed" (I Pet. 2:24).

The idea of an example does not exhaust the meaning of Christ's sufferings. But what does? What do Christ's sufferings mean? The Bible answers: Jesus Christ died to remove sin. He died to satisfy divine justice. He died to reveal God's love.

THE SIN-BEARER

In the first place, Jesus died to remove sin. And He removed it by bearing its penalty Himself. Hebrews 9:26 says, Christ "hath appeared to put away sin by the sacrifice of himself." And Peter is teaching the same thing in the verse just quoted when he says of Christ, "Who his own self bore our sins in his own body on the tree, that we, being dead to sins, should live unto righteousness" (I Pet. 2:24).

This idea sounds strange to modern ears, but it was not strange to Christ's contemporaries. It is an idea drawn from the world of religious sacrifices, and hence it was well known to them. Just as an American would immediately understand a reference to the Boston Tea Party, though it might not be understood by a Russian, and just as a Russian would understand a reference to the battle of Leningrad, though it might not be understood by an Arab, so ancient people understood sacrifices. To them a sacrifice spoke of the removal of sin.

One ceremony enacted in Israel on the Day of Atonement helps us to understand what it means. Early in the day two goats were chosen, one as a sin offering for the sins of the people and one to fill the role of the scapegoat. The high priest was instructed to lay his hands on the head of the scapegoat, thereby identifying himself and his people with it; and he was to confess their sins, symbolically transferring them to the animal which was then led out into the wilderness beyond the city gates to die there. The Bible says, "And Aaron shall lay both his hands upon the head of the live goat, and confess over it all the iniquities of the children of Israel, and all their transgressions in all their sins, putting them upon the head of the goat, and shall send it away by the hand of a fit man into the wilderness. And the goat shall bear upon it all their iniquities unto a land not inhabited" (Lev. 16:21, 22).

This is what Jesus Christ came to do. He came to remove our sin, bearing it in His own person outside the gate of the city. Sin separates men from God. But Jesus removes that sin. He was made sin for us. Paul says, God "hath made him [Christ], who knew no sin, to be sin for us, that we might be made the righteousness of God in him" (II Cor. 5:21). Are your sins upon Him? Has He borne your reproach? Has He suffered for your iniquity? You need only to ask

Him to do it. The Bible says that He will be a sin-bearer for you if you will confess your sin to Him, as Aaron did the sin of the people of Israel, and then trust Him to remove it forever.

GOD SATISFIED

The second reason for Christ's death is that He died to satisfy divine justice. The justice of God calls for the punishment of sin, and the punishment of sin is death. Jesus paid that penalty. He died in our place, satisfying divine justice and leaving nothing for us but God's heaven.

This aspect of the cross of Christ is also taught by a ceremony observed on the Day of Atonement. Leviticus 16 talks about two goats used on the Day of Atonement. One was the scapegoat. But what was the purpose of the other one? The answer is that this goat was used as a sacrifice and that its blood was placed before God within the Holy of Holies in the Jewish temple.

The temples of Solomon and Herod and before that the portable tabernacle of the days of Israel's wandering were composed of two rooms, the outer room just twice the size of the other. The inner room was a square. Within that room was the Ark of the Covenant with its mercy seat, built to the exact specification given to Moses on Sinai. The Ark was a box made of cedar wood and covered with gold. Within it were several objects, the most important being the tables of stone upon which God had written the Ten Commandments. At either end of the Ark facing inward stood the figures of two cherubim. And between them directly over the Ark of the Covenant at the heart of the temple God was understood to dwell. It is a terrifying picture. God's perfect law lies within the Ark, bearing its mute witness against men. God's holy presence rises over the law, poised in judgment and ready to condemn. The scene speaks to us of judgment, and the Ark in this form bears a sentence of death against all people.

But there is more to the symbolism than this. For there was a cover on the Ark of the Covenant called the mercy seat, and upon that cover once a year on the Day of Atonement the high priest placed the blood of the other goat which had just been sacrificed a moment before in the courtyard of the temple. The animal was an innocent substitute. And it was a type of Jesus Christ. Between the law which man had violated and the holy presence of almighty God, symbolized by the space above the Ark, stood the blood. A substitute intervened. The wrath of God was stilled. Consequently, a man might come to God without fear of being devoured by His wrath. In the same way, in Jesus Christ God does not violate His righteousness, but He shows Himself to be a God of great mercy, grace, and love. Jesus satisfies

God's justice. Through faith in His shed blood there is peace with God and access into His presence.

Do you believe that? William Cowper, the great metaphysical poet of the eighteenth century, came to see this meaning of Christ's death as he was reading in the third chapter of Romans. He later wrote, "Immediately I received strength to believe it, and the full beams of the Sun of Righteousness shone upon me. I saw the sufficiency of the atonement he had made, my pardon sealed in his blood, and all the fullness and completeness of his justification. In an instant I believed and received the peace of the Gospel." In 1769 this poet wrote:

> Jesus, where'er Thy people meet,
> There they behold Thy mercy seat;
> Where'er they seek Thee, Thou art found,
> And every place is hallowed ground.

Three years later he wrote these well-known lines:

> There is a fountain filled with blood
> Drawn from Immanuel's veins;
> And sinners, plunged beneath that flood,
> Lose all their guilty stains.

> The dying thief rejoiced to see
> That fountain in his day;
> And there may I, though vile as he,
> Wash all my sins away.

> Dear dying Lamb, Thy precious blood
> Shall never lose its power,
> Till all the ransomed Church of God
> Be saved, to sin no more.

> E'er since, by faith, I saw the stream
> Thy flowing wounds supply,
> Redeeming love has been my theme,
> And shall be till I die.

> Then in a nobler, sweeter song
> I'll sing Thy power to save,
> When this poor lisping, stammering tongue
> Lies silent in the grave.

That is the message of the cross. God's wrath is stilled; man's sin is removed. And the believer is brought rejoicing into God's presence.

THE LOVE OF GOD

There is one more reason for Christ's death. Jesus died to remove sin. Jesus died to satisfy divine justice. But Jesus also died to reveal God's love.

We hear a lot in our day about love — sexual love, selfish love, indulgent love. And generally God is thought to be the author of it. "God is love; God is love," people say. But God is not the author of that kind of love. God's love is not blind love; it is not sinful love. It is a love that sees things as they are and yet moves to punish sin that love might be established in righteousness. This love is seen at the cross. There is hardly a verse in the Bible that speaks of God's love without speaking in the same context, sometimes even in the same sentence, of the cross. "For God so loved the world, that he gave his only begotten Son, that whosoever believeth in him should not perish, but have everlasting life" (John 3:16). "I am crucified with Christ: nevertheless I live; yet not I, but Christ liveth in me; and the life which I now live in the flesh I live by the faith of the Son of God, who loved me and gave himself for me" (Gal. 2:20). "Herein is love, not that we loved God, but that he loved us, and sent his Son to be the propitiation for our sins" (I John 4:10).

The cross is the measure of God's love for you. As you look to the cross you begin to get a feeling of it. From twelve noon until three o'clock when Christ died "there was darkness over the whole land" (Mark 15:33). John Stott says of these hours, "With the darkness came silence, for no eye should see, and no lips could tell, the agony of soul which the spotless Lamb of God endured. The accumulated sins of the whole world and of all history were laid upon Him. Voluntarily He shouldered full responsibility for them. And then in desolate spiritual abandonment that woeful cry was wrung from His lips, 'My God, my God, why hast thou forsaken me?' (Mark 15:34)." * In that moment God the Father turned His back on His beloved Son, and Christ tasted hell for us. That is how much God loves us.

Oh, Christian, look to the cross and marvel at the extent of God's love. If you are uncertain of salvation, look to the cross and find there all that He has done to redeem you. If you are discouraged, look to the cross and see there the height and the depth of His love. If you are apart from Christ and do not yet believe, you also must look to the cross and find there One who has died to remove your sin and to still the demands of God's justice against you forever.

* John R. W. Stott, *Basic Christianity* (Grand Rapids: Wm. B. Eerdmans Publishing Company, 1958), p. 95.

22.

Christ's Greatest Name

(Philippians 2:9-11)

THE FIRST STATEMENTS OF Philippians 2:5-11 cover many of the great doctrines that concern our Lord Jesus Christ. They have taken us from the high point of His glory as the eternal Son of God to the low point of His death on the cross. Paul now moves back up again toward his climax. What is this climax? It is Christ's exaltation; and it is symbolized in a name that is above every name. The name is Lord, the equivalent of God's own name, Jehovah. Paul writes, "Wherefore, God also hath highly exalted him, and given him a name which is above every name, that at the name of Jesus every knee should bow, of things in heaven, and things in earth, and things under the earth, and that every tongue should confess that Jesus Christ is Lord, to the glory of God, the Father" (2:9-11).

A number of commentators have taught that this supreme name given by God is "Jesus." But this is incorrect for several reasons. One writer correctly argues, "First, no name other than Yahweh [Jehovah] has a right to be called 'the name above every name.' Secondly, the movement of verses 9-11 does not stop at the phrase 'gave him the name . . .', but flows straight on to the universal confession that 'Jesus Christ is Lord,' which suggests that the significant thing is the ascription of 'Lord' in *addition* to the names already known. Thirdly, verse 10 is a pretty direct quotation of Isaiah 45:23, where Yahweh [Jehovah], having declared himself to be the only God and the only Savior, vows that he will yet be the object of universal worship and adoration. It is this divine honor that is now bestowed upon the Lord Jesus Christ." *

NAME OF NAMES

The full impact of the truth that Jesus Christ is Lord will be seen only when we realize that the name of Lord is above not only all

---

* J. A. Motyer, *Philippian Studies* (Chicago: Inter-Varsity Press, 1966), pp. 83, 84.

human names but also all of the unique names that have already been given to Jesus.

Suppose that a king was about to bestow an honor on a subject who had never previously distinguished himself. The only names he had ever received from anyone were scoundrel, bum, crook, good-for-nothing, and a dozen others like them. But then he did something that deserved the king's recognition. What would the king say? He would not say, "Arise, Sir Thomas (or whatever his personal name might be)" or "I wish to present you with the Order of Merit." He would say, "Well, you have certainly distinguished yourself. You are a faithful subject." The name "faithful" would be above all of the other names that had previously been given to the man, but it would not be a very great tribute. The title "faithful" would only be one step above nothing. Suppose, however, that there was also a knight of the realm who had already distinguished himself greatly and had been decorated on many occasions. Suppose he had risen to a very high position in the kingdom. And suppose the king wished to honor him. To honor this man the king would need the highest title at his disposal. And it would be especially glorious when measured against the man's other names and honors. Do you see the connection? This is what God did with Jesus. Jesus was abased; now He is honored. Jesus is Lord. And the glory of this title must be measured against His other honors.

Think of the names that have already been bestowed on Jesus. There is the name Messiah, the anointed one. This means that Jesus is the promised deliverer through whom blessing comes to Israel and the Gentile nations. In Him God meets all of the longings of men and brings to fruition all of the currents of history.

Jesus is also the Son of Man. This title was Christ's favorite designation of Himself. Many persons think that this refers only to Christ's humanity, but the phrase means more than that. It refers especially to His coming again in glory. Originally it comes from Daniel, who writes, "I saw in the night visions, and, behold, one like the Son of man came with the clouds of heaven, and came to the Ancient of days, and they brought him near before him. And there was given him dominion, and glory, and a kingdom, that all people, nations, and languages should serve him; his dominion is an everlasting dominion, which shall not pass away, and his kingdom that which shall not be destroyed" (Dan. 7:13, 14). How glorious that Jesus should be called the Son of Man!

Jesus is also called the Son of God. This name points to His divinity. It is the title by which the devil spoke to Jesus (Matt. 4:3, 6); on several occasions it is God's own designation of Him (Matt. 3:17; 17:5); and it is included in Scripture as the high point of the disciples'

verbal confession (Matt. 16:16). John writes, "Whosoever shall confess that Jesus is the Son of God, God dwelleth in him, and he in God"
(I John 4:15).

Jesus is God's Messiah. He is God's Son. He is the Son of Man.
He is our prophet, priest, and king, the Alpha and the Omega, the
door, the Beloved, and many other names. But the title "Lord" is
above them all. It is at the name of Jesus Christ as Lord that every
knee shall bow.

Jesus Is God

Why is the name "Lord" the name that is above every name? Why
not any one of the other titles? Or why not another name entirely?
These questions have several answers, but the most important is that
the title identifies the Lord Jesus Christ with God.

The truth is easily seen in both the Greek and Hebrew usage of the
word. The Greek word for Lord is *kyrios,* the word by which citizens
of the Roman empire acknowledged the divinity of Caesar. This was
an imperial title, and it was never used of the emperors until they
were thought to be deified through a religious ceremony. Therefore, it
was used as a divine title. Within the empire there was a test phrase
used to check the loyalty of the people. It was *Kyrios Kaiser,* and it
meant "Caesar is Lord." By this phrase Christians who would not
say these words were later singled out from pagans and executed.
In those days when a Christian insisted that Jesus is Lord he meant
that Jesus, not Caesar, is divine.

The same meaning is present when the word occurs in Hebrew, only
more so. The Hebrew word is *Adonai,* and it is one of the great
names for God in the Old Testament and in other Jewish writings.
Actually, the name Adonai assumed an extraordinary importance in
Hebrew speech, for in practice it replaced the personal name of God,
Jehovah. No Jew pronounced the word "Jehovah," even when reading
the Bible. Instead he said, "Adonai." In the written Old Testament the
vowel points of the printed word "Jehovah" are even altered to remind the reader to say "Adonai." Against this background it is easy
to see that not only in popular speech but also in Jewish literature
and in the writing and transmission of the Old Testament the word
"Adonai" became almost synonymous with Jehovah, the personal name
of God. Consequently, when the early Christians made their confession
— "Jesus Christ is Lord" — they were actually confessing that Jesus
of Nazareth is the God of Israel, Jehovah, the only true God.

Can you say that about Jesus? Do you know Him as God? Is He
your Lord, your Jehovah? I know that it is not easy for a person to
come to that confession, but it is essential. For all that you will ever

know about God on this earth you will learn as you look to Jesus. Quite a few years ago when my wife was at the University of Pennsylvania she had a friend who acknowledged this verbally but did not understand it. She was not yet a Christian. She began to read the gospel of John together with my wife. They read through three chapters, where Jesus is called God many times, but it was not until the middle of the third chapter and after many weeks of study that the girl suddenly exclaimed, "Why, I see what it means. It means that . . . that . . . Jesus is God." Just think: she had been reading that for weeks and had only at this point come to a full realization of it. Two weeks later she committed her life to the One she now acknowledged to be God.

One more thing must be noted about this word "Adonai." The word contains a personal ending. Adonai does not just mean "Lord" or "God"; it means "my Lord" or "my God." It is the word that Mary used of Jesus in the garden on Easter morning. It is the confession of Thomas, made one week later, that John has used to provide a climax in his gospel. Mary said, "My Lord." Thomas said, "My Lord and my God." In both cases the words were personal. Do you see what this means? It means that it is not enough merely to acknowledge mentally that Jesus Christ is God. The devils also do that and tremble. Jesus must be *your* God. He must be *your* Lord. Is He? If you are to know God, you must receive Jesus Christ as your Lord and personal Savior.

Jesus Is Sovereign

We have already seen one reason why the name Lord is a name that is above every name. It teaches that Jesus is God. But there is another reason also. The name indicates that Jesus Christ is sovereign. Jesus rules as God rules. Today He controls even the smallest things of life. One day He will subdue His enemies forever.

We need to be frank about the Christian life. The Christian life is not an escape from the world's troubles and problems. If it were, God would have taken us out of the world. It is not an escape from temptations. It is not an escape from suffering. The Christian experiences these things, but the Christian life means that he has victory in them. Moreover, he has peace within, knowing that all of these things are in the control of the One who loves him and who does all things well. Paul writes, "And we know that all things work together for good to them that love God, to them who are the called according to his purpose" (Rom. 8:28).

The doctrine of the sovereignty of God or the sovereignty of Jesus Christ has sometimes been called fatalism by enemies of the Gospel.

But it is not fatalism at all. A belief in fatalism or fate is found in the Moslem religion, where it is referred to as "kismet," which means fate. Fate is the impersonal force by which the universe is supposed by Muslims to operate. It is supposed to operate in ways that are totally insensitive to the needs or ends of individuals. This is not the Christian teaching. The Bible teaches that the God who controls all things is not an impersonal deity, but a God who loves us and who orders the events of our lives to lead us forward in line with His perfect and desirable will. It is not meaningless or tragic when difficulties enter your life or when there are temptations. God knows about it. And He has even permitted it to come in order that He might accomplish something in you that will be for your good. In the moments when these things come, as well as in other moments, you must turn to Him and seek His way. As you do, you can be certain that He is making you more and more into the person He would have you be.

JESUS IS COMING AGAIN

There is one other great truth contained in the title "Lord." The title means that Jesus is God. It means that Jesus is sovereign. But it also means that Jesus is coming again. In the second chapter of Hebrews the author of that book says of Jesus that God has put "all things in subjection under his feet. For in that he put all in subjection under him, he left nothing that is not put under him" (Heb. 2:8). This is wonderful, but at this point a break occurs in the thought, and the author adds (as if recognizing what is all too obviously true), "But now we see not yet all things put under him." Jesus is Lord. Jesus is sovereign. But if He is to be Lord completely, He must return to put down the evil that is all too present and to establish His righteous will forever.

Have you ever noticed the names by which Paul refers to Jesus in I Thessalonians 4:13-18, the well-known passage that speaks of Christ's return? Paul has been talking to the Christians in Thessalonica about death, and has argued that since God has raised up Jesus, He will also raise up those who are united to Him by faith. In all of these statements Paul refers to the Lord Jesus Christ by His personal, most human name: Jesus. And that is natural. At this point Paul begins to talk about Christ's return for those who are still living at the end of the Church age. When he starts to speak about Jesus' return, however, he switches the names, no longer referring to Jesus as Jesus but to Jesus as Lord. From this point on the name occurs five times in the verses. "For this we say unto you by the word of the *Lord,* that we who are alive and remain unto the coming of the *Lord* shall not precede them who are asleep. For the *Lord* himself shall descend from heaven with a shout, with the voice of the archangel, and with the trump of God; and the dead in Christ shall rise first; then we who are alive and remain shall be caught up together with them in the clouds, to meet the *Lord* in the air; and so shall we ever be with the *Lord*" (I Thess. 4:15-17). Paul associated the second coming with the fact that Christ is Lord.

Do you look for the Lord's return? The early Christians looked for His coming, and it gave them strength even in their troubles, even in martyrdom. They had a prayer that expressed this hope. It is preserved for us in the Aramaic language at the end of I Corinthians. It is one word, the word *maranatha*. Actually, the word is composed of two Aramaic words run together — the word for "come" and the word for "Lord" — and they can be divided two ways to give two different meanings. The prayer can be read as *"Maran-atha"* which means "Our Lord is coming." Or it can be read as *"Marana-tha"* which means "Our Lord, come!" The second interpretation is the better of the two. The phrase is a prayer. It is a prayer of Christian longing. Moreover, John includes it in that sense in the next to the last verse of the Bible. John writes, "He who testifieth these things saith, Surely, I come quickly. Amen." And he adds, "Even so, *come, Lord Jesus.*"

Is that your prayer? to see Him? to know Him? to see the affairs of the world brought to perfection and to judgment in His own time and in line with His will? It should be. For it has always been the great hope and consolation of Christians.

23.

Every Knee Shall Bow

(Philippians 2:9-11)

ONE EVENING AFTER A CHURCH SERVICE a woman came up to me with a comment on the sermon. I had mentioned Paul in the context of teaching from Romans and she wanted to tell me about him. She said that Paul had always been offensive to her until she had learned something about him from one of her ministers. I said, "What was that?" She said, "Well, that Paul embellished his stories." I said, "What do you mean?" She answered that Paul invented parts of the account of his conversion on the road to Damascus. The first versions of the story were quite simple, according to this woman. There was only a bright light, perhaps a sunstroke. In later versions, she said, Paul added the account of his blindness and the voice of Jesus. She was glad to know this, she said, because it made Paul human.

At this point I began to answer her. I said that her views were not only impossible, they also could not be supported by evidence. A sunstroke does not account for the change that came over the apostle Paul. And there is not even a possibility of spreading out the three accounts of Paul's conversion in Acts over a period of years to document the kind of development about which she was speaking. They were all written years after Paul's conversion, and they are almost identical. At this point the woman broke off the discussion by saying that she preferred to think that Paul was not entirely truthful because it made her feel better in the things she did. I went away thinking how perverse the human heart is when it will not permit the truth even in the face of evidence.

This story sets the background for a study of the final verses of Philippians 2:5-11. Everything up to this point has already happened to the Lord Jesus Christ. It lies in the past. Jesus Christ was in the form of God. He did lay aside His glory and take the form of a man. He died once for man's salvation. He rose again. He ascended into heaven. And He has been given the name that is above every name.

Jesus Christ is Lord. All this has happened, and God has provided men with evidence that these things are so. Still men refuse to admit what God has demonstrated. Like the woman in my story they refuse to acknowledge the facts, preferring their own fantasies to God's truth. And they do this, not from a worthy motive, but because it makes them more comfortable in sin.

Against this attitude of men our text rings out like a thunderclap from heaven. "Wherefore, God also hath highly exalted him, and given him a name which is above every name, that at the name of Jesus every knee should bow, of things in heaven, and things in earth, and things under the earth, and that every tongue should confess that Jesus Christ is Lord, to the glory of God, the Father" (Phil. 2:9-11). According to this verse, the day is coming when the arrogance of men will be ended. Every mouth will be stopped (Rom. 3:19). And everyone will admit that truth is truth, even though he may hate God for it.

DAVID'S LORD

If you read these verses carefully, you will see at once that they are a prophecy. In fact, they are the New Testament equivalent of an Old Testament prophecy: Psalm 110:1 — "The Lord said unto my Lord, Sit thou at my right hand, until I make thine enemies thy footstool." That verse is quoted in the New Testament directly or indirectly at least twenty-seven times. It teaches that the One called David's Lord, the Messiah, will one day reign over all things and that all of His enemies shall be defeated.

Philippians 2:9-11 is the New Testament equivalent of this prophecy. And yet, like most of the revelations given in the New Testament, it tells of things that are not evident in the Old Testament text. First, it tells that the acknowledgment of Christ's rule will take the form of the verbalized confession, "Jesus Christ is Lord." Second, it tells that this confession will be made by all orders of intelligent beings — those in heaven, those on earth, and those under the earth. Finally, it tells that this confession will result in the ascription of glory to the Father.

JESUS CHRIST IS LORD

The acknowledgment of Jesus Christ spoken of in these verses will take the form of the confession, "Jesus Christ is Lord." The title Lord has already been considered in a previous study. It is a name for God (Adonai). Consequently, when it is applied to Jesus Christ it is an acknowledgment that He is God. Jesus Himself said, "He that hath seen me hath seen the Father."

The confession also means that Jesus is the *sovereign* God. The word "Lord" has overtones of rule. Consequently, Jesus is the One who does what is right and who has the power to carry out His decisions.

All of this is true. And yet, the use of the confession in these verses gives to it a slightly different tone simply because it is set in the future at a point in time when the exalted Christ will already have established His rule. There is an illustration of this distinction in Italian history. During the nineteenth century, when Italy was divided into a number of independent states, there was a popular movement for the reunification of Italy under Victor Emmanuel II of Sardinia. He was the first king of the modern state of Italy. But before he became king there was a surge of enthusiasm to drive out the Austrians, keep the French at the borders, and to place this man on the throne. A slogan embodied the hopes of the Italian people during this period. It was composed of the first letters of the Italian phrase meaning "Victor Emmanuel King of Italy." In Italian the phrase is "Victor Emmanuel Re de Italia," and by taking the first letters from each of the Italian words, the patriots produced the slogan VERDI. At this time the great opera composer Giuseppi Verdi was at the apex of his fame. Hence, his name became a symbol of the reunification of Italy. The name was written everywhere just as "Yankee, Go Home" seems to be written everywhere today. In 1861, Victor Emmanuel became king of the united state of Italy, and at the time the word VERDI was still displayed across the country. Now, however, the slogan took on an entirely different meaning. It was no longer a cry of expectation. It was a triumphant acknowledgment of what had already happened.

In exactly the same way the confession "Jesus Christ is Lord" on our lips is expectation, at best an acknowledgment of what is only partially true or true in potential. But the day is coming, the day of which these verses speak, when the confession will stand as a glorious acknowledgment of what has already taken place. Jesus is Lord. But He will then be Lord completely. There will be no more rivals to His throne.

ANGELS, MEN, AND DEMONS

The second important teaching in these verses is the fact that this confession is to be made by every order of intelligent being — by those in heaven, those on earth, and those under the earth.

The King James Version of the Bible uses the word "thing" in each of these phrases, so the verse reads "of things in heaven, and things in earth, and things under the earth." But the word "things" is italicized. Whenever that occurs it means that the word has been added to the English Bible to make what the translators feel is better sense in English, even though there is no corresponding word in Greek. Actually, the three phrases are translations of three adjectives in Greek, and they may refer to either things or people. It is far better to refer them to personalities. In this case the verse means "beings in heaven, beings on earth, and beings under the earth." And it refers to angels, men, and demons. There is great truth in this threefold designation of all intelligent life.

First, the confession will be made by angels. We read about it in more detail in Revelation (chapters 4 and 5). Here we find that there are thousands upon thousands of angels, myriads of angels, that join with the saints in voicing praise to God. I find great encouragement in that. In one of our hymns we sing about the weakness of the praise rendered by men to God. We sing:

> The humbler creation, though feeble their lays,
> With true adoration shall lisp to Thy praise.

Every time we sing that in my church there are members of the congregation who smile. And they smile because it is true. Our praise at best is a lisping. But it is glorious to know that in the day when all of the redeemed stand before God the Father our feeble voices will be swelled by the voices of millions of angels who have seen the great drama of salvation unfold over the ages and who sing out of their great wonder and vast experience.

We also read that this confession will be made by those on the earth: mankind. The book of Revelation seems to imply that this will be an innumerable company of people. There are the twenty-four elders, who symbolize those who believe in Christ during the Church age. There are the 144,000 Jewish converts who believe during the great tribulation. And there are millions of Gentile converts who believe during this same period because of the witness of the Jewish believers. I must admit that when I read these chapters the numbers sometimes seem hard to understand. It seems at times that there are few who believe in Jesus. The number of real believers seems small. And yet, the Bible says that the number is vast.

How can this be? Part of the answer probably comes from a story in the Old Testament. The prophet Elijah was called to perform a dramatic act on Mount Carmel, calling down fire from heaven, and he achieved a great victory. No sooner was the victory won, however, than he began to doubt for his own life and fled into the desert. There he was feeling sorry for himself. He said, "The children of Israel have forsaken thy covenant, thrown down thine altars, and slain thy prophets with the sword; and I, even I only, am left, and they seek my life, to take it away" (I Kings 19:14). The Lord then had to remind him that there were still seven thousand, about whom he did not even know, that had not submitted to the worship of Baal. Perhaps we should remember that. We see at best only a small circle of believers arranged about ourselves, but God has other circles greater than our own and in other places of the world. In every one of these, Christians are bearing witness to what they have learned of Jesus and are praising Him. All of these will one day join with us and with the angels to sing a great paean of praise in heaven.

Verse 10 also says that there is to be a confession of the Lordship of Jesus Christ by those who are under the earth. This means the demons plus those men who have rejected the Gospel and are now confined to Hades. There are different ways of understanding this phrase, of course, and there are commentators who have understood it in terms of the Old Testament saints who were in Paradise in Hades prior to Christ's resurrection. But this has no meaning when we realize that Jesus Christ emptied Paradise in Hades between the moment of His death and the moment of His resurrection and that He took these Old Testament believers to heaven with Him when He ascended to the Father on the first Easter morning. They were the first fruits of His resurrection. Hence, the reference cannot be to these. The reference must be to those who who have rejected the Gospel, and the confession wrung from their lips must be a forced acknowledgment of Jesus.

The word that is used in this verse for "confession" (exomologeo) more often means "to acknowledge" than it does "to confess with thanksgiving." The word occurs eleven times in the New Testament. But out of these eleven instances, four refer to a man confessing his sins, one to Christ's confession of His servants before His Father, and one to Judas' agreeing with the chief priests to betray his master. In each of these cases the word means "to acknowledge" or "to agree." It is in this sense that the word applies to those who have rejected the Gospel. They will not confess that "Jesus Christ is Lord" with gladness, but they will confess it. They will be forced to acknowledge that Jesus Christ is who He said He is — God incarnate, the Savior of the world.

We need to ask ourselves in which way we are going to make that confession. For every one of us will make it some day. You will either make it willingly as you acknowledge Him who is your Savior and Lord, or you will be forced to acknowledge it with bitterness moments before you are banished from God's presence forever. Won't you accept Him now, if you have not already done so? "Now is the accepted time; behold, now is the day of salvation" (II Cor. 6:2).

GOD'S GLORY

A final thought comes from verse 11. Here we read that the confession that will be made will result in glory to God the Father.

This is not true of any honor given to man. If you exalt men, you
dishonor God, whether that means that you exalt yourself or your
merits as a means of salvation, whether you exalt men as mediators
between yourself and God, as saints who win God's favor for you,
whether you exalt human wisdom as that which is able ultimately to
solve the world's problems, whether you place your hopes for the
future in psychiatry, science, systems of world government, or whatever it may be. If you exalt the ability of mankind in any of those
ways, you dishonor God, who declares that all of men's works are
tainted by sin and that men will never solve their own problems or
the problems of others except by turning to Christ and depending
upon His power to do it. The only way to honor God is to give honor
to Jesus Christ.

Do you do that? Do you do that privately? Do you do it publicly?
Just think of the terms by which we are privileged to give glory to
Jesus. Think of His names. Jesus Christ is the one who is the Won-
derful Counselor, the Mighty God, the Everlasting Father, the Prince
of Peace. He is the Messiah, the Lord, the First and the Last, the
Beginning and the End, the Alpha and Omega, the Ancient of Days,
King of kings and Lord of lords, God with us, God our Savior, the
Only Wise God Our Savior, the Lord Which Is, Which Was, Which
Is to Come, the Almighty.

He is called the Door of the Sheep, the Chief Shepherd, the Good
Shepherd, the Great Shepherd, the Shepherd and Bishop of our Souls,
a Lamb Without Spot or Blemish, a Lamb Slain Before the Foundation of the World.

He is the Logos, the Light of the World, the Light of Life, the Tree
of Life, the Word of Life, the Bread That Came Down From Heaven,
the Resurrection, the Way, the Truth, and the Life. He is Immanuel,
God with us; He is the Rock, the Bridegroom, the Wisdom of God,
our Redeemer. He is the Beloved; He is the Head over all things
which is the Church. He is the One Who is Altogether Lovely, the
One in Whom the Father is Well Pleased.

Is Jesus Christ these things to you? He can be. He deserves to be.
If He is these things to you, then in your own heart you praise Him
and in giving Him glory you give glory to God our heavenly Father.

24.

Work Out Your Salvation

(Philippians 2:12, 13)

I DO NOT KNOW WHO IT WAS who first thought that being spiritual means withdrawing from the world, but the idea certainly entered the Christian Church at an early period and has had detrimental effects ever since. In the early days of the Church a Syrian monk named Simon Stylites sat on top of a pillar fifty feet high to avoid contact with the world. The Egyptian hermit Anthony lived most of his life in the desert. And there were others like them. These men were thought to be spiritual primarily because of their withdrawal. They were imitated. But the Bible does not support this view of spirituality.

Of course, no Christian must ever say that spending time alone with God is unnecessary, especially time spent in prayer. Yet the Bible never allows us to think that meditation has achieved its purpose for us unless it results in a practical application. Truth leads to action. And there is no value to a mountain top experience unless it helps us to live in the valleys.

PRACTICAL CHRISTIANITY

In our study of Philippians 2:5-11 we have been looking at some of the most sublime truths in the New Testament, certainly in the book of Philippians. They have concerned the divine and human natures of Jesus Christ, His sacrificial death, and the certainty of His eventual reign over all of creation. And yet these doctrines are introduced into the letter, not for their own sake, but for very practical purposes. They were included first as an example of the role of obedience and humility in the living of the Christian life. And no sooner have they been set forth in these seven verses than Paul returns once more to practical Christianity. He writes, "Wherefore, my beloved, as ye have always obeyed, not as in my presence only but now much more in my absence, work out your own salvation with fear and trembling. For it is God who worketh in you both to will and to do of his good pleasure" (2:12, 13).

161

Bishop Handley Moule writes well of these verses, "We have still in our ears the celestial music, infinitely sweet and full, of the great paragraph of the incarnation, the journey of the Lord of love from glory to glory by the way of the awful cross. May we not now give ourselves awhile wholly to reverie, and feast upon the divine poetry at our leisure? Not so; the immediate sequel is — that we are to be holy. We are *to act* in the light and wonder of so vast an act of love, in the wealth and resource of 'so great salvation.' We are to set spiritually to work."*

Have you ever noticed that Paul uses the word "wherefore" twice in these verses — once in verse nine and once in verse twelve? "Wherefore" means "therefore" or "because of this." And the use of the word points to two parallel results of Christ's conduct. Jesus Christ humbled Himself and became obedient unto death, even the death of the cross, *wherefore* God also hath highly exalted him (verse 9). Jesus showed the course of humility and obedience, *wherefore* the Christian is to work out his salvation (verse 12). The words show that doctrine always leads to practical Christianity.

Working It Out

Unfortunately, Philippians 2:12 is a problem text for many Christians. Some people neglect the context and assume, as a result, that the verse supports the idea of a "self-help" salvation. This is the view that although God has a standard of 100 percent righteousness, He knows that men will never attain it and, therefore, is content with something less, say, 41 percent righteousness or 63 percent righteousness. People who see salvation in these terms take this verse as a statement that salvation can be earned and that we are to work toward it. But the verse does not teach that. On the contrary, it teaches that because you are already saved, because God has already entered your life in the person of the Holy Spirit, because you, therefore, have His power at work within you — because of these things you are now to strive to express this salvation in your conduct.

This should be evident for several reasons. First, it is the clear meaning of the sentence itself. The verse does not say, "Work *for* your salvation" or "work *toward* your salvation" or "work *at* your salvation." It says, "Work *out* your salvation." And no one can work his salvation out unless God has already worked it in.

When a man or a woman first comes to the truth of the Gospel he is not much different from what he was in the moments before he believed. He has heard the Gospel preached and has responded to it.

* H. C. G. Moule, *Philippian Studies* (Glasgow: Pickering & Inglis, n.d.), p. 115.

Before he believed he was filled with misconceptions about God and himself. He had problems that he could not solve. He had wrong patterns of behavior. He was doing many things that were against the will of God. After he believes, these things are usually exactly the same. He still has the same problems, the same misconceptions, the same sins, sometimes even the same doubts. But it now begins to dawn on him that many of these things must change. He now has the Holy Spirit within his heart, and as he responds to the work of the Holy Spirit, he begins to see that the salvation he already has must now express itself in action. It must be seen distinctly in his conduct.

The second reason why this verse refers to the outward conduct of those who have been saved is that there is a clear parallel between Philippians 2:12-15 and the thirty-second chapter of Deuteronomy. The words "children" and "blameless" and the phrase "a crooked and perverse generation" in Philippians 2:15 also occur in Deuteronomy 32: 4, 5. And the context is illuminating. The parallel shows that Paul was thinking of Deuteronomy as he wrote to the Philippians.

The people of Israel had been delivered from Egypt by the hand of God. God had brought them out of Egypt in spite of the fact that there was nothing in them to commend them to God. They were not mighty. They were not wise. They were not more numerous than any other people. But God loved them. And that was the sole reason for God's deliverance. God loved them and called them. If the people had had their way they would have stayed in Egypt, even though they were slaves. In fact, even after they were delivered there were times when they wanted to go back. But God led them out, and He did not change His mind. He had chosen them; He had led them in the wilderness; He had trained them for forty years. And now they were again at the Jordan River, and they were about to go into the land.

Moses knew by this time that he was not to be allowed to enter the land. But before he was taken up into Mount Nebo he wished to give a charge to the people to remind them of their past deliverance and future obligations. Moses knew that God had called them and led them through the wilderness and was with them even then. On this basis he now argues that they are to possess the land and to live there as God's obedient children.

This is why Paul has this chapter in mind. Paul was about to be taken out of this world himself, as Moses was. He did not know whether he would be killed immediately or whether he would be delivered for a short time. But he knew that this would probably be his last charge to his beloved friends at Philippi. What was he to say?

What should he tell them? As he thought along these lines, it must
have come to him that the situation of the Philippians was similar to
that of the Israelites and his was like that of Moses. They had been
dead in their sins and had loved it. They would have stayed in their
sins had God not called them to Himself. But God had called them.
And He had begun to teach them the Christian way of life. Because
of this — because of this deliverance — they were now to work out the
salvation that God had so miraculously given. They were to strive for
the realization of God's love, peace, holiness, goodness, and justice in
their lives.

So are you to strive, if you are a Christian. If you have known God's
great deliverance in your life, then you have entered upon a lifetime
of God's training and encouragement and are to seek to express the
character of God in all that you do. You are to work out this salvation
in your conduct.

God's Working

I have said that we are to work out the salvation that God has
worked in, but to see the whole picture one more thought must be
added: even as we work out our salvation we are to know that it is
actually God in us through His Holy Spirit who does the working.
Paul writes, "Wherefore . . . work out your own salvation with fear
and trembling" (verse 12). But no sooner has he said this than he
immediately adds, "For it is God who worketh in you both to will
and to do of his good pleasure" (verse 13). It is actually God who
does the working.

God's working begins with our wills, for the verse says that God
works in us first to *will* and then to *do* of His good pleasure. Willing
always comes before doing.

No one will ever understand the doctrine of God's working to form
a man's will until he realizes that apart from the work of God in his
heart through Jesus Christ a man does not have free will where spiritual
realities are concerned. I know that someone will want to reply, "What!
Do you mean to tell me that I cannot do anything I want to?" But
my answer is, "Yes; you cannot." Oh, I know that you have free will
to decide certain things, but you do not have free will to decide all
things. And you are most unable to decide the things that are important. For instance, you can decide whether you want to go to
church on Sunday morning or stay at home. You can decide whether
you will take the bus down town or go by car. You can decide whether
you will go to work on Monday morning or pretend you are sick. You
can order turkey or roast beef at a restaurant. You can do these things.
But you cannot exercise your free will in anything that involves your

physical, intellectual, or spiritual capabilities. By your own free will you cannot decide that you are going to have a fifty percent higher I.Q. than you do or that will have a gift for dealing with quantum mechanics. You just cannot do it. You do not have free will to become three inches taller. You do not have free will to make a billion dollars. You do not have free will to run the 100-yard dash in eight seconds. You do not have the free will to look like Burt Lancaster or Steve McQueen, or to look like Raquel Welch if you are a girl. You do not have free will in anything intellectual or physical.

Now just as you do not have free will intellectually and you do not have free will physically, so you do not have free will spiritually. You cannot choose God. Adam had free will, but he lost it. And all men since are without it until it is recreated in them by the Holy Spirit. Let me give you an illustration. It is as if a man were standing on the edge of a muddy pit with slippery sides. As long as he is on the edge he has free will; he can either stay on the bank or jump in. But if he decides to jump in, then his free will is lost as far as getting out of the pit is concerned. He lost his free will in the fall. Oh, he has free will to walk around on the bottom or to sit down. He has the free will to try to scramble up the side or to accept his plight philosophically. He has the free will to cry for help or to be silent, to be angry or complacent. But he does not have free will to be again on the edge of the embankment.

This is what happened in Adam. Adam was created on the edge of the pit. God said, "Of every tree of the garden thou mayest freely eat; but of the tree of the knowledge of good and evil, thou shalt not eat of it; for in the day thou eatest thereof thou shalt surely die" (Gen. 2:16, 17). This was a test case, and Adam had free will to obey or to disobey the commandment. When he disobeyed it he fell away from God. He lost the free will to choose God, and he proved it by running away from God when God came to him in the garden.

Since Adam, all men are born with the same inability to choose Him. Some are complacent; some are angry. Some are silent and philosophical. Some are resigned; some are anxious. But all are unable to come to God. And no one does come to God until God reaches down by grace into the mud pit of human sin and impotence and lifts him up and places him again on the banks and says, "This is the way; walk ye in it."

This is what God does in salvation, and the Bible clearly teaches it. The Bible says, "There is none righteous, no, not one: there is none that understandeth, there is none that seeketh after God" (Rom. 3:10, 11). The Bible says that men are born again "not of blood, nor of the will of the flesh, nor of the will of man, but of God" (John 1:13). And Jesus said, "No man can come unto me, except the Father, who hath sent me, draw him" (John 6:44).

We must face this truth. Even if every generation of mankind and every city and village on earth had a John the Baptist to point to Jesus Christ and to call men to Him, apart from the supernatural work of God in human hearts no one would come. If God rearranged the stars of heaven to spell out, "Believe in the Lord Jesus Christ and be saved," no one would believe. If God sent His angels with the sound of a celestial trumpet to call mankind to repentance, no one would repent. Men come only because God enables them to do it. If you have come to God, it is only because God has first entered your life by His Holy Spirit to quicken your will, to open your eyes to His truth, and to draw you irresistibly to Himself. It is only after this that you are able to choose the path which He sets before you.

Two Kinds of Works

If you have seen this truth, you are ready to see that the proper life of the Christian in which he works out God's salvation is to be lived through the power of God within as He operates through a re-created will. The same God that works in you to *will* now also works in you through that will to *do* of His good pleasure.

I wonder if you have ever noticed that the well-known verses in the second chapter of Ephesians, verses 8-10, speak twice of our works, the things that we do. One kind of work is condemned because it comes out of man and is contaminated by sin. The other kind of work is encouraged because it comes from God as He works within the Christian. The verses say this: "For by grace are ye saved through faith; and that not of yourselves, it is the gift of God — not of *works* [that is, of human working], lest any man should boast. For we are his workmanship, created in Christ Jesus unto good *works* [that is, the result of God's working], which God hath before ordained that we should walk in them." These three verses are really Paul's own commentary upon Philippians 2:12, 13, for they tell us that although God can never be satisfied with any good that comes out of man, He *is* satisfied and pleased with the good that is done by Christians through the power of Jesus Christ within them. Through that power the tyranny of sin is broken, the possibility of choosing for God is restored, and a new life of communion with God and holiness is set before the Christian.

Have you had that experience? Have you felt the power of God within enabling you to do what God desires? You can, for He lives within each Christian leading him to holiness. Charles Wesley knew God's power, and he sang:

> He breaks the power of cancelled sin,
> He sets the prisoner free;
> His blood can make the foulest clean,
> His blood availed for me.

The power of Christ within is a wonderful reality for Christians, for through it we may do of God's good pleasure. We do not boast of ourselves or of human attainments. But we do boast in God. In Him we have all things and are enabled to work out our salvation.

25.

What Are Your Goals?

(Philippians 2:14-16)

ONE SUMMER DURING my college days when my sisters and I were vacationing at a lake in New York state a young boy about ten or eleven years old came to visit our family, and he wanted to water ski. My sisters had taught many people to water ski, and they began to teach him. But it was not easy. The problem was that he did not want to hear their instructions, and the reason he did not want to hear them was that he thought he had learned all about water skiing from books. He knew that you had to crouch back in the water while the line gets tight, keep your knees bent as the boat starts up, and then rise gradually until you are on the surface of the water as the boat goes faster. He did not want to hear their instructions. Finally, when they saw they were not getting anywhere, my sisters said, "All right, try it your way." The boy went down into the water, put on the skis, held the rope, and when the boat started up he went tumbling head over heels. It was just what my sisters expected would happen. And he got so much water in his mouth that he decided not to try it again.

In the same way, some people think they have learned the Christian life from a book while sitting on the sidelines. But the real Christian life is learned in the water, in this case the water of this world. We are not to be of this world, but we are to be in this world. And we are to live for Jesus Christ in the midst of a wicked and ungodly generation. In Philippians 2:14-16, Paul writes, "Do all things without murmurings and disputings, that ye may be blameless and harmless, children of God, without rebuke, in the midst of a crooked and perverse nation, among whom ye shine as lights in the world, holding forth the word of life, that I may rejoice in the day of Christ that I have not run in vain, neither labored in vain."

This was Paul's great desire for the saints at Philippi. And it is God's desire for you and me also. We are not to retreat from the world, but we are to live for God in the world. And we are to do so even though the world is crooked and perverse by God's standards.

LIGHT IN THE DARKNESS

How can we live for Christ in this world? First, I think we must recognize that the world *is* crooked and perverse by God's standards. All too often Christians look at this world, as we might look at the sky on the afternoon of a June day and say, "Oh, the world isn't so dark. It's blue. It's lovely." But the reason for this is that the light of God has been refracted in the atmosphere provided by Christians so that some of the virtues of Christianity are cast about a little and the world does not look quite so bad with this halo. But strip away the halo of the atmosphere of Christianity and its influence, and the blackness that God said is there remains. For this reason Christians must constantly be aware of the darkness and must determine to be a contrast with it.

The world has its goals: pleasure, success, sex, money, esteem. But these are not to be the goals of Christians. Christians know that God grants them pleasure in their lives and are thankful, but that is not to be their goal. Above all they know that pleasure is not to be enjoyed in opposition to God's law. Christians are granted success and are thankful. But personal success is not to be their goal either. They experience a certain amount of wealth, sex, fame, and other things, but these are not to be the goals of Christians.

What are to be the Christian's goals? Paul says three things. He says that the life that is to be lived by Christians in the midst of the world is to be one of *submission to God*. We are to do all things "without murmurings and disputings." Second, this life is one that is to be *blameless before other people*. "Blameless" and "harmless" are the words Paul uses here. Finally, our lives are to be *blameless in the sight of God* also. We are to be without rebuke as His children.

SUBMISSION TO GOD

First of all, we are to be submissive to God. And the token of our submission is to be an attitude of life that does things without murmurings and disputings.

This word "disputings" refers to the inward reasonings of the mind, and is based on the Greek word from which we get our English word "dialogue." Dialogue has become a popular word in our day, and we think well of it. But it is not such a virtue in the Bible, at least not between men and God. God does not want to argue with men. He wants men to listen to Him and to do what He says. In this context the word points to that reasoning that goes on in the human heart in rebellion against God's will.

When such reasoning begins to express itself externally, it becomes murmuring, the second word that Paul uses. Murmurings are mentioned throughout Scripture. The wage earner in Christ's parable murmured against the householder (Matt. 20:1-16). Early in the day the householder hired some men to work in his vineyard, agreeing to pay them a denarius for a day's work. Later in the day he hired another group. About noon he hired a third group of men, and he employed others in the late afternoon. At the end of the day he paid each one a denarius. And the ones who had worked the whole day for the same wages as the others complained; they murmured, and the murmuring was a rebellion against the householder's generosity.

The same word is used in Luke 5:30 of the Pharisees. When they saw Jesus' disciples eating with the tax collectors they were offended and began to "murmur" against His disciples.

In the Old Testament the word "murmurings" often describes the rebellion of the people of Israel during the years of wandering in the wilderness. They were always murmuring. When they were in Egypt they were murmuring because they were in Egypt. When they got out of Egypt, they were murmuring because they were out of Egypt. They murmured because they had nothing to eat. And when God supernaturally provided manna for them to eat they murmured that they did not have meat. They murmured for forty years, and when they got into the promised land they were still murmuring. Many of us are like that. God blesses us, but there is always something we do not like about it. He blesses us more, but there is something we do not like about that, and then there is something else. And we murmur again.

Now all of this is illustrated by the conduct of children, both the disputings that go on in the heart and the murmurings. But in order to see this in the life of a child, it is necessary to know one more thing about "murmuring." Murmuring is one of those curious words that sound like their meaning. The technical term for such words is onomatopoeia. They have the sound of the things they represent, such as "hiss," "buzz," "murmur," and "hum."

The last word sometimes reminds me of a story about a great biologist at Harvard University in the early days of the investigation of bugs and insects. Bugs were the professor's specialty, so one day two of his students thought they would pull a joke on their learned teacher. They caught a beetle and a grasshopper. Then they took wings from the grasshopper and very carefully glued them to the back of the beetle; they added some antennae that did not belong and then brought it to their professor. They said, "Look what we've found. What is it?"

The professor looked at the beetle and then he looked at the boys. He asked "Did you find it in a field where there was lots of grass?" They said, "Yes, that's where we found it." "And as you were out in the field did it come flying along just above the level of the grass?" They said, "Yes, that's just the way it was flying." "And as it flew, did it make a humming noise?" They said, "Yes, it did." And the professor said, "Well, I know what it is, it's a humbug."

Well, "hum" is an onomatopoeic word, and "murmuring" is another. It describes what it sounds like when one murmurs: "Mm . . . mm . . . mm." And it is always associated with rebellion. Take the case of a child. You say to the child, "Go upstairs and get into your pajamas and then come down, and we'll kiss you good-night. It's time to go to bed." And the child stands there silently looking at you. He is disputing in his heart how much he can get away with. He is holding dialogue with himself. Then you say, "Now, go on. It's time to go to bed." And he knows he has to do it. But as he turns to walk out of the door you hear, "Mm . . . mm . . . mm." You say, "What?" And again the child says, "Mm." You say, "What was that?" The child says, "Nothing." And off he goes.

That is what we do. And if you are laughing at that, you are laughing because you know it is true. God says, "I want you to do this." And we are silent because a dialogue is going on inside us. We are saying, "Does God really mean that I have to do it just like that or can I do it in this way?" Or we are saying, "Does God mean that I have to do it now? Maybe I can do it tomorrow, or next year." These are disputings. Then God says, "I mean for you to do it now and do it *My* way." And we say, "Mm." Now Paul says that we are not to do that. We are to live as Christians without murmurings and disputings in the midst of an ungodly world. When God says that we are to do something, we are to do it, and we are to do it because we trust Him and want to obey the One who knows what is really best for His children.

BLAMELESS CHILDREN

The second thing that Paul says is to be characteristic of Christians is that they are to be blameless and harmless in the sight of other people. The word translated "harmless" means innocent, pure, or without mixture. It was used in the vocabulary of primitive metallurgy to talk about pure gold, pure copper, or any metal that did not have impurities. It was also used of the preparation of pure clay for making pottery. In the same sense our lives are to be without mixture before men. We are to be aboveboard in our business dealings. We are not to say one thing and do another. We are not to keep part of the truth back or to misrepresent a case.

And then, we are to be blameless. Just as the inward disputing has an outward expression in murmuring which is bad, so this good inward characteristic of being harmless has an outward expression in being blameless. Because our minds are to be innocent, so is our conduct to be blameless. There is to be nothing that gives occasion for scandal. We are not to be satisfied if we can say, "Well, my strength is as the strength of ten, because my heart is pure." Our conduct must be pure also.

We are to be like Daniel. Daniel lived in the midst of an ungodly world. The Babylon of his day was as ungodly a place as you can imagine. But Daniel lived for God in the very midst of it. He did not live off in a corner somewhere; he lived in the king's palace, and he worked for the king. Moreover, when his enemies tried to do away with him, the only thing about which they could find fault was his worship of Jehovah. And they finally tried to have him executed through a law that stipulated that for a certain period no one could ask a favor of any god or man except of King Darius. When Daniel continued to pray, he became a violator of the law and was thrown to the lions. God delivered Daniel, but not before he had received this testimony: his enemies said, "We shall not find any occasion against this Daniel, except we find it against him concerning the law of his God" (Dan. 6:5). Daniel lived without blame before men. And we are to be blameless also.

Without Rebuke

Finally, Paul says that we are to be blameless before God, for we are to live "without rebuke" as His children. The word used here for "without rebuke" is also used in Ephesians 1:4, where it is translated "without blame." And it refers there, as in Philippians, to a Christian's relationship to God. Paul says that God "hath chosen us in him before the foundation of the world, that we should be holy and *without blame* before him." This does not mean that there will ever come a time in our life when we shall be without sin. Real sanctification lies in the increasing realization of how sinful we are. But it means that our lives will be lived in the sight of God in such a way that they will be open before Him. There will be no barriers between ourselves and God. If we live this way, we shall be able to pray as David prayed, "Search me, O God, and know my heart; try me, and know my thoughts; and see if there be any wicked way in me, and lead me in the way everlasting" (Ps. 139:23, 24).

GROWTH IN THE WAY

Now this is going to be a process that will go on throughout life. And it is not going to be easy. Perhaps you are saying, "Not easy? Why, it's going to be impossible!" Well, no, it is not impossible. For our God is the God of the impossible, and He does things for us and in us that we cannot do for ourselves.

The Bible tells us how this will happen. "I am crucified with Christ: nevertheless I live; yet not I, but Christ liveth in me; and the life which I now live in the flesh I live by the faith of the Son of God, who loved me and gave himself for me" (Gal. 2:20). "For what the law could not do, in that it was weak through the flesh, God sending his own Son, in the likeness of sinful flesh and for sin, condemned sin in the flesh, that the righteousness of the law might be fulfilled in us, who walk not after the flesh, but after the Spirit" (Rom. 8:3, 4). "And be not conformed to this world, but be ye transformed by the renewing of your mind, that ye may prove what is that good, and acceptable, and perfect, will of God" (Rom. 12:2). "Work out your own salvation. . . . For it is God who worketh in you both to will and to do of his good pleasure" (Phil. 2:12, 13).

What do these verses mean? They mean that a man is incapable of living out the kind of life that God requires of him, but that God is capable of living out that life in a man who yields to His Spirit.

It is a matter of spiritual life. God comes to a man who is spiritually unborn. He begins to penetrate his heart with the divine sperm of His Word so that life is conceived and the cell begins to grow. There is a period of incubation before the first cry that announces the arrival of new life, and this is followed by an even longer period of education, guidance, and nurturing in the home. But at last the child goes forth to live in a way that honors His Father. And he goes forth, not as a machine or a computer that only gives back what is fed into it, but as an individual who thinks and decides and responds, and yet thinks and responds as Jesus Christ responds. For the life of God has been reproduced in him.

That is what God wants you to do. You are to submit to His Spirit, allowing Him to make you a light in the darkness of this world. You are to be blameless and harmless both before men and before God. You are to hold forth the word of life to others. And those who have assisted in your spiritual birth and maturing will be able to say, as Paul did of the Philippians, "I rejoice because I have not run or worked in vain."

26.

Partners for Christ

(Philippians 2:17-24)

EVERY NOW AND THEN people object to living the normal Christian life on the ground that what is required of a Christian is impossible. And it is easy to see why this is so. Suppose you are a salesman who was responsible for fifty thousand dollars' worth of sales last year. The boss comes to you and says, "Well, you did very well last year; fifty thousand dollars was a good figure. But we should like to increase that by five thousand this year." You take a deep breath and say, "All right, I'll do my best." But if the boss comes to you and says, "Fifty thousand was a terrible figure; we should like to make that five hundred thousand this year," you are very likely going to quit your job and get another.

This is the way the Christian life often strikes people when they first begin to realize what is required of them as Christians. When you first become a Christian you have a pretty high opinion of yourself. You say, "After all, I believed, and that's something; and the Lord has brought me this far." You think you have arrived. Then you begin to study the Bible and realize that God wants you to be conformed to the image of Jesus Christ. You get a glimpse of His love, His compassion, His wisdom, His understanding, His holiness, and all of His other perfections. And, like the salesman, you say, "Well, that's impossible. I can't do it. I guess I'll just have to be content to live as I am."

That is wrong. It is true that in this life you will never be completely like Christ and that much of your sanctification will consist in realizing how much unlike Him you are. But yet, you *are* to become more like Him. The Bible teaches that although God's standards are high, and thus seem impossible, God provides supernatural resources to meet them. God helps the Christian to put the highest of these principles into practice.

174

Faith in Action

All this is taught in the second chapter of Philippians. The previous chapters have shown us that the central theme of the chapter is the Christian life. In the opening verses Paul writes that the Philippians were to let nothing be done through strife or vainglory, but in lowliness of mind each was to think better of the other Christian than of himself. They were to be humble. And they were to be obedient to God. Jesus Christ showed the way of such humility and obedience in His path from the throne of heaven to the cross, and the Christian is to copy Him in that. Then the argument goes on. Because the Philippians are the children of God, they are to do things pleasing to God without rebellious murmurs and internal disputes. They are to be without blame in the midst of a wicked and perverse nation, among whom they are to shine as lights in the world, holding forth the Word of Life. That is to be their high and unwavering standard.

At this point, however, someone is bound to say, "Well, that might be all right in theory, but it is pretty hard to do in practice. How can we do it? How can a Christian meet such standards?" Paul replies that although it is hard, very hard, it is not impossible. And to prove that it is possible — not only in theory, but also in practice — Paul presents three human examples. Who are these examples? They are Paul himself, Timothy, and Epaphroditus — an apostle, a young minister, and a layman. In the remainder of the chapter Paul uses these persons to show that all of the things he has been talking about *are* possible for the one who will surrender his life to God. We are going to look at the first two examples in this study.

The Apostle

The first example Paul uses is himself, although he does so only briefly. In fact, he uses only one verse to describe his own attitude and conduct as opposed to six verses each for Timothy and Epaphroditus. Of himself Paul says, "And if I be offered upon the sacrifice and service of your faith, I joy, and rejoice with you all" (Phil. 2:17).

To understand this verse we need to realize that Paul is using a potent image in it. The verb that is translated in the first line as "offered" actually means "poured out," and it is a technical word for a certain part of a pagan sacrificial offering. If we were to have watched a Greek or a Roman perform such an offering, we would have seen him arrive at an altar with his sacrifice. It would have been a living animal, and it would have been valuable. The animal would have been killed, and after it had been killed it would have been burned on the altar, giving off a sweet fragrance in the process. At this point the ancient worshiper would have made an additional offering called a libation. He would have taken a cup of wine and poured it upon the altar, thus pouring it upon the sacrifice that was already burning. Because the altar was hot, the libation would immediately disappear in a puff of steam and be gone.

Paul is referring to this offering. And he is saying this: "I know that you are worried about me because I am in prison in Rome and my life may soon be offered up upon a pagan altar. But my life is not the important thing. The important thing is your faith. The faith is the substantial and valuable offering. And it is itself a sweet fragrance to God. When my life is poured out it will only be the drink offering poured out upon the far greater offering of your faith." Do you see what this means? It means that Paul was placing his own achievements, even his own martyrdom, at a very low point on the scale of Christian service. And he was holding up the faith and achievements of his converts for admiration. This is an example of the very humility and obedience to Jesus Christ about which Paul was speaking. Do you show such humility as you meet with other Christians? If not, you need to apply Paul's self-evaluation to yourself and not reckon your own achievements too highly.

Now if you are to do this properly — and I include myself in the recommendation — you must realize that Paul's frame of mind was not something that came about in an instant. Paul's genuine humility was the product of a long relationship with God. Suppose for a minute that there is a small boy in your home who has seen a number of space spectaculars on television and who is determined to grow up to be a space engineer and to plot the course of future rocket ships to planets. He shares this desire with his father. It is a commendable ambition. But if he is wise, the father will point out that the job he is thinking of requires great knowledge and long years of training, and that if he is serious about such a career, he should begin by mastering his multiplication tables and the basic lessons of the physical sciences.

It is the same spiritually. In these verses Paul is brought forward as a strong example to Christians. We see that a life of true humility and obedience is not impossible. But if we would emulate him in his self-effacement, we must be prepared to start at the beginning. We must learn small lessons in humility before there can be large ones.

The Youthful Minister

The second of Paul's examples is Timothy, the young man whom Paul had found in the area of Derbe and Lystra in Asia Minor, and whom he had often taken with him on his various missionary journeys.

Paul speaks quite eloquently of him: "But I trust in the Lord Jesus to send Timothy shortly unto you, that I also may be of good comfort, when I know your state. For I have no man likeminded, who will naturally care for your state. For all seek their own, not the things which are Jesus Christ's. But ye know the proof of him, that, as a son with the father, he hath served with me in the gospel" (Phil. 2: 19-22).

These verses say four things about Timothy. First, they say that he was likeminded with Paul: "for I have no man likeminded, who will naturally care for your state." This phrase — "no man likeminded" — is ambiguous in Greek, for it could mean several different things. It could mean that Timothy was unique; that is, "I have no one quite like him." It could mean that there was no one else who could do Timothy's particular job. Or it could mean that Timothy was like Paul. I believe that in this context it probably means the latter. Paul had just been talking about the attitude of mind that thinks humbly of itself and much of others, and he has mentioned himself as an example. Now there is Timothy also, for Timothy too is likeminded. Paul had found that he too was self-effacing in his Christian conduct.

Second, Paul says that Timothy was concerned for others. He cared for them naturally. In fact, he served them with the disposition of a true shepherd who was faithful in the care and protection of his flock.

There is a literal example of such a person in Jacob, one of the Old Testament patriarchs. Jacob was not a very praiseworthy character. He was a liar and a cheat. And he was impatient. He was what we would call a mama's boy. But in one respect he was eminently praiseworthy. Jacob was a shepherd, and he was faithful in his care of the flocks. On one occasion, when his uncle Laban reproached him for starting off suddenly with all of his flocks for Palestine, Jacob said, "That which was torn of beasts I brought not unto thee; I bore the loss of it. . . . Thus I was; in the day the drought consumed me, and the frost by night; and my sleep departed from mine eyes. Thus have I been twenty years in thy house" (Gen. 31: 39-41). And Jacob spoke the truth. He had been a good shepherd, and Laban could not contradict him.

On another occasion, when he had returned to his home and had met his brother Esau, Esau wanted him to hurry on to the place where he was living. But Jacob was concerned for the children of his household and the flocks. He said, "My lord knoweth that the children are tender, and the flocks and herds with young are with me: and if men should overdrive them one day, all the flock will die. Let my lord, I pray thee, pass over before his servant: and I will lead on softly, according as the cattle that goeth before me and the children be able to endure" (Gen. 33:13, 14).

Timothy was like that. He had great concern for God's people, and he led them gently. Do you? Do you guide your family, your children, your Sunday school class, your church gently? Or do you drive them on regardless of their individual condition and of their ability to travel with you? To lead them gently is the task of a good shepherd.

The third thing for which Paul praises Timothy is his concern for Jesus Christ. Timothy put Christ first. And in this he stood head and shoulders above those who were around him. It is so easy to put other things first. You can put your own reputation first. You can put your pleasure first. You can give first place to your plans, or your family, or success, or any number of other things. But if you do, all of these things will be distorted, and you will miss life's greatest blessings. Timothy put Christ first, together with Christ's interests, and the other things fell into place naturally.

The final thing for which the young man Timothy is praised is that he had learned to work with others. Paul says of him, "But ye know the proof of him, that, as a son with the father, he hath served with me in the gospel" (vs. 22). How often we want to be independent! We want to serve God, but the work must be our work. It must be our job, and it must be run according to our conception of things. A real mark of Christian maturity is the ability to work with others cooperatively under the banner and for the cause of Jesus Christ.

Working Together

That verse also says as much about Paul and about his ability to work with others as it does about Timothy. Paul had referred to Timothy's service as the service of a son with his father. But this is not the expression one would normally expect in antiquity, or today either, for that matter. The normal duty of a son is to obey his father and to serve him. And any of Paul's readers would have expected the verse to say, "And as a son with the father, so hath he served *me* in the gospel." Instead of this Paul alters the sentence to include the small word "with," and thereby indicates that the service of himself and Timothy was a joint service in the Lord.

This is the real answer to the problems of what we have come to call the generation gap. We talk as if the generation gap were something new. But anyone who knows history well knows that it is not. Euripides described the hippies of his day, the girls from Sparta, like this: "No Spartan girl could ever live clean even if she wanted. They are always out on the street in scanty outfits, making a great display of naked limbs. . . . Abominable's the word. It is little wonder Sparta is hardly famous for chaste women" (*Andromache,* translated by John Frederick Nims).

Socrates said this, "Our youth now loves luxury. They have bad manners, contempt for authority, disrespect for older people. Children nowadays are tyrants. They no longer rise when their elders enter the room. They contradict their parents, chatter before company, gobble their food, and tyrannize their teachers." Moreover, the Bible is full of examples of the difficulties between fathers and their children. I and II Samuel in the Old Testament alone contain half a dozen examples.

All of the problems that can arise between the generations could have arisen between Paul and his faithful but younger co-worker Timothy. There could have been jealousies, misunderstandings, diversities of purpose, rebellion, tyranny, and many other things. But none of these occurred. Instead of this, they served together as partners in the spread of the Gospel, each taking his standard and instructions from the Lord.

Do you do that? If you are a member of the generation under twenty-five, do you see the calling to which God has called you? It is not to rebellion against your parents or against the older generation in general. It is to work with them in a mutual service to the Lord. You will be able to do that as you learn to serve Christ's interests and not merely your own.

And this verse speaks also to the parents. You have the duty of raising your children. You are to lead them to become faithful disciples of Jesus Christ. You are to encourage them to follow Jesus, to learn the truth of the Gospel, to emulate Christ's character. You have a role of supervision. But you must never forget that you actually serve with them as bondslaves of Jesus Christ. And whatever standards you would set for them and whatever patterns of obedience you would seek to instill in them must also become real for you and be part of your service. You must remember that the ultimate loyalty of your children is not to you but to the Lord Jesus Christ.

Do you recognize their devotion to the Lord? And do you know the freedom of serving Him also? If so, then you will be able to work with them, not only for secular ends, but also to proclaim the Gospel of salvation to their friends and yours. I know of many parents who have found the means of bringing young people to the Lord through the testimony of their children and the contacts that their children have. In this they encourage each other, and they shine as ever brighter examples of what the Christian life can be.

27.

The Man Whom God Honors

(Philippians 2:25-30)

OF ALL THE MEN PAUL HONORS in his epistle to the Philippians, it is a layman named Epaphroditus who gets the most attention. Here is a man who is almost unknown to us, and yet Paul selects him — Epaphroditus — as deserving highest honor. Paul writes, "Receive him, therefore, in the Lord with all gladness, and hold such in reputation, because, for the work of Christ, he was near unto death, not regarding his life, to supply your lack of service toward me" (Phil. 2:29, 30).

Why was Epaphroditus to be held in good repute? Why was he to be honored? He was to be honored because of his self-effacing service to another Christian. Paul spells it out more clearly in the first verse that mentions him: "I thought it necessary to send to you Epaphroditus, my brother and companion in labor, and fellow soldier, but your messenger, and him that ministered to my need" (Phil. 2:25).

These phrases are arranged to make a crescendo climaxing in the last phrase, the phrase dealing with Epaphroditus' ministry on behalf of the Philippian Christians. It is as if a nominating speech were being given at a political convention and the person making it were to say, "Ladies and gentlemen and delegates, I present to you a man who is a good father to a wonderful and happy family, a man who is prominent in the affairs of his city, a successful lawyer, a distinguished civil servant, former governor of the state, the distinguished vice-president of the United States, and the next president of the United States." The eulogy builds toward that climax.

It is the same here. Epaphroditus was said to have been four things. He was a brother, a fellow-worker, a fellow soldier; and he was a messenger of the Philippian Christians and a minister in their absence to Paul's needs. These things build toward the final statement. To gether they are an important summary of what the Christian life should be.

180

A Brother

In the first place, Paul calls his Christian friend a brother. And this is striking, simply because the ideal of brotherhood was such a new thing in Paul's day.

To be sure, some aspects of ancient life and culture bore a faint resemblance to Christian brotherhood; but these, even at their best, were exclusive. Roman soldiers knew a form of fellowship that was the natural outgrowth of the dangers they faced together. There were political associations organized somewhat like our Masonic lodges and other service organizations, but they were united only for particular political and social objectives. For the most part the anicent world was sharply divided between slaves and free men, Greeks and Romans, Jews and Gentiles, aristocrats and plebeians, citizens and soldiers. And there was nothing that genuinely united all branches of this great-ly polarized society.

Into this world came the Gospel of Jesus Christ and with it Chris-tian brotherhood. Christians knew that they had all been under the curse of God because of sin and had now been brought into a new relationship to God through their relationship to Christ. They also knew that this affected the way they were to look at one another. In the days of the apostles the Christians did not talk much about the Christian brotherhood, but it was there. And it was real. All of the divisions of the Roman world were potentially within the Church because of the social, national, or religious backgrounds of the Chris-tians. But the Christians simply overlooked them. There was nothing exclusive about the early Christians.

Do we have such brotherhood in the Church of Jesus Christ today? If it exists, can men and women see it as they saw the brotherhood of the earliest Christians? Can they see that there is a unity among people who profess Christ but who, from the world's point of view, should be divided because of their various backgrounds? I am sure such a brotherhood exists. But I am not sure that it exists as much as it ought to, or is as visible as it should be.

We live, too, in a world of imitations. And there are imitations of the brotherhood which came through Christianity. Communism is one of them. Racial exclusiveness, whether black or white, is another. Blacks speak of a brotherhood of soul. Whites talk of their Anglo-Saxon heritage. But these things are substitutes for Christianity. And their defenders achieve a fellowship by throwing up barriers instead of tearing them down. Paul says that Christ has "broken down the middle wall of partition between us" (Eph. 2:14).

CO-WORKERS FOR CHRIST

Paul uses a second word to praise Epaphroditus. He says that he had proved himself to be a fellow-worker. The word reminds us of the praise Jesus Christ had for the little church at Ephesus recorded in the second chapter of Revelation. This was a working church, and it was praised for it. Jesus said, I know how thou ". . . hast borne, and hast patience, and for my name's sake hast labored, and hast not fainted" (Rev. 2:3). Epaphroditus was this kind of worker.

There is a sense in which our churches sometimes have almost stopped working. Years ago now there was an article in *Christianity Today* entitled "Did Success Spoil American Protestantism?" The question of the title was answered in the affirmative, "Yes, it did." And I am convinced that the thesis of the article was a correct one. As Protestantism won its great cultural victories in America, particularly in the nineteenth century, the Protestant church entered a period of internal decline that we see clearly today and will undoubtedly see more clearly in the years ahead. By its numerical and financial success, Protestantism became increasingly identified with American culture and so became unable to speak prophetically to it, except in a few rare instances. Because of its very success the Protestant church became complacent. It became lazy. It lost its intellectual and cultural dynamic. And in far too many instances it largely abandoned a forthright proclamation of the Gospel.

We need to reconstitute a working church in our day. And we can, God helping us. Let me suggest three areas where true believers must work hard. First, we need to work hard in the intellectual areas. It is simply distressing to scout the shelves of modern-day works on theology, biblical exegesis, literature, and social criticism, and find that the overwhelming proportion of the space is taken up by the works of those who deny the fundamental doctrines of Christianity. And there are not many great works from an evangelical perspective to be placed beside them. We need clear thinkers, winsome writers, and persuasive apologists who can reverse the trends we see around us and who can publish works of lasting value that will in time trickle down through the professors, seminaries, and pastors to the churches and to society at large. Nothing will accomplish this but hard work.

Second, we need to recapture a spirit of hard work in the social realm, for this is where the greatest action is taking place in our day. It was the strength of the evangelical Christians united behind Wilberforce that led to the abolishing of slavery in the British dominions in the last century. Evangelicals have led some of the great movements to abolish child labor and to introduce better working conditions into

factories. Evangelicals launched the great social work conducted by
the Salvation Army. And evangelicals have staffed and supported
great missions. Unfortunately, in this country much of the cutting
edge of the evangelicals' social concern has been blunted, and the
social arm of the church stands in need of resharpening. This, too,
will require the work of dedicated Christians.

We also need to work with renewed vigor in the area of evangelism.
Evangelism has always been the one area of concern in which the
conservative churches will cooperate. And yet, there has been a great
falling short on this level also. People are not flocking to the churches
today, even when they are welcome. Many will not even enter a
Christian church. So if they are to be won, we must win them individually. You must win them, and you must do it on a one-to-one
basis. You must make friends with those who are not real believers.
You must come to know their problems. And you must be ready to
apply Christian truths to them.

Perhaps you are saying that this is too much work for you and that
you cannot possibly handle their problems. That may be true. But
that is why we are to work with other Christians. We need help in
such a ministry. Epaphroditus is not termed merely a worker. He
was a fellow-worker with Paul and Timothy. Perhaps you should ask
the Lord to enable you to become a fellow-worker in these areas with
other Christians.

FELLOW-SOLDIERS

The third word that Paul uses of Epaphroditus is "fellow-soldier."
It was not only that Epaphroditus worked with Paul; he fought side
by side with him also. When Paul uses this word he recognizes that
the work they were doing was more like a battle than the normal
labor of a citizen in peacetime. The Bible says, "For we wrestle not
against flesh and blood, but against principalities, against powers,
against the rulers of the darkness of this world, against spiritual
wickedness in high places" (Eph. 6:12). This was the battle. This
warfare requires the shoulder-to-shoulder, aggressive forward motion
of all Christians.

A shoulder-to-shoulder fighting accounted for the success of Rome's
armies. Prior to the triumph of Rome, men fought mostly as individuals.
They often dressed alike and were armed alike, but they did not fight
side by side with each other. The Roman armies did, and as a result
the phalanxes of the legions were the terror of the ancient world.
The soldiers marched abreast behind a solid wall of shields. And as
they marched they struck their shields with their spears in unison and

sang their battle songs. In such a way we are to advance in harmony against the spiritual powers arrayed against us.

The climactic phrase of Paul's tribute to Epaphroditus tells us that he was the messenger of the church at Philippi and a minister to Paul's needs. The word translated "minister" in this verse is the same one that is translated "service" in verse 30: "Because, for the work of Christ, he was near unto death, not regarding his life, to supply your lack of *service* toward me." Paul is saying that Epaphroditus nearly died in fulfilling this ministry.

This fact leads to some interesting thoughts on the sickness that many Christians have endured in Christ's service. Some people have taught that health is a birthright of Christians and that sickness is the result of sin or of a lack of strong faith. Others, like Job's comforters, have said that sickness is always a sign of God's chastening. These thoughts are not true, and the case of Epaphroditus refutes them. Epaphroditus was a man who, Paul says, was to be held in the highest honor. Yet he grew sick in the midst of the most unselfish Christian service. Moreover, he was sick for some time. Philippi was about 800 miles from Rome, a traveling distance of not less than six weeks by ancient means of travel. And we are told that he was sick long enough for news of his sickness to get to Philippi and for the fact that they had heard about it to get back to Epaphroditus. That is, he was sick for at least three months. And even though he was with Paul, the apostle had no indications from the Lord to heal him.

Dr. H. A. Ironside writes about this passage:

> Let it be noted that the apostle did not consider he had any right to demand physical healing even for so faithful a laborer as Epaphroditus. Paul recognized it as simply the mercy of God, not as that to which saints have a right. This is true divine healing. And let it be remembered that sickness may be as really from God as health. It is clear that Paul never held or taught "healing in the atonement," and therefore the birth-right privilege of all Christians. Nor do we ever read of him or his fellow-laborers being miraculously healed. Paul himself, Trophimus, Timothy and Epaphroditus, all bear witness to the contrary. The apostle urges the saints to receive their messenger, when he should return to them, with all gladness, and commands them to hold such in reputation, because for the work of Christ he had been sick, nigh unto death, not regarding his life in order to serve Paul in their stead. Such are the men whom God delights to honor. *

* H. A. Ironside, *Philippians* (Neptune, N.J.: Loizeaux Bros., 1922), p. 65.

You and I must think of illness like that. And if the case of Epaphroditus is to teach us anything, it must teach us that sickness is often a badge of honor for God's children.

LIVING FOR OTHERS

This was the high point of Paul's praise for his friend Epaphroditus — praise for the kind of life that sacrifices its own interests for others — but we must not think that Paul was praising a type of life that he himself did not practice. Paul was in prison. Most of his friends had deserted him. Only Timothy and Epaphroditus were left. The first was without a peer. The second was a model of selfless Christian service. These men were in Rome to help Paul. And yet, what does Paul say he is doing with them? He writes that he is going to send Timothy back to the Philippians because he thinks it is necessary for *their* well-being. He is willing to give him up. And he is sending Epaphroditus back also, even though he thinks most highly of him.

What was Paul thinking about during the dark days before his execution? About himself? About his future? Not at all! He was thinking about the needs of his fellow-Christians, and he was willing to sacrifice his own interests for theirs. Are you? Are you willing to sacrifice your own interests for the concerns of other Christians? If not, you must remember that this is your calling, for you are called to follow the Lord Jesus Christ. Jesus laid aside His glory and became man, taking to Himself all of the suffering and weakness that is part of our humanity. Then He died on the cross for your salvation. Jesus lived for others. And He will teach you to live for others also, just as He taught the apostle Paul and his friends — Timothy and Epaphroditus.

28.

Better Than Happiness

(Philippians 3:1-3)

THE THIRD CHAPTER OF Philippians is probably the most beloved chapter of Paul's letter. In it he sets forth many of the cardinal doctrines of the Christian life and unveils in stirring language his own personal desire to know and to serve the Lord Jesus. It is interesting, however, that these doctrines are included not so much for their own sake but as a natural outgrowth of a challenge to the Christians at Philippi to be joyful. Paul writes, "Finally, my brethren, rejoice in the Lord. To write the same things to you, to me indeed is not irksome but for you it is safe. Beware of dogs, beware of evil workers, beware of the concision. For we are the circumcision, who worship God in the spirit, and rejoice in Christ Jesus, and have no confidence in the flesh" (Phil. 3:1-3). The verses suggest that joy is founded to a very large degree on sound doctrine.

JOY IN SUFFERING

It is a great privilege for me as the pastor of a large congregation to visit Christians who are confined to hospitals and nursing homes through illness and who yet give evidence of a supernatural joy even in the midst of their suffering. I visited one woman who had been confined to a home for incurables for many years. She had a form of acute, crippling arthritis that had left her unable to walk or even to move freely. She was unable to care for herself in many simple but necessary things. At times she was in almost unbearable pain. And yet she spoke of the goodness and grace of God, not only to herself, but also to many others who were with her in the hospital. She knew real joy, and she showed it even in the midst of her suffering.

I visited a man who was in the hospital with a serious coronary thrombosis. Instead of complaining about his condition, about the medical service, or some similar thing, he was thinking of all that the Lord had done for him in past days. And he was praying for those who were with him in the same room of the hospital. This man knew what it meant to rejoice in the Lord always. And both he and my other friend were exercising a supernatural joy that was their birthright as Christians.

As I have been with them I have often remembered that Jesus promised joy for those who followed Him. The angel who announced His birth to the shepherds said, "Behold, I bring you good tidings of great joy, which shall be to all people. For unto you is born this day in the city of David a Savior, who is Christ the Lord" (Luke 2:10, 11). Jesus said, "These things have I spoken unto you, that my joy might remain in you, and that your joy might be full" (John 15:11). And in John 17 Jesus prayed to His Father "that they might have my joy fulfilled in themselves" (John 17:13). This joy is the birthright of all true believers. And it was this joy that Paul wished to see in the little congregation at Philippi.

What is joy? Joy is a supernatural delight in God and God's goodness. And it is a very different thing from happiness. Every Christian virtue has its counterpart in a so-called virtue of the world. The world has sex; Christians have love. The world strives for security; Christians have trust. The world seeks self-gratification; Christians know peace. The world seeks happiness; the Christian's counterpart is joy. Happiness is our translation of the Latin word *fortuna,* and it is closely related to chance. Thus, if things happen to work out in a way which we approve, we are happy. If they do not so happen, we are unhappy. Happiness is circumstantial, but not joy. Joy is an inner quality of delight in God, or gladness, and it is meant to spring up within the Christian in a way totally unrelated to the adversities or circumstantial blessings of this life.

When Joy Is Gone

Unfortunately, it is impossible to speak of the supernatural qualities of Christian joy without saying at the same time that many Christians fail to experience this joy as they ought. Or they lose it after the initial joy of their salvation. Circumstances get them down. And instead of the victory all Christians should experience, they suffer depression. One of our great hymns speaks of such victory even in death:

> When through the deep waters I call thee to go,
> The rivers of sorrow shall not overflow;
> For I will be with thee thy troubles to bless,
> And sanctify to thee thy deepest distress.

But other hymns tell of the loss of joy that is characteristic of the life of many Christians. A hymn-writer once wrote:

> Look how we grovel here below,
> Fond of these trifling toys;
> Our souls can neither fly nor go
> To reach eternal joys!

And another songwriter has added:

> How tedious and tasteless the hours
> When Jesus no longer I see!
> Sweet prospects, sweet birds, and sweet flowers
> Have all lost their sweetness for me.

It is a sad confession. And it is doubly sad because it is true of many Christians. This should not be. For instead of depression there should be a joy in the Lord that goes beyond our circumstances.

Do you know this joy? Perhaps you are saying, "I know that I should have it, and I would like to rejoice in the Lord always. But circumstances still get me down. What can I do? How can this joy be sustained?" Well, the answer is in God's Word, and we must follow it as we would a doctor's prescription. If you see a doctor about feeling tired and run down and he prescribes exercise and an increase of vitamin B, you go to the drugstore and buy vitamins. And if you are disciplined, you see that some exercise is planned into your day. In the same way, if we lack Christian joy, we need to adhere to God's remedy. What is this remedy? I believe it can be summed up in several principles.

God's Remedy

The first principle is that you must begin by becoming a Christian. I know that it seems obvious to say this, but it is my experience that at least two classes of people need to face this squarely. The first class is composed of those who are not Christians and know it but who think that the fruits of Christianity can be grown without the life of Christianity, the life that comes from the Lord Jesus Christ. If you are such a person, you need to recognize the fact that joy is supernatural and that it is only given to those who have surrendered their lives to Him.

The second class of persons is composed of those who are not Christians but who *think* they are, perhaps because they have been raised in a religious home or because they attend church. They think they are Christians, but they do not understand the heart of the Gospel and have not actually committed their lives to Jesus Christ. Hence, they cannot understand their failure to experience the fruits of such commitment. If you are this type of person, then you must begin with the first principle also.

Let me explain it as plainly as I am able. Before you become a Christian you stand before God as one who has fallen short of His standards. You come to Him with all of your good works and fine resolutions. You have your own insight and all of your best traits of character. But as you stand before God you realize that even the best of these things is imperfect and thus is a failure to God. You hear God say, "You come to me with all that is human; but what is human is tainted by sin, and I cannot work with that. That is a foundation upon which I cannot build. You must turn from it."

And you do. You lay these things aside, you count them as loss, and you come to the cross to receive God's righteousness. You say to God, "I admit that everything I do falls short of your standard, and I recognize your verdict upon it. I lay it aside. I do not deserve anything from you, but I come empty-handed to receive what you have promised to give through faith in Christ Jesus. I come to receive your righteousness by which I am accounted righteous. I come to receive the Holy Spirit by whom I will have power to live the Christian life. And I ask you to help me to live it for Jesus' sake. Amen."

If you have done that, you have taken the first step to experiencing the joy that is to characterize the Christian life.

Righteousness and Peace

The second step is this: if you are to experience God's joy, you must first know His righteousness and peace. And this means that a life of holiness and trust are prerequisites. The order of these things is set forth in Romans 14:17: "For the kingdom of God is not food and drink, but righteousness, and peace, and joy in the Holy Spirit."

Many Christians do not know the joy that could be theirs because their lives are not holy and because they do not trust God for their future. I know of one girl who would not trust God in regard to marriage. Instead of admitting that God's plan for her was best, whatever it may have been, she was intent on getting married. And her determination to get married led her into many situations which clearly were not God's will for her. They actually led her into sin. She had her way, but she was not happy. And she was the first to admit that she certainly was not experiencing God's joy.

Sin keeps us from God, who is the source of joy. And anxiety also works against joy. Instead of sin and anxiety in his life, the believer in Jesus Christ should experience a life of holiness and peace. And he should realize God's peace as he submits all aspects of his future to Him. In the following chapter Paul writes, "Be anxious for nothing, but in everything, by prayer and supplication with thanksgiving, let your requests be made known unto God. And the peace of God, which passeth all understanding, shall keep your hearts and minds through Christ Jesus" (Phil. 4:6, 7).

JOY IN SOUND DOCTRINE

The third step to a life of continuous, supernatural joy is to steep ourselves in the teachings of the Bible. When I first began to study what the Bible has to say about joy I was surprised to discover how many times joy is associated with a mature knowledge of God's Word. David said, "The statutes of the Lord are right, rejoicing the heart" (Ps. 19:8). Psalm 119 declares, "I have rejoiced in the way of thy testimonies, as much as in all riches" (verse 14). Jesus said, "If ye keep my commandments, ye shall abide in my love, even as I have kept my Father's commandments, and abide in his love. These things have I spoken unto you, that my joy might remain in you, and that your joy might be full" (John 15:10, 11). All of these verses teach that joy is to be found in a knowledge of God's character and commandments and that these are to be found in His Word. If you have not known much of this joy, the reason may be a neglect of a study of Scripture.

What place should the Bible have in your life as a Christian? The place it should have is illustrated by an interesting custom of Old Testament times. In the days of the New Testament and for hundreds of years before that, pious Jews wore a small device on their foreheads that contained some words of Scripture. Some still do today. It was called a frontlet. Actually, they memorized the Scripture, but the frontlet was worn as an object lesson to remind them that God's Word was always to be the object of their deepest meditations and the source of the principles by which they were to order their lives.

The command to wear frontlets occurs three times in the Old Testament, and in each case the practice is related to one of the cardinal doctrines of the Scriptures.

The first mention of this custom is in Exodus 13:9. This chapter contains a summary of the events that took place in Egypt at the first Passover, when the lambs were killed, one for each household, and when the angel of death passed over those Jewish families whose homes were marked by the blood of the innocent animal. The Passover was an illustration of the way in which God would later pass over those whose sins were covered by the death of Jesus Christ and deliver them from judgment. After a summation of these events the chapter says, "And it shall be for a sign unto thee upon thine hand, and for a memorial between thine eyes, that the Lord's law may be in thy mouth; for with a strong hand hath the Lord brought thee out of Egypt." The first great doctrine that they were to have before their eyes was the doctrine of the atonement, the doctrine of salvation through the shedding of blood.

The second time the frontlets are mentioned is in Deuteronomy 6: 4-8. These verses contain a summary of the character and requirements of God. "Hear, O Israel: The Lord our God is one Lord: And thou shalt love the Lord thy God with all thine heart, and with all thy soul, and with all thy might, And these words, which I command thee this day, shall be in thine heart, And thou shalt teach them diligently unto thy children, and shalt talk of them when thou sittest in thine house, and when thou walkest by the way, and when thou liest down, and when thou risest up. And thou shalt bind them for a sign upon thine hand, and they shall be as frontlets between thine eyes." The second great doctrine was the nature of God and a man's responsibility to Him. They were to love Him with all their heart, and with all their soul, and with all their might.

The third mention of frontlets occurs five chapters later, in Deuteronomy 11:18. In this chapter God is setting forth the principle by which He will bless the life of any individual or nation. The principle is obedience. Where there is obedience God says He will give blessing. Where there is disobedience He will send judgment. After a statement of this principle we read, "Therefore shall ye lay up these my words in your heart and in your soul, and bind them for a sign upon your hand, that they may be as frontlets between your eyes. . . . That your days may be multiplied, and the days of your children, in the land which the Lord swore unto your fathers to give them" (Deut. 11:18, 21). The third great doctrine is the need for obedience, and it is to characterize all of our lives as God's people.

CLOSENESS TO GOD

I do not believe that in this life you or I will ever master all of the great truths of Scripture. The Word of God is inexhaustible, like God Himself, and if our joy depended upon such a mastery, we would never actually experience it. Our joy does not depend on that. Our joy depends upon our relationship to God and our life with Him. But if there is ever to be the joy in the Christian life that there ought to be, there must be a deep and growing experience of the basic truths upon which that life is founded. We must understand the nature of the atonement made for us by Christ. We must strive to know God better and to love Him. And we must attempt to live obediently before Him as His children.

There is a great deal of unrest in this world, and there will always be unrest for those who do not know Jesus. Apart from Him there is no true peace, no joy, and no real happiness either. But this should never be the case with a Christian. If you are a Christian, you should draw close to God. You must feed on Scripture. And God will "fill you with all joy and peace in believing" (Rom. 15:13).

29.

Profits and Loss

(Philippians 3:4-8)

IN THE THIRD CHAPTER of Philippians Paul says that he has learned
to count all human effort as loss that he might win Christ. To state
these truths he uses the figure of a balance sheet, showing assets and
liabilities. He says that he has learned, when keeping the records of
his life, to reckon all of the assets that he had earned before he knew
Christ as liabilities and to enter into his new column of assets the
name of Jesus Christ alone. He writes, "If any other man thinketh
that he hath reasons for which he might trust in the flesh, I more: circumcised the eighth day, of the stock of Israel, of the tribe of Benjamin,
an Hebrew of the Hebrews; as touching the law, a Pharisee; concerning zeal, persecuting the church; touching the righteousness which is
in the law, blameless. But what things were gain to me, those I counted
loss for Christ. Yea doubtless, and I count all things but loss for the
excellency of the knowledge of Christ Jesus, my Lord; for whom I
have suffered the loss of all things, and do count them but refuse,
that I may win Christ" (Phil. 3:4-8).

TWO SETS OF BOOKS

In our society almost everyone keeps records. Businessmen keep
records of their business. Taxpayers keep records of their income and
expenses. Housewives keep records of where the money goes so that
when their husbands say, "What! Is the money gone already?" they
can say, "Yes, I spent it to get your shirts laundered or your suit
pressed." And government keeps records on almost everyone.

In the spiritual realm, too, there are records. Men keep records with
God; God keeps records with men. And the whole problem is that
God's methods of bookkeeping are not the same as man's methods of
bookkeeping. God writes that men are sinners. For "there is none
righteous, no, not one: there is none that understandeth, there is none
that seeketh after God. They are all gone out of the way, they are

together become unprofitable; there is none that doeth good, no, not one" (Rom. 3:10-12). And men write that although that may be true of other men, it is certainly not true of them. Men measure themselves by other men while God measures men by His own standard of moral perfection.

In the last century the corporation of Harvard University was building a new philosophy building, and the plans came for approval to the president. This man was a Christian. He approved the plans, but made one change. Over the door of the building of philosophy the designers had made room for the inscription: "Man is the measure of all things." When the plans came back from the President's office, the plans were approved in every detail except for the inscription. Where it had said, "Man is the measure of all things," it now said, "What is man, that thou art mindful of him?" a quotation from Psalm 8:4. That is God's point of view; the other is man's point of view. There is a difference, and all men apart from Jesus Christ are interested in having God come around to their way of thinking. They want God to adopt their bookkeeping.

In his successful book, *How to Win Friends and Influence People,* Dale Carnegie tells a story from his own experience that will further illustrate this truth. Carnegie had been renting the grand ballroom of a certain New York hotel for years in order to give his lectures. At the beginning of one season, after the tickets had been printed and the announcements had been made, the manager of the hotel suddenly informed him that the rent for the ballroom was being raised 300 percent. Carnegie did not want to pay the increase. So he waited a few days and then went to see the manager.

"I was a bit shocked when I got your letter," he said, "but I don't blame you at all. If I had been in your position, I should probably have written a similar letter myself. But let's take a piece of paper and write down the advantages and disadvantages that will accrue to you if you insist on this increase in rent."

Carnegie then drew a line through the center of a piece of paper and labeled one column "Advantages" and the other "Disadvantages." Under "Advantages" he wrote, "Ballroom Free." And he explained that this was a real advantage, for the rental of the ballroom for dances and conventions would undoubtedly bring in more money than a series of lectures. He then turned to the disadvantages.

"First," he said, "instead of increasing your income from me, you are going to decrease it. In fact, you are going to wipe it out entirely because I cannot pay the rent you are asking." Then he said, "There is another disadvantage to you also. These lectures attract crowds of

educated and cultured people to your hotel. And that's good advertising for you, isn't it? In fact, if you spent $5,000 advertising in the
newspapers, you couldn't bring as many people to look at your hotel
as I can bring by these lectures. Now I wish you would carefully
consider both the advantages and disadvantages that are going to accrue to you, then give me your final decision." The next day he received a letter informing him that his rent would be increased only
50 percent instead of 300 percent.

That is what men try to do with God. God says, "This is the
standard: perfection; this is My way of bookkeeping." And men come
to Him and say, "Now look, God, let's take a sheet of paper and
draw a line on it and list the advantages and disadvantages that accrue
to you if you insist on your bookkeeping. In the first place, you will
be able to say that you're the boss. That's an advantage. But there
are disadvantages also. You will lose my support because I will not
do things your way. And you will lose my income and my influence
because I certainly will not point anyone to a God who is so obstinate
where human righteousness is concerned." And thus men try to persuade God Almighty.

How arrogant! And how devilish! It may be true that the hotel
manager was charging Dale Carnegie too much, but the God who is
the only true Judge of the universe rules righteously; and His standards
are righteous. And it is nothing but devilish impudence for a man
to think that he can dicker with God Almighty. No man can get God
to change His standards.

MAN'S RUIN

If a person is to accept this truth he must realize that human righteousness is nothing when measured against the righteousness of God
revealed in Jesus Christ, and that God is right to insist upon His
standards. In the first place, man's righteousness falls short of the
standards set by God, and anything short of those standards is unrighteousness. Righteousness is one of those things, like perfection or
wholeness, that loses its meaning entirely if you divide it. Perfection
is a whole. You cannot be half-perfect. To be half-perfect is to be
imperfect; it is not perfection at all. You cannot have a whole half of
an orange. You either have a whole orange or you have part of an
orange. Righteousness is exactly the same. You are either completely
righteous by God's definition or you are not righteous at all. Jesus
Christ said in what is undoubtedly the most important single verse
in the Sermon on the Mount, "Be ye, therefore, perfect, even as your
Father, who is in heaven, is perfect" (Matt. 5:48). And that is the

standard. All men fall short of it, and falling short of it, they miss it all. If you have a boat tied up to a dock by a chain that has ten links in it, how many links do you have to break to set it adrift? Just one. And if you have a churning cataract fifty yards down river, the boat will go over it and be destroyed just as easily with one link broken as with all ten. It is the same spiritually. Some men break all the links of God's law, and we call them criminals or murderers. We put them in prison if we can catch them. Other people carefully pry open just one of the links, and we try to overlook it since all of us are at least that guilty. But all are adrift and headed toward the cataract. That is what is meant when we say that all men are equally unrighteous from God's point of view.

There is a second reason why human righteousness is not adequate when measured against the goodness of God. Human goodness, even at best, is polluted by sin. When I lived in Switzerland, I read a newspaper headline one day that said that an epidemic of typhoid had broken out in Zermatt. It was very acute because the hotel managers had tried to keep it quiet for some time to protect the tourist business. Zermatt is one of those beautiful mountain villages nestled at the foot of the Matterhorn. The road is too steep for cars, and the only entry to the valley is by cog-wheel railroad. Everything is peaceful in the village. It is idyllic. If there was ever Paradise on earth, it is there at Zermatt. But typhoid had broken out, and it was some time before they found out the source of the trouble. The water main passing through the town had a crack in it, and the animal refuse from the fields was dripping into the crack and from there into the main water supply. The typhoid bacillus had bred there, and the pipe was contaminated. Now a person who did not understand the nature of disease might say, "But you cannot have any better water than the water that comes from the mountains. That is beautiful water; it comes from the melting glaciers." Yes, but the pipe that carried it was contaminated by typhoid, and consequently any water that went through it was contaminated also.

So, too, with human righteousness. We do good things, but all of our good deeds, even the best of them, are contaminated by sin. And because sin is there, sin can always break forth into death. That is why the noblest ideals and most sublime ideologies of men often lead to the most devilish actions in practice. Human righteousness leads away from God. And God must pronounce a curse upon it in order that true righteousness might be established in a man through the work of Jesus Christ.

PAUL'S ASSETS

In Philippians 3, verses 4-8, Paul illustrates these principles from his own experience. Humanly speaking he had acquired all of the assets that anyone could imagine. He was a Jew, and the Jews had always had a special place in God's dealings with the human race. These were real advantages. But in terms of salvation Paul had come to admit that all of these things had actually kept him from God. He writes, "But what things were gain to me, those I counted loss for Christ. Yea doubtless, and I count all things but loss for the excellency of the knowledge of Christ Jesus, my Lord" (Phil. 3:7, 8).

Paul lists seven achievements in these verses, and they fall into two categories — those that were inherited and those that were earned. The first of the inherited assets was the fact that Paul had been born into a Jewish family and had been circumcised according to Jewish law on the eighth day of life. He was not a proselyte, who had been circumcised in later life, nor an Ishmaelite, who was circumcised when he was 13 years old. He was *a pure-blooded Jew,* born of Jewish parents ("a Hebrew of the Hebrews"); he had been born a Jew from the cradle.

Moreover, he was an Israelite. Israel is the covenant name of God's people, just as the word "Jew" emphasizes their racial origins. Hence, Paul claims to be a member of the *covenant* people.

He was also of the tribe of *Benjamin.* When the civil war came that divided Judah from Israel after the death of Solomon, Benjamin was the one tribe that remained with Judah in the south. The northern tribes had separated from God's revealed religion and had set up schismatic altars where blood sacrifices were performed in direct violation of Leviticus 17. That chapter says that sacrifices were to be offered only at the great altar in Jerusalem. Benjamin had resisted this and had remained loyal to the house of David. Thus, Paul took justifiable pride in this ancestry.

Then, too, Paul cites the advantages that he had won for himself. First, in regard to the law he was a *Pharisee.* This was a matter of choice. The Pharisees constituted the most faithful of all Jewish sects in their adherence to the law. They set a hedge about it *(Pirke Aboth* 1:1), constructed of additional commandments, and Paul writes that he was blameless where the law was concerned. Moreover, Paul was a *zealous* Pharisee. His zeal is seen in the fact that he was a persecutor of the Church. In fact, he was so zealous for the law that he killed people who disagreed with his conception of it. And he was present at the stoning of Stephen, consenting to his death.

That is a real list of assets from a man's point of view. But the day came when Paul saw what this was in the sight of the righteous God. I suppose that the most important word in the entire third chapter of Philippians is the word that begins verse seven — "But." That "but" marks Paul's experience on the road to Damascus when Paul first saw Jesus and learned what God's righteousness was. He thought before this that he had attained righteousness by keeping the law. But then he saw Christ and he knew that all his righteousnesses were as filthy rags. He had said, "As touching the righteousness that is in the law, I am blameless;" but when he saw Christ he came to say, "I am the chief of sinners."

That is the work of God in a man's heart. Paul came to the point where he opened his ledger book. And after he had looked at all of the things that he had accumulated by inheritance and by his efforts, he reflected that these things had actually kept him from Christ. He then took the entire list and placed it where it belonged — under the list of liabilities. He called it "loss." And under assets he wrote, "Jesus Christ alone."

It should be noted that he did not count them loss merely for Christianity. Dr. H. A. Ironside writes, "He was not simply exchanging one religion for another; it was not one system of rites and ceremonies giving place to a superior system; or one set of doctrines, rules and regulations making way for a better one. . . . He had come in contact with a divine person, the once crucified, but now glorified Christ of God. He had been won by that Person forever, and for his sake he counted all else but loss. . . . Christ, and Christ alone, meets every need of the soul. His work has satisfied God, and it satisfies the one who trusts in him." *

CHRIST OUR RIGHTEOUSNESS

Is that true of you? Have you exchanged your assets for Christ? Or are you trusting in the kind of goodness that will never be accepted by God? If you are, let me give you a warning. That goodness will take you to hell. Hell is full of it. But if you will lay your goodness aside, counting it loss, God will credit Jesus Christ to your account "who of God is made unto us wisdom, and righteousness, and sanctification, and redemption" (I Cor. 1:30).

This has always been the heart of Christian experience, and it has been embodied in many of our hymns. One of them says:

Nothing in my hands I bring,
Simply to Thy cross I cling;

* H. A. Ironside, *Philippians* (Neptune, N.J.: Loizeaux Bros., 1922), pp. 79, 80.

> Naked, come to Thee for dress,
> Helpless, look to Thee for grace;
> Foul, I to the fountain fly;
> Wash me, Savior, or I die.
>
> Rock of ages, cleft for me,
> Let me hide myself in Thee.

Will you pray that prayer? If you do, God will provide the washing, and Christ will be reckoned as your one sufficient asset forever.

30.

Your Goodness or God's?

(Philippians 3:9)

PHILIPPIANS 3:9 IS A ONE-VERSE SUMMARY of the book of Romans, for it deals with the heart of salvation in a capsule form. What is salvation? Paul writes that it is to "be found in him [Christ], not having mine own righteousness, which is of the law, but that which is through the faith of Christ, the righteousness which is of God by faith." The principles involved are these: first, there are two kinds of righteousness: the righteousness that comes from men and the righteousness that comes from God. Second, God cannot be satisfied with any righteousness that comes from men. And third, God *is* satisfied with His own righteousness, which He offers freely to all who believe in Jesus Christ. For those who do believe, this is the objective basis of salvation.

TWO KINDS OF RIGHTEOUSNESS

It is not easy to describe the righteousness of God because it is an aspect of His character and sin limits our knowledge of Him. And yet we know that the righteousness of God is related to the holiness of God and that both are seen in the law of the Old Testament and in the ethical teachings of Jesus Christ. The law is not God's righteousness; but it is an expression of it, just as a coin is an expression of the die in the mint that produced it. In the law we see the impression of God's purity, holiness, love, integrity, and perfection.

The righteousness of God is also seen in Jesus Christ. We see God's power in nature. We see God's principles in the law. But we see God's personality in Jesus. And it is infused with righteousness. Jesus said to His enemies, "Which of you convicteth me of sin?" (John 8:46), and they were silent. A few verses earlier He had said of God His Father, "I do always those things that please him" (John 8:29).

Now it is important to emphasize that this righteousness, the righteousness of God that is seen in the law and in Jesus Christ, is different from human righteousness. Men would like to think that they can attain God's standard of righteousness merely by adding to their own, but if the two kinds of righteousness are different in nature — and they are — this is impossible. Most people believe that all goodness may be placed on a scale. On the bottom are those whose righteousness is on a very low level. These are the murderers, thieves, and perverts. There are others whose righteousness is a bit higher. These are average citizens. There are a few whose righteousness is very high indeed. And then, so they think, there is God, whose righteousness is the highest of all. Actually, it is not this way. God teaches that there are two kinds of righteousness — His righteousness and man's righteousness — and that the accumulation of human righteousness, no matter how diligent, will never take a man to heaven.

The accumulation of human righteousness is a bit like playing Monopoly. The game has beautiful money. The least valuable bills are the one-dollar bills; they are white. The most valuable are the five-hundreds; they are gold. The object of the game is to collect as much money and property as you can. The game is enjoyable, but only a fool would take his Monopoly earnings and go into town to buy groceries. A different kind of currency is used in the real world. It is the same spiritually. And yet, although this is true, there are people who think they are collecting assets before God when they are only collecting human righteousness. And God tells us that we must leave the play currency to deal in His goodness. Man's goodness has no value in heaven.

ALL ARE CONDEMNED

Unfortunately, most people will not believe that. And for that reason much of the Bible is given over to showing why human goodness will never please God. The book of Romans is the primary example. Like a doctor's diagnosis, the opening chapters of this book probe to the depths of man's sin, exposing his spiritual illness and indicating why human remedies will not heal man's soul. There are three types of men, Paul says. And each one needs God's righteousness.

You know, I am sure, that the way you categorize things determines the number of categories you get. If you classify trees on the basis of whether they keep their leaves the year around or lose them each fall, you get two classes: evergeen and deciduous. If you classify the same trees by their bark, leaves, habitat, height, and so on, you get hundreds of classes. It is the same way with persons. If you classify men on the basis of their income, you can have as many levels as there are brackets on the Internal Revenue scale. If you classify them by intellect, you get as many brackets as there are points on the Intelligence Quota scale. But if you classify men spiritually, which is

our concern here, you get only three types. These three brackets include all men. And it is these that are discussed in Romans.

The first type of man is described in Romans 1:18-32. He is what
we would call a hedonist. This is the man who says, "The only standards of conduct that I recognize are those that I devise for myself.
And I determine to live for myself and for whatever pleasure I can
find." Paul says that this man needs the Gospel because he is on a
path that is leading him from God.

What is this path? Paul describes it clearly in verses 21-28: "When
they knew God, they glorified him not as God, neither were thankful,
but became vain in their imaginations, and their foolish heart was
darkened. Professing themselves to be wise, they became fools, and
changed the glory of the incorruptible God into an image made like
corruptible man, and birds, and four-footed beasts, and creeping things.
Wherefore, God also gave them up to uncleanness . . . unto vile affections . . . [and] to a reprobate mind."

The first step along this path is described as a vanity of the imagination that results from turning from God. The word "imagination" is
a translation of a Greek word from which we also get our popular
English word "dialogue." It occurs ten times in the New Testament
and each time with a bad connotation. It is that activity of the human
personality that exalts its own reasoning against God. In another place
Paul says that this way of thinking is to be resisted by Christians.
They are to live by "casting down imaginations, and every high thing
that exalteth itself against the knowledge of God, and bringing into
captivity every thought to the obedience of Christ" (II Cor. 10:5). In
spiritual things men must submit to God's wisdom.

The second step along the path of the man who lives only for himself and by his own standards is that his heart is darkened. God is not
only truth; God is light. And when men turn from Him they walk in
darkness, just as a man walks in his own shadow when he turns his
back to the sun. The farther he gets from the light the longer the
shadow becomes and the darker his journey.

Third, "professing themselves to be wise, they became foolish." No
one who turns to his own reason instead of to God's truth and thus
has his heart darkened says, "I am living only by my depraved human
reasoning and my foolish heart is darkened." Oh no! He says, "I am
becoming wise. It is the believers in Jesus Christ who are foolish."
This is acute self-deception. It was actually the way in which the devil
induced Eve to sin, for he said, "Your eyes shall be opened, and ye
shall be as God, knowing good and evil" (Gen. 3:5).

The final step along the path of the natural man is a perversion of
the worship of God which leads to an abasement of man himself.

The Bible says that he changes "the glory of the incorruptible God into an image made like corruptible men, and birds, and four-footed beasts, and creeping things." This means that if a man will not allow Jesus Christ to begin to make him like God through grace, that man will attempt to make God like man. And since this debases God it will inevitably debase man also. If a man will not worship the true God, he will construct something else in God's place. And the substitute will become more and more repellent the farther he gets from the holy, just, loving and altogether beautiful God. This has happened again and again in man's history.

If you come to a fork while driving down the road and take the wrong turn, the only sensible thing to do is turn around and go back. It is the same spiritually. Some men go gently down the road I have just described, never going very far and frequently stopping to fool around with sin. Some men go down the same road at a terrific speed and are miles away when the others are just beginning to round the first bend. But it is the same road, and the cure is identical. All must first stop. This is called repentance. And then they must turn themselves around and go back. This is the true meaning of conversion. The hedonist needs the Gospel because his own way takes him from God.

The Moral Man

The second type of man described in Romans, who also needs the Gospel, is the man who leads an ethically superior life. He is the moral man, and his case is set forth in Romans 2:1-16. Perhaps you are like this. He is the man who would say, "Well, all of what you have said is true — about the hedonist. But I am not like that. I do not live only to myself. I pursue high standards. In fact, I pursue the highest standards I know. Therefore, your call to repentance does not apply to me." And Paul's answer is, "Yes, yes it does. And it does for two excellent reasons."

The first reason is that no matter how high your standards may be they still fall short of God's standards. That is the difference between playing with Monopoly money and using real currency. The second reason is that you fall short of your own standards no matter how high or how low they may be.

What is your ethical standard? You may say, "Well, my standard is the Sermon on the Mount." Do you live up to that standard? Of course you do not, for Jesus said, "Be ye, therefore, perfect, even as your Father, who is in heaven, is perfect" (Matt. 5:48). And no one is perfect. Perhaps your standard is the Ten Commandments. Do you keep them? Of course not, for you covet most of the days of your life, things that other people have, and you break many of the other commandments also. Is your standard the Golden Rule? If so, you break that, for no one always does for the other person what he would like to have done for himself. Perhaps your standard is merely the lowest common denominator of human relationships — the standard of fair play. Well, do you do that? Not always! And so you stand condemned by even the lowest of the ethical standards.

One day when that great man King David was on his roof in the heart of the city of Jerusalem he saw a girl who was bathing on a roof not far away. Her name was Bathsheba. After discovering who she was, David invited her to the palace and made love to her. Bathsheba was married. And when it was discovered that she was pregnant David arranged to have her husband killed in battle so that he could marry her, which he did. This was a great sin, the greatest sin of David's life, and the time came when God sent the prophet Nathan to him to expose the crime. Nathan first asked for his judgment on a hypothetical problem. Nathan said, "There were two men who owned sheep, one poor and one rich. The rich man had many sheep, and the poor man had just one. One day a stranger came to the house of the rich man seeking hospitality, and the rich man did not want to feed him by diminishing his own herd. He therefore took the sheep of the poor man and served it." At this point in the story David grew angry and declared, "The man who hath done this thing shall surely die." And Nathan replied, "Thou art the man."

Be careful when you erect a standard of your own, of your righteousness, and say you will live by that. You will be condemned by that standard, whatever it may be. You must disabuse yourself of the idea that you can earn heaven, and you must admit that you, too, need God's righteousness.

The Religious Man

There is only one more type of man discussed in Romans, and he is handled in Romans 2:17-29. He is the religious man. He says, "Yes, I know that all of the things you have said are true and that they are true of me. I fall short of those standards. But I am religious, and I place my trust there. I have been baptized and confirmed; I take communion; I give toward the church's support." And Paul says, "Well, good for you. But you need the Gospel of Jesus Christ also." "Why?" "Because God is not interested in outward things alone — church membership, the sacraments, and stewardship — He is interested in what is within." The Bible says, "Man looketh on the outward appearance, but the Lord looketh on the heart" (I Sam. 16:7).

In the city of Basel, Switzerland, each year there is a carnival that takes place at the beginning of Lent. It is much like the Mardi Gras except for the fact that Basel is a Protestant city and shows it by having its carnival after Lent begins instead of before Lent like all other cities. Mardi Gras actually means "fat Tuesday" because it is celebrated on the day before Lent begins, and Lent always begins on a Wednesday. Well, Basel's carnival begins after that, and it is always a wild affair with all of the debauchery that one associates with a carnival season. And everyone knows what goes on, even though they may not know exactly who does it because the people wear masks. Each year the Salvation Army uses the carnival season to advertise the Gospel. And it does so in a striking way. All around the city the Army places billboards and posters containing the German words, *"Gott sieht hinter deine maske!"* This means, "God sees behind your mask." And the point is that God knows what is going on within. Man looks on the outward appearance, but the Lord looks on the heart.

God is looking on your heart and mine. What does He see? Does He see deeds, even religious deeds, that are not backed up by the divine life within? Or does He see His own righteousness, imparted to you and beginning to work its way out into your conduct? You cannot fool God with human righteousness. If you are trusting this, He must say to you as He says to all men, "There is none righteous, no, not one: there is none that understandeth, there is none that seeketh after God. They are all gone out of the way, they are together become unprofitable; there is none that doeth good, no, not one" (Rom. 3:10-12). You must turn from your goodness to God's.

GOD'S RIGHTEOUSNESS

The problem is whether or not you will accept God's verdict upon your goodness and turn to Him for that righteousness which He gives you by grace. This Paul did, for he says that his desire was to be found in Christ "not having mine own righteousness, which is of the law, but that which is through the faith of Christ, the righteousness which is of God by faith."

Are you sensitive to what God has to say about your character? Quite a few years ago a man was brought into the emergency room of the general hospital in McKeesport, Pennsylvania, with a dislocated spine. My father, who is an orthopedic surgeon, was on duty, and he saw at a glance that the man had been partially paralyzed. He had been in a serious accident, and there was much wrong with him. His legs had been broken. There were deep lacerations over much of his body. But he could not feel these things because a nerve had been pinched by the spine, and he had no sensation in the lower part of his body. My father began to operate on him, using a local anesthetic and occasionally asking if the man could feel anything from his injuries. The questioning went like this: "Do you feel anything?" "No." "Do you feel anything now?" "No." At last my father came to a piece of splintered bone that was pressing on the nerves. This time, as he asked the question "Can you feel anything?" my father removed the bone, and the answer came back loudly, "Yes, yes I can feel it." It was a cry of pain. But it was a pleasing cry, for it was the first step in the man's complete recovery.

It may be the same for you. God's verdict upon the human race includes all men — the hedonist, the moralist, the most religious person, and you, whatever you may be — and it is one that declares all human righteousness unable to satisfy the righteous standards of God. You are included in that judgment. But you may not be able to feel that the things God is saying about you are true. Are you sensitive to God's verdict? Do you feel the truth of His statements? If not, there is a spiritual disorder in your life. And God must begin to operate on it before you will come to Him.

Perhaps He is doing that now! You may be feeling the most acute spiritual pain because of it, but you must know that your new sensitivity is the first step in your spiritual recovery. Your recovery will take place completely as you come to God to receive a righteousness that comes from God Himself and is entirely untainted by sin. That righteousness comes by faith in Jesus Christ. You must come to God through Him.

31.

What Is Faith?

(Philippians 3:9)

ALL TRUE TEACHING OF the Word of God must stress that God alone is responsible for our salvation. But when this is said, any person may quite properly ask: "How, then, does this apply to me? What makes the death of Jesus personal? You say that God offers His righteousness to men who lack that righteousness; how, then, do I receive it? What must I do? By what means does this wonderful salvation become mine?" The answer to all of these questions is that God's righteousness becomes yours personally through faith. The letter to the Hebrews says, "Without *faith* it is impossible to please Him" (Heb. 11:6). Romans tells us that "the righteousness of God [is] revealed *from faith to faith*" (Rom. 1:17). And Ephesians says, "For by grace are ye saved *through faith*" (Eph. 2:8).

In Philippians Paul echoes that teaching. He writes of his wish to be found in Christ, "not having mine own righteousness, which is of the law, but that which is through the faith of Christ, the righteousness which is of God *by faith*" (Phil. 3:9). "The faith of Christ" and "righteousness . . . by faith"! These phrases speak of the human side of our salvation.

THE NATURE OF FAITH

Unfortunately, many people are puzzled about this thing called faith, although there is no need to be puzzled by it. Faith is simply belief. If you believe in a thing, you have faith in it. Thus, faith is one of the most common realities of life. It is far more common, for instance, than romantic love, artistic insight, exceptional intelligence, and similar things. These things are true for only some people. But faith is a reality which all men experience.

In spite of this truth there have been many attempts to discredit faith by turning it into something that is not really faith at all. Every attempt to define faith as believing something you know is not true is an example of this distortion, for in this case faith becomes *delusion*. When one of the many sects that cling to the edge of true Christianity tries to teach that sin, evil, and sickness do not exist and that faith can overcome them by denying their reality, such faith is not true faith. And those who follow this nonsense will be disappointed both in this life and in the life to come.

Another substitute for faith is *credulity*. Credulity is the attitude of a man who will accept something as true apart from evidence, simply because he earnestly wishes it to be true. Rumors of miraculous cures for some generally incurable disease encourage this attitude in many unfortunate people. But credulity is not faith either.

The most common distortion of faith in our day is the attempt to make belief *subjective*. This is the faith of existentialism, and it is at the heart of all religious feeling that is divorced from the objective truth of Scripture. Once a man told me that he firmly believed that he was a Christian. As we probed a bit further during our conversation I discovered that he did not believe in Christ's divinity. He did not believe that Jesus died for his sin or that the New Testament contained an accurate record of His life and ministry. He did not acknowledge Christ as Lord of his life. And when I pointed out that all of these things are involved in the true definition of a Christian, he answered that in spite of these things he believed deep in his heart that he was a Christian. The thing that he called faith was grounded only in his feelings.

Against all of these distortions the Christian must reply that real faith is far more tangible than this and is not at all based on a person's individual feelings. When you drive your car across a bridge, you have faith that the bridge will hold you up. You have faith in the engineers who designed it, in the men who built and maintain it, in the inspectors who guarantee its safety. If you have doubts about the safety of the bridge on any of these counts, you do not drive across it. If you step onto a bus to go home at night, you have faith that the bus is safe, that the driver is an employee of the transportation company, and that the sign on the bus is a true indication of where the bus is going. If you buy a ticket to a sports show, you have faith that the show will be held as advertised and that the ticket will gain you admission. In every one of these examples faith is believing something on the basis of evidence and then acting upon it.

By far the greatest example of faith is the way in which a man and a woman will commit themselves to each other in marriage. The man says, "Will you marry me?" And the woman says, "Yes." The whole conversation only takes five words. But between two persons who know and trust each other the words constitute a pledge of faith that can last until death. Such faith is personal. And it is no accident that the pledge of a man to a woman and of a woman to a man has been taken both in Scripture and in Christian poetry as an illustration of that bond in faith that exists between a Christian and his Lord. In Ephesians Paul speaks of marriage as an illustration of Christ's love for us: "This is a great mystery, but I speak concerning Christ and the church" (Eph. 5:32). One of our hymn writers has beautifully written:

> I am the Lord's! O joy beyond expression,
> O sweet response to voice of love Divine;
> Faith's joyous "Yes" to the assuring whisper,
> "Fear not! I have redeem'd thee; thou art mine."

> I am the Lord's! It is the glad confession,
> Wherewith the Bride recalls the happy day,
> When love's "I will" accepted Him forever,
> "The Lord's," to love, to honor and obey.

> I am the Lord's! Yet teach me all it meaneth,
> All it involves of love and loyalty,
> Of holy service, absolute surrender,
> And unreserved obedience unto Thee.

> I am the Lord's! Yes; body, soul and spirit,
> O seal them irrecoverably Thine;
> As Thou, Beloved, in Thy grace and fulness
> Forever and forevermore art mine.

SAVING FAITH

At this point of our study I anticipate an objection. For someone is going to ask whether we have not shifted the subject by moving from the common faith that all men exercise every day of their lives to religious or saving faith. "Aren't they two different things?" someone will ask. And the answer to that is, "No, they are not, so long as you are speaking about the nature of faith itself," and "Yes, they are, if you are speaking about the object of belief and the evidence for it." Faith is believing in someone or something and acting upon it. And we can believe God exactly as we believe men. The only difference between the kind of faith that men exercise every day and saving faith is that saving faith is absolutely certain, for it is faith in the only One in the universe who is absolutely faithful and who never breaks His promises. James, the Lord's brother, wrote, "Every good gift and every perfect gift is from above, and cometh down from the Father of lights, with whom is no variableness, neither shadow of turning" (James 1: 17).

This is taught in a striking verse from I John. The apostle John was very much interested in evidence. His gospel speaks of seven types of witnesses to the revelation of God the Father in Jesus Christ. His first epistle begins with a reminder that he speaks as an historical witness to that "which we have heard, which we have seen with our eyes, which we have looked upon, and our hands have handled, of the Word of Life" (I John 1:1). And he ends the epistle with the statement that he has written these things to Christians that they might be certain of their salvation (I John 5:13). John was certainly interested in evidence. "All right, John," we might ask, "you have been speaking about the evidence for faith. What is the greatest evidence?" And we hear John answer: "If we receive the witness of men, the witness of God is greater; for this is the witness of God which he hath testified of his Son. He that believeth on the Son of God hath the witness in himself; he that believeth not God hath made him a liar, because he believeth not the record that God gave of his Son" (I John 5:9, 10).

Does that statement seem excessive to you? It is not, if we understand what God is saying. What does God most want from men? God wants to be believed. We believe men. We trust men with our lives, our health, our families, our fortunes every day of our lives. Why should we not believe God? At the best, men are partially reliable. They can be trusted partially. But God is entirely reliable. He is eminently trustworthy. He is the only personality in the universe whose word is always His bond. And He calls upon us to believe that He gives eternal life to everyone who will believe on His Son.

WHAT WE BELIEVE

What does God call upon us to believe? First of all, God demands that we admit without reservation that we are less perfect than Himself and that we should, therefore, be separated from His presence forever. God is perfect, and anyone who fails to meet that standard deserves to be separated from Him.

This principle is hard for the non-Christian to accept. But it should not be, for we recognize the principle in many things that are accepted naturally. Take medicine as an example. No one would question the right of a state's government to make the requirements for the practice of medicine as high as is reasonably possible. The state sets the standards, and anyone who wants to be a doctor must meet them. If you want to be a doctor, you must first graduate from college and hold either a Bachelor of Science or Bachelor of Arts degree. After that you must graduate from medical school and hold an M.D. This must be followed by a one-year internship under the supervision of competent doctors. And after this you must pass an examination which leads to licensing by the state. No sane person would want to trust himself to a man who claims to be able to practice medicine but who has not passed these requirements.

In the same way, God has a right to His requirements. They are summed up as perfection. The only difference between this demand and the demands of the state boards of medicine is that no one has ever met God's standards. And no one will. God says that "all have sinned, and come short of the glory of God" (Rom. 3:23). Consequently, men deserve separation from God as surely as quacks should be barred from the medical profession.

The second thing that God asks men to believe is that He loves them in spite of their sin and that He has acted in Jesus Christ to remove that sin and to restore fellowship between Himself and those who believe. Romans 5:8 says, "But God commendeth his love toward us in that, while we were yet sinners, Christ died for us." John 3:16 says, "For God so loved the world, that he gave his only begotten Son, that whosoever believeth in him should not perish, but have everlasting life."

There are two parts to this transaction. On the one hand, we are sinners, and sin must be punished. God says that Christ died to bear that punishment. The second part is that on the basis of Christ's death God now comes to us and offers us His righteousness, entirely as a free gift. Before, we were clothed in sin; now, we are clothed in righteousness. Before, we were no people; now, we are God's people. Before, we were aliens; now, we are citizens of heaven. Before, we were separated from God; now, we have fellowship with Him and our life here and now is transformed by His presence. That is salvation.

Do you believe these things? Do you believe that you are less perfect than God? Do you accept His verdict that your lack of perfection should bring judgment and that it bars you even now from His presence? Do you believe that God sent Jesus Christ to bear the just penalty for your sin and that He offers you His righteousness? If you do not believe these things, you will be condemned to an eternity without God. If you do believe them, then God will remove your sin and enter your heart through His Holy Spirit; and God will begin that moment-by-moment transformation of your life that is His perfect will for you and which will lead in God's own time to the final transformation of your person when you will be made like Jesus Christ forever.

The Steps of Faith

Now there is one more thing to be said. We have considered the initial moment of saving faith, when faith first seizes upon the facts of God's salvation. This is of tremendous importance. But we must never think that faith stops here. Faith is an aspect of life, and it is certainly a continuing aspect of the life of the Christian. Faith is belief. And belief grows stronger as it comes to know the nature of the one it trusts.

Faith does not start strong. But it is meant to become strong. The faith of Abraham is the great illustration of this principle. When the call of God came to Abraham to leave Ur of the Chaldees and go into a land that he would afterwards inherit, the book of Hebrews says that "Abraham . . . obeyed; and he went out, not knowing where he went" (11:8). This was faith, but such faith did not need to be strong. It was only belief in the ability of God to lead the patriarch into the land. Yet Hebrews goes on to say, "By faith he sojourned in the land of promise, as in a foreign country, dwelling in tents with Isaac and Jacob, the heirs with him of the same promise" (11:9). Such faith was stronger, for it was a belief exercised in the face of famine, danger, and the delay in God's complete fulfillment of the promise. Two verses further on the chapter speaks of the faith through which Sarah received strength to bear a son when she was past the age of child-bearing. By this point faith was strong, for it had come to know the God of the promise as the God of miracles. In the last verses we read of a faith that conquers doubt even in the midst of great emotional suffering and the seeming contradiction of all that had been believed previously. "By faith Abraham, when he was tested, offered up Isaac; and he that had received the promises offered up his only begotten son, of whom it was said, In Isaac shall thy seed be called; accounting that God was able to raise him up, even from the dead, from which also he received him in a figure" (11:17-19). Abraham believed that God was able to perform a resurrection. And it is in reference to this last event that God says of Abraham in Romans, "He staggered not at the promise of God through unbelief, but was strong in faith, giving glory to God, and being fully persuaded that, what he had promised, he was able also to perform" (Rom. 4:20, 21).

Such is the normal growth of faith. If you are a new Christian, you are somewhere at the beginning of the road that Abraham walked. If you are a more mature Christian, you are farther along that road. Your faith may be weak. Your faith may be strong. But the overriding fact is that your faith is in God the Father and in His Son, our Lord Jesus Christ. God cannot fail. Come to know God. Spend time with

Jesus. And you will find, as God intends you to find, that your faith will go on from strength to strength. And the glory of it all is that the strength of your faith will lie, not in you, but in faith's object. It will lie in God, in the One you are coming increasingly to know.

32.

Knowing the Living Christ

(Philippians 3:10, 11)

THERE ARE MANY THINGS that distinguish Christianity from other world religions, but one of the most significant distinctions is this: Christians believe that Jesus rose again from the dead after having been crucified and that He lives today to be known by those who trust Him. The Jesus who was born in Bethlehem 1900 years ago, who lived, who died, and who rose again, still lives. Consequently, to know Him personally, intimately, and experientially is the first and greatest goal of the believer's life.

This was Paul's goal also, and Philippians 3:10, 11 is a great expression of it. Paul has spoken of his initial faith in Christ. He now speaks of the goal of Christian living: "That I may know him, and the power of his resurrection, and the fellowship of his sufferings, being made conformable unto his death, if by any means I might attain unto the resurrection of the dead." Paul wanted to know Jesus. And, as he writes about his desire, the nature of that knowledge is plain. First, it is to be experiential. Second, it is to be a knowledge of God's power. Third, it is to be learned in suffering. And fourth, it is to result in a life that is a preview of the life of eternity.

EXPERIENTIAL KNOWLEDGE

In the first place, the knowledge Paul sought was experiential. We must see this aspect of his statement clearly, for without this understanding of Paul's desire the verses themselves are meaningless. Here is the great apostle to the Gentiles, through whom we have learned about Jesus, with all of his great rabbinical and historical knowledge, writing of his desire to know Him. And if we do not understand his meaning, we might well ask, "What do you mean, 'That I may know him'? We are believers in Jesus, but it is from you that we have learned much of what we know. You have written of His life, death, and resurrection. You have explained the meaning of the Gospel; you have

214

defended it against the attacks of Jewish legalists and against the gnostics. You have understood these things better perhaps than anyone we know. What do you mean when you say, 'That I may know him'?" And Paul would answer, "You have misunderstood me if you refer my statement to such knowledge. I did not say, 'That I may know *about* Him.' I said, 'That I may know *Him.*' And between the two statements is all the difference in the world."

We recognize, of course, that the word "know" has several different meanings in English, as also in other languages. It can mean "to have learned by serious study." This is the way one knows analytical geometry or calculus. It can mean "to have learned by intuition." This is the way we use the word when we say, "Oh, I know what's going on." It can refer to "understanding." It can even refer to a type of head knowledge that Paul told the Corinthians was detrimental to the Christian faith. For he wrote, "Knowledge puffs up, but love builds up. If anyone imagines that he knows something, he does not yet know as he ought to know" (I Cor. 8:1, 2, RSV). Such knowledge was not what Paul was seeking. Paul wanted to know Jesus in the truest biblical sense — personally and experientially. And he wanted this to affect his day-by-day living.

J. A. Motyer has seen this truth clearly. He writes, "We have largely lost the biblical dimensions of the word 'knowledge' in our customary use of it. We confine it almost to 'the contents of the brain.' The Bible would not resist this meaning, but neither would it accept it as a complete definition. First, it would add a practical dimension. Nothing is truly known unless it is being practiced in daily life, or in some way (according to its nature) allowed to control the conduct of the person concerned — 'to depart from evil is understanding' (Job 28:28). Secondly, in knowledge between persons, to 'know' is to enter into the deepest personal intimacy and contact. Thus the Bible does not say that 'Adam knew Eve' (Gen. 4:1) because it is too shy to speak openly about sexual matters, but because this is what knowledge between persons is — deep, intimate union. Consequently, having been saved wholly and solely by Christ, Paul wants to enter into the deepest possible union with Him." *

Do you have that desire? To know Jesus? To know Him intimately? To awake with Him in the morning and to live each day with Him and in His presence? There is only one inexhaustible person, and that is the Lord Jesus Christ. Men will disappoint us, but Jesus never. It is entirely satisfying to know Him.

* J. A. Motyer, *Philippian Studies* (Chicago: Inter-Varsity Press, 1966), pp. 132, 133.

RESURRECTION POWER

Now we must also notice that Paul's desire did not stop merely with the knowledge of Christ. He also wished to know His power. Paul writes, "That I may know him, and the power of his resurrection." Paul is not speaking here of an abstract knowledge about the resurrection any more than He is speaking of an abstract knowledge of Christ. Paul knew all about the resurrection. He knew the evidence for it. He had talked to the witnesses. He believed it as a fact. He even proclaimed it wherever he went in his preaching. This is not his present interest, however. Here Paul speaks of experience. And he states that, in addition to knowing about the resurrection, he also wants to experience its power.

How did Paul wish to experience this power? Above all, in the living of a godly life. Paul knew that a life lived with Jesus meant a life of holiness. But he also knew that such a life was impossible if it depended upon his own natural powers. He knew that the natural man cannot even understand spiritual things, "for they are foolishness unto him, neither can he know them, because they are spiritually discerned" (I Cor. 2:14). And he had learned by experience his own inability to live as God intended. In Romans seven he writes, "For the good that I would, I do not; but the evil which I would not, that I do. . . . I delight in the law of God after the inward man; but I see another law in my members, warring against the law of my mind, and bringing me into captivity to the law of sin which is in my members. Oh, wretched man that I am! Who shall deliver me from the body of this death?" (Rom. 7:19, 22-24). Paul longed for deliverance from such defeat through Christ's resurrection power.

Paul was sensitive to power, as were many of his contemporaries. His world was a world of power, most of it originating in Rome and controlled by the Roman authorities. The Jew was proud of his religious heritage. The Greek was proud of his wisdom. But the Roman was proud of his power. To him it was the greatest reality in the world. This was Paul's environment, and Paul had a genuine respect for Rome's power. He appealed to it on several occasions. But Paul knew that at best it was only the third strongest power in the world. The second strongest power was sin, for it held men in a vice-like grip through a tyranny far more terrible than Rome's. And the strongest power was the resurrection power of Jesus — God's power. He knew that this power could overcome sin and death and that it was far more potent than Rome's armies.

This knowledge enabled him to write, "There is, therefore, now no condemnation to them who are in Christ Jesus. For the law of the

Spirit of life in Christ Jesus hath made me free from the law of sin
and death. For what the law could not do, in that it was weak through
the flesh, God sending his own Son, in the likeness of sinful flesh and
for sin, condemned sin in the flesh, that the righteousness of the law
might be fulfilled in us, who walk not after the flesh, but after the
Spirit" (Rom. 8:1-4).

The power of Jesus Christ is a great reality. And many have come
to know it. That is why so many Christians sing:

> He breaks the power of cancelled sin,
> He sets the prisoner free;
> His blood can make the foulest clean —
> His blood availed for me.

Above all, Paul wanted to experience the resurrection power of Jesus
Christ over sin daily as he strived to live a holy life before God.

FELLOWSHIP IN SUFFERING

The third thing that Paul says he wished to know of Jesus Christ
was "the fellowship of his sufferings." This does not mean that Paul
wished to suffer for human sin, for only Jesus Christ could do that.
He alone suffered innocently and therefore for others. Paul wished
to join in Christ's sufferings in a different sense. He wished to stand
with Christ in such an indivisible union that when the abuses and.
persecution that Christ suffered also fell on him, as he knew they
would, he could receive them as Jesus did. He wanted to react like
Jesus, for he knew that abuse received like this would actually draw
him closer to his Lord.

Such sufferings will always come to the Christian. Peter wrote to the
believers of his day, "Beloved, think it not strange concerning the
fiery trial which is to test you, as though some strange thing happened
unto you, but rejoice, inasmuch as ye are partakers of Christ's sufferings" (I Pet. 4:12, 13). And Paul wrote to Timothy that "all that will
live godly in Christ Jesus shall suffer persecution" (II Tim. 3:12). Such
persecutions will come to you, if you seek to live as God commands
you. But they need not be tragic. On the contrary, they can draw you
closer to Jesus while allowing His life to be clearly seen in you.

I must add, however, that the knowledge of Christ's sufferings comes
at a very high price, the price of total obedience. Hence, Paul writes
of "being made conformable unto his death."

To understand this phrase we must go back to chapter two of the
letter, where Paul speaks of Christ's obedience in death and holds it
up as a pattern for all Christian conduct. He argues that Jesus was

so careful to obey his Father that He laid aside His outward mantle of glory and took to Himself man's form and nature, enduring all the sufferings of this world, and that He even died as a man in obedience to His Father's will. The fellowship of Christ's sufferings is won at the price of such radical and total obedience.

Are you like Jesus in that? Are you careful to obey God completely, even at the expense of open persecution and real suffering? I am afraid that many of us are like the man who wrote to the Bureau of Internal Revenue stating: "I can't sleep; my conscience is bothering me. Enclosed find a check for $50. If I still can't sleep, I'll send you the balance." This is not obedience. This is compromise. And it does not lead us to the fellowship of Christ's sufferings. If we are to know Him, really know Him, we must obey Him completely.

A Present Resurrection

In the last phrase of this great expression of Paul's goals Paul tells why he desires to know Christ so completely and to be conformed to His death. It is that he might "attain unto the resurrection of the dead."

We must not understand this to mean that Paul was afraid for his eternal security. The one who wrote in Romans, "For I am persuaded that neither death, nor life, nor angels, nor principalities, nor powers, nor things present, nor things to come, nor height, nor depth, nor any other creation, shall be able to separate us from the love of God, which is in Christ Jesus, our Lord" (Rom. 8:38, 39), and who said just two chapters earlier in Philippians, "Being confident of this very thing, that he who hath begun a good work in you will keep on performing it until the day of Jesus Christ" (Phil. 1:6) — such a one is not worried about his eternal security. He knows that God will bring him safely to heaven. Paul is not thinking in these terms. He is thinking about something else. Actually, he is saying that he wished to be so much like Christ in the way he lived that people would think of him as a resurrected person even now, even before his physical death.

Dr. Ralph L. Keiper puts it this way: "What then does Paul mean when he desires to 'attain unto the resurrection of the dead'? There is a clue in the Greek text. The word for resurrection in verse 11 differs from the word resurrection in verse 10. In verse 11 the word has a little preposition in front of it — the preposition *ek* which is equivalent to our word 'out.' The word resurrection literally means to 'place' or 'stand up.' To the Greek mind, living people were standing up, dead people were lying down. So, making a Greek pun, Paul says, 'I want to know Him, and the power of His resurrection, and the fellowship of His suffering that I may give the spiritually dead a preview of eternal life in action as I am standing up outstandingly among those who are spiritually on their backs — spiritually dead.'

"Or to put it still more colloquially, 'As I walk your streets, as I walk into your homes, as I walk into your stores, as I walk into your offices, as I mingle among the sons of men, I want to be so living for Christ, so outstanding for Him that you can see that I am a living one among the dead ones'" (*Eternity*, March, 1961, p. 21).

Is that your desire? To be so living for Christ that you will appear as a resurrected person among those who are spiritually dead? It should be, for it is God's desire for you.

In one of his books Dr. H. A. Ironside tells of the unusual conversion of a Hopi Indian man. "Little Rattlesnake" was his Indian name. And it was apt, for his life was not lived on the highest moral plain. In his youth he had gone to a government school in Carlisle, Pennsylvania, but he had returned home scorning the white man's religion because of his wicked ways. In time he found some wicked ways of his own. One night years later, he had a dream in which he imagined the Christians of his Indian village being snatched up to heaven while the others were left behind. And this so disturbed him that he sought out a Christian conference where Dr. Ironside happened to be speaking. There he was soundly converted. A great change came over him. He began to witness boldly to those with whom he had formerly consorted. His upright life began to demonstrate the reality of his profession. His wife became a Christian, and together they began to raise their children in the love and knowledge of the Lord. To the Indians, both believers and non-believers, "Little Rattlesnake," the pagan, became known as "Frank, the Christian preacher."

This was an example of the reality about which Paul was speaking. It was his desire. And, of course, it was God's desire both for him and for you. Can such a change occur in you? Of course, it can, for God does the changing. He can turn Saul into Paul; Simon, "the braggart," into Peter "the Rock"; John, "the Son of Thunder," into John the Evangelist; Little Rattlesnake into Frank, the Christian preacher; and you — whoever and whatever you may be — into the kind of person in whom Christ's holy and loving character may be seen. This is God's greatest purpose in saving you.

33.

Following the Living Christ

(Philippians 3:12)

I AM NOT SURE what humorist it was who first defined an ideal as "something that everyone is expected to honor but nobody is expected to attain," but many people think of Christian discipleship in this way, and the fact is unfortunate. The goals of discipleship are not unattainable ideals. And the Bible does not allow us to escape the demands of Christian discipleship by the excuse that the standards of that calling are too high.

Our study of Philippians has already brought us to two verses that were an expression of Paul's great and life-long desire to know Jesus Christ. He wrote of his desire to "know him, and the power of his resurrection, and the fellowship of his sufferings, being made conformable unto his death." Paul lived this desire. But as he wrote these words the great apostle must have realized that there would be some among his readers at Philippi, as there are today also, who would dimiss them as something that no Christian could possibly be expected to accomplish. They would admit that the ideal was a good one, but they would call it totally unpractical.

Paul does not allow this kind of thinking to continue. He immediately adds that although even he has not realized the goal in its entirety, he is still trying; and (we must understand him to be implying this) his readers should be trying also. He writes, "Not as though I had already attained, either were already perfect; but I follow after, if that I may apprehend that for which also I am apprehended of Christ Jesus" (Phil. 3:12).

Paul's confession is not only a statement of the demands of Christian discipleship. It is also an announcement of the principles by which this calling should be realized. First, Paul acknowledges that he was apprehended, or called, by Christ Jesus. Second, he notes that God had a purpose in calling him. And third, he acknowledges that this puts an obligation on himself — the obligation to follow after Jesus.

If you and I are to be disciples, these principles must also be a part of our goals and Christian understanding.

The God of Beginning

It is very important to recognize that all discipleship begins with God's call or, as Paul says, with being "apprehended of Christ Jesus." God's call must be foremost, for nothing can take place spiritually in a man's life until this happens. Actually, it involves the creation of spiritual life. It would be foolish for a man to enter a funeral home to encourage the corpses to lead an upright life. The corpses are dead. And if the words were to have any purpose, the corpses would first have to be made alive. In the same way, the call to discipleship must begin with the power of God to make a spiritually dead man alive, for only then are the standards of that calling significant.

This is what the new birth means. Before conversion God says that a man is dead in his trespasses and sins. The man is alive physically and intellectually, but he is not alive spiritually. Hence, he cannot respond to spiritual stimuli. While he is in this state the Word of God is a hidden book to him, and the Gospel of Jesus Christ is nonsense. But then God touches his life. God's touch brings life out of death, the life of the spirit, and the man then believes in Jesus Christ and begins to understand the Bible. This is what it means to be apprehended by God. And this must happen first before there can be any true discipleship. Jesus said, "Ye have not chosen me, but I have chosen you, and ordained you, that ye should go and bring forth fruit, and that your fruit should remain" (John 15:16).

We find examples of this throughout the Bible. Abraham was apprehended by God. Did Abraham choose God? Oh, no! He was perfectly satisfied where he was in the Mesopotamian river valley in a pagan culture, but God called him and sent him on his way to Palestine.

Moses was apprehended by God. And he was apprehended when he was still a baby floating in the Nile in a basket. God said, "I am going to deliver my people from Egypt, and I am going to do it by means of this baby. I am going to protect him from Pharaoh. I am going to give him the best of this world's training and education. And I am going to do many miracles through him." And God did these things through Moses.

There is also the story of David. God put His stamp upon the future King David when David was still out protecting the sheep. God sent the prophet Samuel to David's home to anoint one of the sons in the family of the future king. The father brought out all of his sons in order, except David. Samuel looked at the boys and thought how good a king the oldest son, Eliab, would make. But before Samuel could anoint him God indicated that he was not the one. Next came Abinadab, who was not the future king either. And then there was Shammah, and so on until seven of Jesse's sons were presented. But Samuel said, "The Lord hath not chosen these." Then Samuel asked, "Are all thy children here?" And Jesse answered, "There remaineth yet the youngest, and, behold, he keepeth the sheep." Samuel said, "Send and fetch him; for we will not sit down till he come here." When David had come the Lord said, "Arise, anoint him; for this is he." The Bible says, "Then Samuel took the horn of oil, and anointed him in the midst of his brethren; and the Spirit of the Lord came upon David from that day onward" (I Sam. 16:11-13). Once again, it was God who apprehended David.

We come to the New Testament, and we find that God chose John the Baptist before he was born. Jesus apprehended His disciples while they were still fishermen. God apprehended Paul when he was in the process of persecuting Christians. And in every case the call of God was primary. This has always been the foundation stone of true discipleship.

Is that true of you? Are you one of God's children? Has He picked you up and made you His? Has He given you spiritual life so that you can now understand His love, His grace, and other biblical doctrines? Or are you just pretending Christianity? If you are only pretending, then you must begin where all of the others have begun. You must begin by acknowledging God's call to you in Christ Jesus and your need for Him. And you must commit yourself to Him.

God's Purpose

The second step in becoming an effective disciple of Jesus Christ is to be aware of the purpose for which He has called you. Paul says, "I follow after, if that I may apprehend *that for which I am apprehended* of Christ Jesus." What is that thing for which the apostle Paul and we ourselves, if we are Christians, have been apprehended?

The answer is spelled out in Romans 8:28 and 29. Most Christians know the first of these verses, as we noted earlier in the chapter on Philippians 1:6. It says, "And we know that all things work together for good to them that love God, to them who are the called according to his purpose." It says that God has a purpose in saving us. But not many Christians know the verse that follows this, in spite of the fact that it goes on to tell what the purpose is. "For whom he did foreknow, he also did predestinate to be conformed to the image of his Son, that he might be the firstborn among many brethren." What was God's purpose in saving you? His purpose was that you might be conformed to the image of Jesus Christ. If you are a Christian, God saved you to make you as holy, pure, gracious, and loving as Jesus.

At this point I can almost hear someone saying, "Well, if that is the case, I'll just wait for God to do it. I'll enjoy that holiness in heaven." But this is not the way in which Paul means it. Paul had a great sense of the *present* demands of discipleship. Spiritually speaking he belonged to the *now* generation. And everything he mentions in this chapter has to do with the Christian's present conduct.

When Paul speaks of knowing Jesus Christ, in verse 10, he is speaking of knowing Him *now*. He wants to experience Christ even in the midst of life's sufferings. When he speaks of attaining unto the resurrection of the dead, in verse 11, he is speaking of a spiritual resurrection *now*. It is the attainment of a kind of life so filled with Christ that those who do not know Him will regard it as the life of eternity. Verses 13 and 14 speak of a present striving for the best that God has for him *now*. Our present text is similar. Paul is saying that he wishes to be conformed to the image of Jesus Christ *now*.

Is that your desire? It should be. If it is not, it will become your desire more and more as you begin to realize that this was God's greatest purpose in calling you to faith in the Lord Jesus.

Following Christ

The first two of these points now lead to a very practical conclusion, for Paul writes that because God has apprehended him and because He has done so for a purpose, he himself must determine to follow after Jesus. And this means that God's calling always puts an obligation on His children.

This is a personal thing. Discipleship is always personal. Remember how it was with Peter. Peter frequently avoided the personal contact with Jesus by speaking impetuously and often on behalf of the Twelve. But when Jesus came to recommission him after Peter's denial there was no escaping a personal response. Jesus asked a very simple question, "Simon, son of Jonah, lovest thou me more than these?" And Peter had to answer for himself, "Yea, Lord, thou knowest that I love thee." It happened three times, and each time Peter answered, "Yea, Lord, thou knowest that I love thee." At this point Peter's mind turned to someone else. He noticed John, the beloved disciple, standing nearby and asked Jesus about him: "Lord, and what shall this man do?" Jesus answered, "If I will that he tarry till I come, what is that to thee? . . . Follow thou me" (John 21:15-22). For Peter, discipleship was personal. And it is personal for you and me also. Discipleship can never be conditioned upon God's plans for some other Christian. It is personal. Christ's call is always the personal one to "Follow me."

It is also true that discipleship is costly. In fact, it costs a man his all. There are always Christians who think that they can be Christ's disciples piecemeal. They think that they can follow Him an inch at a time after first assuring themselves that there is no danger and that the inch also conforms to their own plans for themselves and their future. But this is not discipleship at all. Discipleship means abandoning your sin, your past, your own conception of yourself, your plans for your own future, even at times your friends or your family, if that is God's will for you, and following Jesus.

Now I know that you may be saying, "Oh, but isn't that hard? To give up all of the things I treasure?" Well, it is true that it is hard sometimes. But it is also true that there is a far greater sense in which we really never give anything up in the service of our Lord. We give things up, but Christ gives us more. And even the things we surrender are so arranged by God that they work for our spiritual well-being.

Peter learned this once in his life in a conversation that he had with Jesus. Mark tells us that just before Christ's final journey to Jerusalem there was a point when Peter was bragging as usual, in this case reminding the Lord of his sacrifices in order to serve Him. He said, "Lo, we have left all, and have followed thee." In other words, Peter was reminding the Lord that he was an ideal disciple and that his discipleship had proved costly. What nonsense this was! Peter had left hardly anything. And there were many things that he still had not left. For one thing, he had certainly not left behind his own idea of what Christ's ministry was to be, for he was constantly trying to tell Jesus how to go about it. His claim was presumptuous. It was egotistical. And Jesus had this answer for Peter. He said, "Verily I say unto you, There is no man that hath left house, or brethren, or sisters, or father, or mother, or wife, or children, or lands, for my sake and the gospel's, but he shall receive an hundredfold now in this time, houses, and brethren, and sisters, and mothers, and children, and lands, with persecutions; and in the age to come eternal life" (Mark 10:29, 30). Jesus was teaching that the disciple suffers no loss for which God will not abundantly compensate.

In one of his most popular works the American novelist and writer Mark Twain told the story of a prince and a pauper. The two boys came from entirely different circumstances, but they looked alike. And one day, when chance had accidentally thrown them together, they decided to put on each other's clothes. The prince donned the pauper's rags. The poor boy put on the rich one's finery. Unfortunately (or fortunately, as it eventually turned out), the boys were then separated. The pauper was mistaken for the prince and taken to live in the palace, while the prince was turned back to the poor streets of London where he suffered great indignities before he eventually regained his rightful place and the throne.

In the same way, the Lord Jesus Christ took on our poverty, while we have been clothed in His finery. The Bible says, "For ye know the grace of our Lord Jesus Christ, that, though he was rich, yet for your sakes he became poor, that ye through his poverty might be rich" (II Cor. 8:9). He became poor as we were so that we might be clothed in His righteousness. He endured suffering and death that we might become like Him — sons of God and co-heirs with Him of God's glory.

Oh, it is true that the paupers must give up their rags. But there is no comparison between our rags and God's glory. And Jesus has told us that there is nothing given up in this life that is not replaced a hundredfold by spiritual treasure, and not only in this world but in eternity also.

Quite a few years ago, the son of a wealthy American family graduated from Yale University and decided to go out to China as a missionary for Jesus Christ. His name was William Borden. Many of his friends thought him foolish to give up so much of this world's goods and his future here to go. But Borden of Yale loved the Lord Jesus Christ, and he wished to serve Him. After only a short time on the field, and before he even reached China, Borden contracted a fatal disease and died. He had given up everything to follow Jesus. But at his bedside his friends found a note that he had written as he lay dying: "No reserve, no retreat, and no regrets." Borden of Yale had given up everything, but he had found a treasure that was beyond words.

Perhaps there is something that God has been asking you to lay aside in order that you might be a more effective witness for Him. I do not know what it is. The thing that is a hindrance for one disciple is often entirely different for another. I shall probably never know what it is. But whatever it is, you know it. At this point in your life, for you it is the touchstone of your discipleship. Will you cast it aside to follow Jesus? If you do, you will grow in your Christian discipleship. And God will bring great blessing into your life, and through you also into the lives of others.

34.

Striving for the Living Christ

(Philippians 3:13, 14)

SEVERAL YEARS AGO an Englishman named C. Northcote Parkinson wrote a humorous book on the functioning of corporations called *Parkinson's Law*. One chapter in the book set about to analyze the disease that has affected a corporation in which, according to Parkinson, "the higher officials are plodding and dull, those less senior are active only in intrigue against each other, and the junior men are frustrated or frivolous." The disease goes through stages, he says, from the point at which a person appears in the organization's hierarchy who combines in himself "a high concentration of incompetence and jealousy," to the point at which the whole corporation is characterized by smugness and apathy. At this point little is attempted and nothing is achieved. In a humorous way Parkinson calls the disease *injelititis*, and he defines it as induced inferiority or paralysis. In our terms it is complacency or the absence of the urge to shoot high.

I wondered as I read the book if something of the sort is not found in the lives of many Christians. In this case, of course, it would be a spiritual smugness or spiritual apathy. And it would be seen most clearly in complacency regarding spiritual things. I think spiritual injelititis is found widely. And it may be found in you. Have you lost your vision for God's future blessing on your life? Or have you ceased to work hard in His service? If so, you have caught the disease. And the words of our text should be a rousing challenge to your apathy.

Paul writes about his goals, setting himself as an example: "Brethren, I count not myself to have apprehended; but this one thing I do, forgetting those things which are behind, and reaching forth unto those things which are before, I press toward the mark for the prize of the high calling of God in Christ Jesus" (Phil. 3:13, 14). Paul was not complacent. And neither should we be complacent. Instead of smugness Paul knew a sanctified ambition, and he threw himself eagerly into the race that God had set before him.

Paul says that he had learned to press ahead in three ways. First, he forgets those things which are behind. Second, he looks forward to those things which are before. And third, he presses on toward the mark of the prize of God's calling. In Paul's mind there was a sanctified forgetting, a sanctified remembering, and a sanctified striving for that to which God had called him.

FORGETTING THE PAST

In the first place, Paul says that he forgets those things that are behind. What are they? Well, he certainly did not forget his knowledge of the Bible and Christian doctrine; the letter he had just written proves that. Some of the greatest truths of the Christian faith are given in this very chapter in shorthand form. Moreover, he certainly did not forget God's grace and God's great mercies, because he had been talking about them throughout the letter. He knew that all he had of value in his life came through the grace of God manifested in Jesus Christ.

What is the nature of this forgetting then? I believe that it is the kind of forgetting that occurs when we cease to let things that are in the past overshadow the present, that lets the past be past, both the good and the bad, and that constantly looks forward to the work that God still has for us.

There is an illustration of the opposite of this attitude in the Old Testament. When God led the people of Israel out of Egypt toward the promised land, He provided everything that they needed for their journey. They had shade by day and light by night. They had water to drink and manna to eat. The time came, however, when the people ceased to look forward to the land that God was giving them and instead looked back to their life in Egypt. They said, "We remember the fish which we did eat in Egypt freely; the cucumbers, and the melons, and the leeks, and the onions, and the garlic. But now our soul is dried away; there is nothing at all, besides this manna, before our eyes" (Num. 11:5, 6). The people of Israel began to hunger for these things, and God taught them a great lesson by giving them the things they asked for. He gave them quail until they grew sick of it. The point of the illustration, however, is that they began to look back and failed to trust God for their present and future blessings. You and I are not to do that as Christians.

This does not mean, of course, that we are not to be thankful for the past blessings. If we had been among the people of Israel when they were in Egypt and we had been able to buy the cucumber, and the melon, and the leeks, and the onion, and the garlic, it would have been quite proper to thank God for them, especially if we had been slaves. It would have been proper to remember years later how gracious God had been. These things would have been right. But it would have been entirely wrong to long for these things after God had begun to lead us into new paths and had set new and greater blessings before us.

Unfortunately there are many leeks-and-garlic Christians among us. And you are one if you are constantly looking to the past. If your Christian testimony is entirely taken up with what God did for you thirty or forty years ago, or if you are constantly talking about the good old days when God's blessing on your life seemed great, then you are looking to the past. You can never do that and move forward. One of my good friends describes old age as the point in life when a person ceases to look forward and looks back. If that is accurate, then there are certainly a lot of old or middle-aged Christians — and I do not mean in terms of their years. They are living a leeks-and-garlic type of Christianity, and Paul warns against it. He would say, "Look! Past blessings are fine. We have received them from God's hands, and we should be thankful for them. We rejoice in everything that He has done in our lives. But now we must let those things lie in the past and move forward. There can be no progress without this proper forgetting."

REACHING FORWARD

The second thing that Paul claims to have done is to have fixed his gaze on the many things that God would yet be doing. For he speaks of himself as "forgetting those things which are behind and *reaching forth* unto those things which are before." Someone once said to David Livingstone when he was back in England briefly after having worked for many years in Africa, "Well, Dr. Livingstone, where are you ready to go now?" And Livingstone answered, "I am ready to go anywhere, provided it be forward." That was what Paul would say also. Paul's sense of the Lord's leading was always linked to his awareness of open doors, and he did not spend a lot of time asking the Lord to open them. Paul expected the Lord to open doors, and when He did, Paul went through them instantly. Through those doors Paul was constantly reaching forth unto those things that were before.

I think that it is precisely at this point that these verses are often misunderstood. When verse 14 speaks of the "mark" and the "prize" of God's high calling, most readers of the letter think naturally of a prize received in heaven, and then interpret verse 13 as a description of Paul's striving for a heavenly reward. But this is not the true meaning of the verses. It is true that the prize is probably a prize received in heaven; but the prize is achieved, as in a long race, not by pressing toward the prize itself but by pressing on to one mark after another along the long race course of the Christian life. Actually, Paul says that he is striving to achieve this aspect of his calling.

This is evident in the text in three ways. First, the verse speaks of the "upward" calling of God in Christ Jesus. This throws the emphasis of the verse upon the ascent. Second, Paul mentions God's "call." In the New Testament when this word is used of a Christian it almost always refers to God's calling to be conformed day by day to the image of Jesus Christ. That, too, is a reference to the present. The third indication that these verses speak of present goals is the fact that Paul speaks of the "things" (plural) for which he is reaching. He is not thinking of a single thing to be reached at the end of the road — the prize — but of the many things he is striving to reach along it.

Do we run our race like that as Christians? We can err in two ways in the running of the Christian life. We can err by looking only at the past; this is sin, for it is a lack of faith in God's future blessing. But we can also err by looking only at so distant a future that we miss the more immediate blessings that God has in store for this life.

Instead of either of these, you and I should run our race reaching forth to each new task before us. We should awake in the morning to say, "Lord, here is a new day that you have given me. I know that there are new things to be done and new lessons to be learned. Help me to use this day as well as I possibly can — to raise my children properly, to do well at my job, to help my neighbor." And when we go to bed that night we can pray, "Lord, I have not done anything today as well as I should have, and I missed many of Your blessings. But thank You for being with me. Help me now to place today's experiences behind and rest well that I may serve You better tomorrow." And God will do it. For He is anxious to lead us onward in our experience and our service for Him.

There is a third point to Paul's statement in these verses. The life Paul wishes to live involves not only a forgetting of the past and not only a looking forward to the things that lie ahead. It also involves a striving for these things. And this means effort. It involves perseverance, discipline, and concentration. Do you concentrate on the Christian life, or is your mind filled with the things of this world? Do you fix your mind on the things God has for you, or do the temporary, passing, and insignificant things of this world crowd out things that are eternal?

THE CHRISTIAN'S WARFARE

Now it is evident that if we are really to engage in that great struggle for God's best about which Paul is speaking, then we must also be prepared for vigorous spiritual conflict. For our striving is not only against ourselves or against circumstances but against the spiritual forces of this world that would seek to hinder us. Paul calls them principalities and powers, the rulers of the darkness of this world.

Satan's attacks are directed against Jesus Christ, and he does not care much about a believer who is far away from his Lord. If you want an easy time as a Christian, all you have to do is to get far away from Jesus Christ — move away to the periphery of the battle. If you are out there, Satan is not going to bother you much. That is where he wants you. However, if you draw close to the Lord, as Paul wished to do, and join with Him in the battle, then Satan's arrows will start coming at you too. The battle will be hard. And you will find it necessary to use God's weapons for the conflict.

All too often Christians arm themselves with the weapons of the world instead of with God's armor. In Ephesians 6 Paul speaks of God's weapons as truth, righteousness, the Gospel, faith, salvation, and the Word of God. But how often do believers prefer the world's armor: wisdom, self-confidence, financial security, success, and popularity! This is not the armor that God has prepared for His warriors.

What is the armor? The first part is truth, for Paul writes, "Stand, therefore, having your loins girded about with truth." Pilate asked Jesus about the truth, but he did not wait for an answer. If he had, he would have learned that Christ is the truth and that God's Word is truth (John 14:6; 17:17). If we are to stand fast as Christians, we must first be armed with the truth about Christ and with the great, energizing principles of God's Word.

We are also to have on the breastplate of righteousness. This is not the righteousness with which we are clothed by God when we believe on Jesus Christ. It is not the divine righteousness that Paul is talking about here. If we are believers in Christ, we already have that righteousness and there is no need to admonish the Christian to put it on. The righteousness mentioned here is a practical righteousness that is meant to characterize the life of the individual. Christians are to live holy lives. They must not allow their conduct to damage their testimony.

Then, too, we are to have our feet shod with the preparation of the Gospel of peace. This means that we are to have mastered the heart of the Gospel of God's grace to man in Jesus Christ and to be ready to explain it to others. In the same way, Peter admonished his readers to "be ready always to give an answer to every man that asketh you a reason of the hope that is in you, with meekness and fear" (I Pet. 3:15).

We are also to take the shield of faith. This is not the faith we exercised in believing Jesus Christ originally, but a present faith that does not doubt in the midst of God's current dealings with us. Does it seem to you that events have turned against you? Do you see what appear to be uncontrollable setbacks in your work or in your relationships to other people? Well, here is where the shield of faith must be raised against all attacks of Satan. You must learn to say of God as Job did, "Though he slay me, yet will I trust him."

There is also the helmet of salvation. How wonderful to know that the center of our being is protected by the great and eternal salvation that God has worked out for us!

Finally, we are to take the sword of the Spirit, which is the Word of God. What is this Word? It is interesting to note that a special Greek word is used for the term "word" in this verse (verse 17), for this gives the verse a slightly different meaning from the previous admonition in verse 14 to be armed with the truth. This word is not the normal Greek noun *logos* which would refer to the Word of God in its entirety. It is the more restrictive word *hrema*, which really means "a saying." Paul is saying that we are to be armed with specific sayings of Scripture, specific verses, and that we are to be able to draw on them in every circumstance and in every spiritual engagement.

As we engage in the battles of the Christian life which result from our striving for the victories that God sets before us, we can take confidence in the fact that the victory of Jesus Christ has already guaranteed the outcome. In that great Greek classic written by Xenophon, the *Anabasis*, there is a section that tells of a crucial battle between the forces of the Greeks invading Persia and the Persian armies. The armies were arrayed against each other over a long front, and when the call to battle was given the Hellenes struck first, driving into the middle of the Persian forces and potentially turning the tide of the battle. Unfortunately, they did not profit by it. The length of the Greek lines prohibited the other Greeks from seeing the crucial advance, and when the battle proved hard for them — and Cyrus, the Greek commander, was killed — the mass of the Greeks turned back and thereby yielded the field to the enemy.

It should not be that way for Christians. For not only has the victory been won for us by Jesus, we are also informed of that victory, for the Bible exists to tell us about it. By His death and resurrection Jesus Christ decisively defeated Satan and the forces of darkness, and we now advance under His banner to enforce His conquest. We are to wear His weapons. And as we go we are to echo Paul's challenge: "Brethren, I count not myself to have apprehended; but this one thing I do, forgetting those things which are behind, and reaching forth unto those things which are before, I press toward the mark for the prize of the high calling of God in Christ Jesus."

35.

How to Know the Will of God

(Philippians 3:15)

How CAN YOU KNOW God's will? How is it possible for a man to know the mind of God? If God has a plan for your life, how does He reveal it to you? How can you find that plan? How does a sinful, finite human being come to know what a holy and infinite God desires?

Our starting point for finding the biblical answers to these questions, is the text to which we have now come in our exposition of the book of Philippians. In the verses immediately preceding this one, verses 13 and 14, Paul has written of the aspirations that should characterize our Christian conduct. And he has spelled out his statements personally lest we should think that he is recommending for others what he has not applied to himself. He has written of his desire to forget the past and to press on in his upward calling, "reaching forth unto those things which are before . . . for the prize of the high calling of God in Christ Jesus." At this point, however, he turns directly to his readers and admonishes them to be "thus minded." And he adds, "And if in anything ye be otherwise minded, God shall reveal even this unto you" (verse 15). In this verse Paul says that in spiritual things the Philippians could be totally certain of God's guidance.

I believe that this verse can be rightly applied to every aspect of our lives, for all of life bears on God's calling. Several years ago an amateur pilot explained to me how airliners are kept on their course by radar. A pilot cannot always see what is coming, particularly in bad weather. At best he can see only about a hundred miles. And yet he can fly his aircraft safely in all kinds of weather, for the course is marked out by radar. If he deviates either to the right or to the left, the radar warns him accordingly. It is thus that God guides us. Our text does not mean that we shall always be able to see more than one step ahead in our Christian lives. It does not mean that we shall even always be able to see ahead at all. But it does mean that God has a

plan for our lives — for your life and mine — and that He promises to
reveal the steps of that plan to us.

THE NATURE OF GOD

The basis for this assurance lies in the nature of God. For it is God's
nature to reveal Himself and His purposes to man. Quite a few years
ago when I was in seminary I learned the famous definition of God
contained in the Westminster Shorter Catechism: "God is a Spirit, infinite, eternal, and unchangeable, in His being, wisdom, power, holiness, justice, goodness, and truth." The first time a person hears that
definition I suppose he inevitably thinks that just about everything that
could possibly be said about God is wrapped up in it, for the definition
is so long. And yet, as I began to memorize and study it, I learned
that it was far from comprehensive. For one thing, there is no mention
of God's being love. And God is certainly infinite, eternal, and unchangeable in His love. Moreover, today I believe I should also like
to see God's desire to reveal Himself to man included. I should like
to say, "God is a Spirit, infinite, eternal, and unchangeable, in His
being, wisdom, power, holiness, justice, goodness, truth, love, and desire to reveal Himself to man."

In one sense all that God has ever done has been directed to this
end. When God made the world it was to reveal Himself to those who
would eventually live on it. Creation reveals God. Hence, Paul tells
us that "the invisible things of him from the creation of the world are
clearly seen, being understood by the things that are made, even his
eternal power and Godhead, so that they are without excuse" (Rom.
1:20). When God caused the Scriptures of the Old and New Testa-
ments to be written, this too was to reveal Himself to man. Finally,
just as God revealed His power in nature and His purposes in Scripture, so did He reveal His personality in His Son, the Lord Jesus Christ.
That is why Jesus could properly say, "He that hath seen me hath
seen the Father" (John 14:9).

It is God's nature to reveal Himself. And God's revelation always
involves a disclosure of His will for the individual person. On this
basis Dr. Donald Grey Barnhouse used to say that it was actually
impossible for a Christian who wanted to know the will of God for his
life not to know it.

WANTING TO DO IT

This statement by Dr. Barnhouse also brings us to the first of the
great biblical principles by which a Christian may unquestionably
come to know God's will. For the Bible teaches that if you really want
to know God's will, you must be willing to do His will even before you

know what it is. This is clearly taught in John 7:17: "If any man will do his will [and the phrase means 'wants to do it'], he shall know of the doctrine, whether it be of God, or whether I speak of myself." In this verse, although Jesus was speaking literally of the rejection of His doctrine by the Jewish leaders, He was actually teaching the greater principle that knowing the will of God consists largely in being willing to do it.

Now if we are going to come to the point where we are willing in advance to do God's will, we must recognize first that in ourselves we do not want to do it. If you are saying to yourself, "Oh, but I have always wanted to do the Lord's will," you are kidding yourself. For "the carnal mind is enmity against God; for it is not subject to the law of God, neither, indeed, can be" (Rom. 8:7). And there is a great deal of the carnal mind in all of us.

In ourselves we are a bit like the Israelites when they first came out of Egypt. They were a huge company. The Bible says that there were 600,000 men, and in addition to that there were the women and children. So the total must have been in the neighborhood of two million. This great host had been led into the desert where the temperature goes above 100 degrees in the day-time and often falls below freezing at night. When I was in Egypt one summer, the temperature was 140° F. at Luxor. And it was even hotter in the middle of the desert. In these circumstances the people would have perished from the extremes of temperature if God had not performed a great miracle to save them.

The miracle was the miracle of the cloud which signified God's presence with the people and led them in their wanderings. The cloud was large enough to spread out over the camp of the Israelites. It provided shade during the day-time; and it gave warmth by night, when it turned into a pillar of fire. It was the banner by which they regulated their march. When the cloud moved the people moved, and when the cloud stopped they stopped. One of our great hymns describes it by saying,

> Round each habitation hovering,
>   See the fire and cloud appear,
> For a glory and a covering,
>   Showing that the Lord is near.
> Thus, deriving from their banner
>   Light by night and shade by day,
> Safe they feed upon the manna,
>   Which he gives them when they pray.

The cloud was the single most distinguishing feature of their encampment.

Now we must imagine how it would be when the cloud moved forward and how weary the people would have become of following it. We read in the final verses of Exodus, "When the cloud was taken up from over the tabernacle, the children of Israel went onward in all their journeys; but if the cloud were not taken up, then they journeyed not till the day that it was taken up" (Exod. 40:36, 37). Sometimes it moved often, at others times not at all. We may imagine a family coming to a stop under the cloud's guidance in the middle of a hot afternoon and immediately beginning to unpack their baggage. They take down their bedding and set up their tent. And then, no sooner has it all been arranged, than someone cries out, "The cloud is moving." And so they repack their baggage and start to go on again. One hour later the cloud stops. They say, "We'll just leave our things packed this time and sleep on the ground." Well, they do. And the cloud stays that night and all the next day and all that week. And as they are going into the second week the family says, "Well, we might as well get it over with." They upack. And immediately the cloud begins to move again.

The people must have hated the moving of the cloud by which God guided them. But no matter how much they hated the cloud they still had to follow its guidance. If someone had said, "I don't care if the cloud is moving; I'm going to stay right here," the cloud would have gone on, and he would have died in the heat of the desert, or he would have frozen at night. They hated God's leading. But by this means God was molding a nation of rabble, of slaves, into a disciplined force that would one day be able to conquer the land of Canaan. And He was teaching them absolute obedience.

It is the same with us. Neither you nor I naturally want God's will. We want our will. We will always hate God's way, and particularly His way of training us to be soldiers. But we must go through it. For through that training we must learn to say, "Father, even though I do not naturally want Your will, nevertheless, I know that it is the best thing for me; and it is necessary for my spiritual training. Lead me in the way I should go." And God will do that. For to know God's will we must come to the point where we first want to do it.

WALKING BY GOD'S WORD

The second great principle for knowing the will of God is that nothing can be the will of God that is contrary to the Word of God. The God who is leading you now is the God who inspired the Bible then, and He is not contradictory in His commandments. Consequently, nothing can be the will of God for you that is not in accordance with His Word.

God's will is expressed in great principles. Take John 6:40, for instance. I call this verse the will of God for all unbelievers. It says, "And this is the will of him that sent me, that everyone who seeth the Son, and believeth on him, may have everlasting life; and I will raise him up at the last day." If you are not a Christian, God is not at all interested in telling you whether you should accept a job with General Motors or with Du Pont. He is not interested in telling you whether you should marry Sally or Mary, or Henry or John, or whether you should enlist in the army. He is interested in whether or not you will believe in Jesus Christ and receive Him as your personal Savior. God's will for you starts at this point. This is His will. And you must accept this demand before you can begin to go forward on any other level.

Another passage is Romans 12:1, 2. It is an expression of God's will for the Christian. "I beseech you therefore, brethren, by the mercies of God, that ye present your bodies a living sacrifice, holy, acceptable unto God, which is your reasonable service. And be not conformed to this world, but be ye transformed by the renewing of your mind, that ye may prove what is that good, and acceptable, and perfect, will of God." If you are a Christian, you can take it as an unchangeable principle that anything that contributes to your growth in holiness is an aspect of God's will for you. And anything that hinders your growth in holiness is not His will. God is interested in having you become like His Son, the Lord Jesus.

Colossians 3:23 is an expression of God's will for your work. It says, "And whatever ye do, do it heartily, as to the Lord, and not unto men." I think this is especially applicable to young people. A member of my congregation once remarked that all too often young people interpret a difficulty in their work or their schooling as being an indication that what they are doing is not God's will for them; actually, she said, it is probably God's indication that they should work harder at it. This verse tells us that God wants us to do well everything that we have to do.

A principle that is closely related to this one is found in Ephesians 6:5, 6: "Servants, be obedient to them that are your masters according to the flesh, with fear and trembling, in singleness of your heart, as unto Christ; not with eyeservice, as menpleasers, but as the servants of Christ, doing the will of God from the heart." This is for you if you have a difficult boss, or a difficult teacher. The Bible says that it is God's will that you should avoid gossiping about him or her and, instead, work as well as you are able under his guidance. And you should do it, not only when he is watching, but when he is not watching — as unto the Lord and not unto men.

Perhaps you are saying, "Well, these principles are good, but they do not touch the small things with which I am wrestling." You want to know whether you should go to the movies as a Christian, join a bridge club, make friends with the people at work, join in social drinking, or some other thing. Well, let me give you a final principle that covers most of these. Philippians 4:8: "Finally, brethren, whatever things are true, whatever things are honest, whatever things are just, whatever things are pure, whatever things are lovely, whatever things are of good report; if there be any virtue, and if there be any praise, think on these things." Do you see the instruction? God says that you are to pursue the best things in life. If these things are the best things for you, then do them. If not, you are to go another way. Just be sure that you take your guide lines from Scripture.

Looking to the Lord

The third principle is also important. It is the principle of daily and even hourly fellowship with the Lord. Psalm 32:8 states it this way: "I will instruct thee and teach thee in the way which thou shalt go; I will guide thee with mine eye." Clearly, if God is to guide us with His eye, He must first catch our eye. And this means that we must look to Him regularly throughout the day.

Let me illustrate this by a story. I have a good friend who is a gospel singer and who for many years was a bachelor. He once said, "You know, Jim, it is always easy to find a Christian girl to marry. And it is always easy to find a beautiful girl to marry. But it is not always so easy to find a beautiful, Christian girl to marry." I suppose he was partly right. At any rate, he eventually found a beautiful, Christian girl and married her. And she was perfect in every way but one. The one imperfection lay in the fact that at times she talked with a very shrill voice, especially in the presence of company. And because he was a great baritone singer, her voice often grated on his ears. This was the making of a serious problem in their marriage.

Well, the Lord had given him a great deal of tact, along with his many other talents, and he used his tact to go about the problem in this way. One day he came to his wife and said to her, "Look, dear, you know the first thing that a drama coach teaches an actress when she begins training?" His wife said, "No." "He teaches her to lower her voice. By nature a woman's voice is shrill, but it becomes warm and pleasing when it is lowered about an octave. A drama coach will teach an actress to say a phrase, count down eight notes, repeat it again, and then practice that repeatedly. I think your voice would be improved if you would do that." When my friend's wife agreed, they arranged a signal by which she would be reminded to lower her voice in the presence of company. The signal was for him to tuck in his chin.

My friend told me that there were times when this produced the funniest effect you could imagine. There they would be, sitting around the dining room table talking, and his wife's voice would be rising higher and higher. He would tuck in his chin and look at her. And then, often right in the middle of one of her sentences, she would catch his eye. She would notice his chin, and her voice would drop like a lead marshmallow and then go on at a pitch one octave lower.

She saw the sign when she looked at her husband. It must be the same in our daily walk with the Lord. The Lord knows that we shall go astray. It is our nature to go astray. Our speech will become unpleasing, or our conduct. And we will always do things that displease Him. But we must get into the habit of looking to Him often — in church, in our quiet time, in the various periods of our day — to catch His eye, to notice His sign. For if we do, we shall find Him watching. He will direct us. And He will guide us with His eye.

God's Paths

There is only one more point that I need to make, and it is not difficult at all. If you are serious about knowing the Lord's will and honestly seeking it, then you must be prepared for the Lord to guide you into new ways. If there is one thing that I have most learned about the Lord's guidance it is that He does not often lead us in old ways. God is creative. He is infinite. And He is infinite in His plans for His children.

David Wilkerson, the author of *The Cross and the Switchblade* and a minister who has been greatly blessed in a unique ministry to teenagers in New York City, tells in the opening chapter of his book how he was led in new paths in his ministry. He had been a Pentecostal preacher in central Pennsylvania, and by his personal standards he was doing quite well. The church had grown. There were several new buildings. And yet he was discontented. One day he decided to spend the late evening hours praying instead of watching television. He sold the television set after much hesitation and began to spend time with the Lord. He did this for some time. Eventually, out of these times of prayer he was led to begin his work helping the youth caught up in drug addiction and delinquency in Manhattan. God's will for David Wilkerson meant leading a country preacher into the heart and the heartbreak of the city.

It will also be true for you. If you will seek God's will, determining to do it even before you know what it is, if you will look to Him while responding to His voice in the Bible, then God will reveal His way and direct you in ever widening and ever more interesting paths. He will be close to you, and He will lead you in the way that you should go.

36.

Walking With the Living Christ
(Philippians 3:16-19)

HAVE YOU EVER NOTICED that the way a man walks quite often reveals his character? A proud man will walk erect, his head held high. A coward will often slink away or perhaps walk along with a smug, blustery air. Sometimes novelists make use of this fact to describe their characters. Heroes walk like heroes; villains slouch, sneak, creep, or swagger. The need to describe such forms of walking has even enriched our language. Roget's *Thesaurus* lists dozens of English synonyms for walking. And the Zulu language, according to Dr. Eugene A. Nida of the American Bible Society, contains at least 120 distinct words for similar ideas — to walk pompously, to walk with a swagger, to walk crouched down as when hunting, to walk in tight clothes, and so on. These truths are an acknowledgment that the way a man walks reveals something of his ambition, state of mind, and values.

It is for this reason, perhaps, that Christians are called to an exemplary walk in the Bible. They are told to "walk worthy of the vocation to which [they] are called" (Eph. 4:1). They are to walk "circumspectly" (Eph. 5:15), "honestly" (I Thess. 4:12), and "in the light" (I John 1:7).

In Philippians Paul writes in the same vein, "Nevertheless, as to that which we have already attained, let us *walk* by the same rule, let us mind the same thing. Brethren, be followers together of me, and mark them who *walk* even as ye have us for an example. For many *walk*, of whom I have told you often, and now tell you even weeping, that they are the enemies of the cross of Christ, whose end is destruction, whose God is their appetite, and whose glory is in their shame, who mind earthly things" (Phil. 3:16-19). In these verses Paul speaks twice of the Christian's walk and once of the unbeliever's walk. And he teaches that the walk of the believer in Jesus Christ is to reveal the true nature of his calling.

240

OUR FORMER WALK

The first thing that we must understand about the walk of the Christian is that it is to be entirely opposed to the walk he had before he became Christ's follower. In other words, the standards you had before you became a Christian are to be replaced by new standards now. Why is it that Paul speaks here of those who are enemies of the cross of Christ? It is not simply because he knew such people and thought of them just at this moment in the writing of the letter. It is because he knew that this is the way we all were before we became followers of Jesus Christ, and he wished to stress it. He wanted his readers to know that their new calling was to be entirely different.

Paul says that the non-Christian is first an enemy of the cross of Christ. That means that he is an opponent of the Christian Gospel. He resists it and wants others to resist it also. Second, his end is destruction. This means that his path does not lead to peace, happiness, success, or self-satisfaction — in spite of what the unbelievers think — but to misery, discontent, unrest, and eventually to a permanent separation from God. Third, his God is his belly. The old King James and the Revised Standard versions say "belly." The New Scofield Bible says "appetite." But the meaning is identical. The phrase points to one who is possessed by his own selfish appetites and who sees no need for God as a higher principle beyond them. Fourth, the non-Christian takes pride in things that should be his shame. This means that his values are reversed, and he finds himself declaring good what God calls evil and calling evil that which God calls good (cf. Isa. 5:20).

Moreover, these words are intensely practical. For they are seen in the history of the world and in our own contemporary standards. In our day America is preoccupied with sex and the self; it is committed to a materialism designed to satisfy the individual's selfish desires. Our values are becoming so reversed that honesty is increasingly novel, chastity is despised and mocked, and a word in behalf of law, justice, or personal integrity is often ignored or laughed down. This is the way things are, but it should not be surprising. The Bible says that this is the natural walk of the man apart from Christ — although Christian values or other high ethical standards sometimes temper it — and it is away from this natural walk and to Christ that God calls the Christian.

This is the true meaning of conversion. Some people speak of conversion as if it were synonymous with justification or being born again. But actually it means to turn around. And it implies not only regeneration but discipleship as well. Before you believed you were going down a path that led away from God. It led to destruction, as Paul

says. Then God saved you. He reached down and in grace turned
you around, reversing your values to His values, and setting you on a
path of His choosing. Because of this reorientation "old things are
passed away . . . all things are become new" (II Cor. 5:17). If you
are to walk as a Christian, you must begin with this primary reversal
of your standards.

WALKING WITH OTHERS

A second important thought about the proper walk of a Christian
occurs in Phil. 3:17. Paul writes, "Brethren, be followers *together* of
me." Here the great apostle to the Gentiles says as clearly as he can
that the walk of the believer must always be a walk with, and therefore in harmony with, other Christians.

The same truth is taught in verse 16, although it is somewhat hidden
by the English translation. Paul's charge to the Philippians to "walk
by the same rule" is conveyed in a phrase based on the colorful Greek
word *stoichein* which means to walk in a row. The masculine noun
of this word means a "row," as a row of houses, a rank of soldiers,
a line of ships, a wall of trees, and so on. And the feminine noun
stoicheia was the word used for the alphabet, for it was composed of
an orderly row of letters. In all of these instances the words imply
an ordered and harmonious arrangement. Hence, when Paul speaks in
this way to Christians he is implying that their life together should
also be harmonious. The successful walk of the Christian depends not
only upon his own goals or upon his own doctrine. It also depends
upon the success of his walk with other Christians.

One of the great illustrations of the late C. S. Lewis makes this
transparently clear. Lewis imagines the Church of Jesus Christ to be
something like a fleet of ships sailing in formation. To sail well they
need a common goal. For instance, if the fleet is headed for Calcutta,
each ship must be headed for Calcutta. And a ship that is headed for
New York has no place in the formation. Spiritually this means that
the goal must first be set for the Christian by the Lord Jesus Christ
and that the Christian must always be conscious of it. Then, too, each
individual ship must be in order. This corresponds to the Christian's
personal morality. And it is also essential. Third, each ship must be
managed in such a way that it does not collide with the others or get
in their way. This last point is the one made in this part of Philippians. The ships must sail together. Or, as Paul would say, they are
to sail by the same rule, minding the same thing.

None of this means that the Christian ceases to be an individual
before God, of course. But it does mean that he must be conscious of

the other individuals. He must be concerned for them and cooperate with them in all of the common Christian objectives.

THE LORD'S COMPANY

But then we must also walk with the Lord, for we take our orders from Him and not from one another. The Roman soldier did not take his instructions from the man who was marching beside him, but from his commander. The ship sailing in formation does not take its directions from the ship beside it but from the admiral on the deck of the flagship. Similarly, Christians must take their orders from the Lord Jesus Christ.

This will not come through a mystical experience. It will come only through a knowledge of God's Word. The psalmist had learned this and said, "Blessed is the man who walketh not in the counsel of the ungodly, nor standeth in the way of sinners, nor sitteth in the seat of the scornful. But his delight is in the law of the Lord; and in his law doth he meditate day and night" (Ps. 1:1, 2).

Think of the blessings that are promised to an individual as the result of a personal and prayerful study of God's Word. We become Christians by exposure to the truths in the Bible. Peter said that we are "born again, not of corruptible seed, but of incorruptible, by the word of God, which liveth and abideth forever" (I Pet. 1:23). What does Peter mean when he says, "Born again not of corruptible seed, but of incorruptible"? Well, he is using the facts of sex as an image, saying that the Word of God operates upon our heart as the male sperm does upon the ova in the uterus of a woman. The uterus is our heart. The ova is faith. And the sperm of God's Word penetrates our hearts to bring forth the life of eternity.

Has God's Word done that in you? Nothing else will do it, not the word of a person, however wise, not philosophy, not history, not science. God's Word says, "That which is born of the flesh is flesh; and that which is born of the Spirit is spirit." If you are to experience the divine life, you must experience it in the only way it can come — through the Bible as the Holy Spirit penetrates your heart through Scripture. This is the first great blessing of Bible study.

The second is our sanctification, for it is by a study of the Bible and fellowship with God that we are made increasingly as He would have us to be. John 17:17 says, "Sanctify them through thy truth; thy word is truth." The verb "to sanctify" means "to make holy"; so when Jesus asked God to sanctify His followers through God's truth, He was actually praying that they might become holy through a study of God's Word. Unfortunately, Christians often seek holiness anywhere but here. They seek it through reading other literature, by attending religious services, by special emotional experiences, even at times through mysticism. But holiness does not come by these. Sometimes these things are helpful — some of them more than others. But they are not the straight path to an upright and holy life. God's methods of sanctification are all wrapped up in Scripture.

Third, the Word of God is the primary means by which God reveals His will to us. God's Word contains unshakable facts and great principles, and through these God teaches us that certain things are His will for us and that other things are not.

I have often been struck personally by how relevant Scripture can be to a particular problem. Take St. Augustine as an example. In his youth Augustine's greatest problem was immorality, and although he wanted deliverance from his sins he knew that he did not want it until he had satisfied his sexual appetite completely. In his *Confessions* he tells that he prayed, "Lord, make me chaste," while he knew that he was actually adding under his breath, "but not quite yet." This was his problem, and he wrestled with this hindrance to his belief for years. At last while Augustine was near Milan in Italy, God brought him to the end of his resistance and spoke to him through two verses that were uniquely directed to his need. They were Romans 13:13, 14; and he came upon them quite suddenly by what the world would call chance. "Let us walk honestly, as in the day; not in reveling and drunkenness, not in immorality and wantonness, not in strife and envying. But put ye on the Lord Jesus Christ, and make not provision for the flesh, to fulfill its lusts." God used these words to speak directly to the heart of St. Augustine.

Another case comes from my own experience. During my years of graduate study in Switzerland my wife and I attended a Bible study that met each week in our home. Anyone was invited to these studies, and sometimes those who came regularly would be able to bring a non-Christian friend. One of these, who attended for only one night, was a girl named Diane whom we all knew was having serious marital problems. Her problem was not simply that she and her husband had arguments or misunderstandings. They often had prolonged and violent fights in which the two would actually strike one another. And, of course, Diane often got the worst of the battle. The night she attended was a night when we were studying the Sermon on the Mount. We had gone through most of Matthew 5 and had come to the verse, "But I say unto you that ye resist not evil, but whosoever shall smite thee on thy right cheek, turn to him the other also." We read it, and there was a great pause. It was the longest pause I had ever heard in a Bible study. And at last the girl said, quietly, "My, that's an interesting verse. I think I understand what it means. Just suppose, as an example, that someone should hit you. If you hit him back, he'll probably hit you again. But if you don't hit back, then he'll probably quit." There were a few inner smiles. And then she added a very profound word, "But it isn't so easy to do, is it?"

How relevant the Bible was to her problem! And she found it increasingly relevant as she came to know it better. Months later I learned that she had become a Christian in England as the result of attending a Billy Graham crusade and that she eventually came to know that what was impossible for her before her conversion became increasingly possible after it. She wrote a friend that she was becoming able to forgive her former husband, from whom by that time she was divorced; and she was beginning to make a new life for her son.

Do you want to know how relevant the Bible can be to your life and how God can use it to reveal His will to you? Then you must spend time reading it daily. If you are a Christian, God has a path marked out for you. You will find it only as you discover His will for you through Scripture.

A final function of God's Word, as we fellowship with Him in it, is to keep us from the counterfeits of truth in our day. Whenever the truth of the Gospel is preached the devil will immediately set about to erect a counterfeit beside it, an idol that looks like the real thing but which is dead because it omits the life-giving heart of the Gospel. And many are taken in by such idols.

It seems to me that the author of the book of Hebrews faced a similar problem as he wrote to the people of his day. He was writing to people who had some knowledge of true Christianity but who were still clinging to a form of Judaism which taught that a man is made pleasing to God by good works. They knew some of the Bible, but they did not know it well. And hence, they were not only fooled by the counterfeits; they were also unable to receive the deeper teaching that the author of the book wished to share with them. At length he says, "Of whom [that is, Jesus] we have many things to say, and hard to be uttered, seeing ye are dull of hearing. For when for the time ye ought to be teachers, ye have need that one teach you again the first principles of the oracles of God, and are become such as have need of milk, and not of solid food. For everyone that useth milk is unskillful in the word of righteousness; for he is a babe. But solid food belongeth to them that are of full age, even those who by reason of use have their senses exercised to discern both good and evil" (Heb. 5:11-14).

Unfortunately, we are almost all in the first of those categories. And there is much that we all need to know. But we do have the Bible. Shall we neglect it or not? Christian friend, let us fill up our souls with the Bible. For only then shall we continue to walk as we ought to walk with God. And only then shall we see clearly the way in which we should go.

37.

Our Blessed Hope

(Philippians 3:20)

IN THE EARLY DAYS OF the Christian Church the doctrine of the last things had three great points of focus: the return of Jesus Christ, the resurrection of the body, and the final judgment. And of the three the most significant was Jesus Christ's return. This was the blessed hope of Christians. For this they prayed. And with this thought they comforted one another in the face of sorrow, persecutions, death, and martyrdom.

The expectation of the Lord's personal and imminent return gave joy and power to the early Christians and to the Christian communities. We must imagine that as they lay in prison, suffering and tormented, often near death, they looked for His coming and thought that perhaps in an instant and without warning Jesus would appear and call them home. As they entered the arena to face the lions or looked up in their cell to face their executioner, many would have thought with joy in their hearts, "Perhaps this is the moment in which Jesus will return; and even now, before the beasts can spring or the ax can fall, I shall be caught up to meet Him. And the world will find this cell or this arena empty."

Unfortunately, in our day belief in the second coming of Jesus Christ has faded into a remote and sometimes irrelevant doctrine in many large segments of the Christian Church. And it is entirely possible that our present lack of courage and lack of joy flow from this attitude.

A BIBLICAL DOCTRINE

We are told today by many, some of them within the Church, that belief in the return of Jesus Christ is a preposterous doctrine or at best a "pie in the sky" philosophy. But it is hard to see how any professing Christian can dismiss it.

The return of Jesus Christ is mentioned in every one of the New Testament books except Galatians (which was written with a particular

247

and quite different problem in view) and the very short books such as II and III John and Philemon. Jesus quite often spoke of His return. Mark records Him as saying, "Whosoever, therefore, shall be ashamed of me and of my words in this adulterous and sinful generation, of him also shall the Son of man be ashamed, when he cometh in the glory of his Father, with the holy angels" (Mark 8:38). Again, "Then shall they see the Son of man coming in the clouds, with great power and glory. And then shall he send his angels, and shall gather together his elect from the four winds, from the uttermost part of the earth to the uttermost part of heaven" (Mark 13:26, 27). John tells us that Christ's last words to His disciples included the promise: "I go to prepare a place for you. And if I go and prepare a place for you, I will come again, and receive you unto myself, that where I am, there ye may be also" (John 14:2, 3).

Paul's letters are also full of the doctrine. To the Christians at Thessalonica he wrote, "For the Lord himself shall descend from heaven with a shout, with the voice of the archangel, and with the trump of God; and the dead in Christ shall rise first; then we who are alive and remain shall be caught up together with them in the clouds, to meet the Lord in the air; and so shall we ever be with the Lord" (I Thess. 4:16, 17). Peter called the return of Jesus Christ our "living hope" (I Pet. 1:3). Paul called it our "blessed hope" (Titus 2:13). And John wrote, "Behold, he cometh with clouds, and every eye shall see him" (Rev. 1:7).

It is the same in the verse which is our text in Philippians. "For our citizenship is in heaven, from where also we look for the Savior, the Lord Jesus Christ, who shall change our lowly body, that it may be fashioned like his glorious body, according to the working by which he is able even to subdue all things unto himself" (3:20, 21). In these verses and in many others the early Christians expressed their belief in a personal return of Jesus, a return that was to be closely associated with a period of great wickedness on earth, the resurrection and transformation of their own bodies, an earthly rule of the glorified Jesus, and a final judgment of individuals and nations. And they acknowledged that their lives should be lived on a higher plane because of it.

CHANGED CONDUCT

The personal return of Jesus Christ should have a profound bearing on our own life and conduct. Lord Shaftesbury, the great English social reformer, said near the end of his life, "I do not think that in the last 40 years I have lived one conscious hour that was not influenced by the thought of our Lord's return." It is certain that this conviction was one of the strongest motives behind his social programs.

If you are expecting the Lord's return, then this conviction ought to alter your concern for social issues as well as other things. At the height of the race crisis in the United States in the early 1960's two signs hung on the wall of a restaurant in Decatur, Georgia. The first sign read, "Jesus is coming again!" The second sign, directly below it, said, "We reserve the right to refuse service to anybody!" The juxtaposition of the two signs was unintentionally humorous, for at least two reasons. First, because they implied that the owner, who apparently was looking for the return of Jesus Christ, might refuse Him service. And second, because the entire idea of racial discrimination which was involved proved incongruous in the light of Christ's imminent presence.

Are you looking for Jesus' return? If you are motivated by prejudice against other Christians or others in general, whether they are black or white, rich or poor, cultured or culturally naive, or whatever they may be — then the return of Jesus Christ has not made its proper impression on you. If you are contemplating some sin, perhaps a dishonest act in business, perhaps trifling with sex outside of marriage, perhaps cheating on your income tax return — then the return of Jesus Christ has not made its proper impression on you. If your life is marked by a contentious, divisive spirit in which you seek to tear down the work of another person instead of building it up — then the return of Jesus Christ has not made its proper impression on you. If you first protect your own interests and neglect to give food, water, or clothing to the needy as we are instructed to do in Christ's name — then the return of Jesus Christ has not made its proper impression on you.

John wrote, "Beloved, now are we the children of God, and it doth not yet appear what we shall be, but we know that, when he shall appear, we shall be like him; for we shall see him as he is. And every man that hath this hope in him purifieth himself even as he is pure" (I John 3:2, 3). The greatest consequence of belief in the return of the Lord Jesus Christ should be a purification of our conduct.

HOPE IN SUFFERING

Another consequence of a firm belief in the return of Jesus Christ should be a transformed understanding of suffering. For suffering strengthens our hope and makes our present fellowship with Jesus more wonderful. This is why Paul writes of the believer's hope in Romans saying, "And not only so, but we glory in tribulations also, knowing that tribulation worketh patience; and patience, experience; and experience, hope" (Rom. 5:3, 4). In Paul's experience hope had transformed suffering, and suffering had intensified his hope.

The word "tribulation," which occurs in this verse, means any sufferings, persecution, or hardship — like that which Paul lists of himself in II Corinthians: stripes, imprisonments, stoning, shipwreck, perils, weariness, thirst, and hunger. And it includes the cruelest of oppressions. To understand this we must recognize that the word carried the most vivid of images in Paul's day, both in the Greek language and in the Latin translation. The Greek word which Paul used was *thlipsis,* which means the kind of oppression that a conquered people would receive from a cruel conqueror. The Latin word for tribulation was based on the noun *tribulum,* which meant a threshing sled, and implied severe torture. A *tribulum* was generally several feet wide and five or six feet long and was studded with sharp spikes on the bottom; it was pulled over the grain on a threshing floor by an animal. Apparently such an instument was known in the east in pre-Roman times, for Amos speaks of the people of Damascus having threshed Gilead with threshing instruments of iron (Amos 1:3). The Latin word *tribulare* in itself compared oppression to experiencing such threshing.

It is easy to see how the Christians thus conceived of their suffering. They knew themselves to be often pressed under as wheat while the tribulums of the world passed over them. They knew the feel of the spikes and the lash of the flail. But they endured such suffering. They had learned that it was the way in which God separated the wheat in their lives from the chaff and by which He made them more useful and more obedient servants.

I believe that all of God's children come to learn this sooner or later. Certainly it was known by the persecuted prophet Jeremiah. What had persecutions done for Jeremiah? Well, in Jeremiah 17 he intimates that they had actually drawn him closer to the Lord and strengthened him for his work. He is contrasting two types of men. The first is the person who trusts in man and thereby departs from the Lord. Jeremiah asks what will happen to him. And he answers, "For he shall be like the shrub in the desert, and shall not see when good cometh, but shall inhabit the parched places in the wilderness, in a salt land and not inhabited." The other type of man is the one who trusts God and whose hope is in Him. What is he like? Well, says Jeremiah, "He shall be like a tree planted by the waters, and that spreadeth out her roots by the river, and shall not see when heat cometh, but her leaf shall be green; and shall not be anxious in the year of drought, neither shall cease from yielding fruit" (Jer. 17:6, 8). In other words, Jeremiah had found that tribulation had strengthened his roots and had actually drawn him closer to his Lord.

All Christians should experience that. Tribulations will come. Job spoke truthfully when he said, "Yet man is born unto trouble, as the sparks fly upward" (Job 5:7). But the Christian can have a hope in the midst of them that transforms suffering and is strengthened by it.

DAY OF JUDGMENT

Everything written up to this point has been encouraging. It has been intended for Christians. But there is a somber side also. And it is somber for those who do not know Christ and who therefore do not expect Him. Christ is coming. His coming will be a joy for Christians. But oh, my friend, it will also mean the beginning of Christ's judgments. And these will be terrible for those who do not know Him.

Christians acknowledge this every time they recite the Apostles' Creed, for they say that Jesus shall come again from heaven "to judge the living and the dead." And Paul told the Athenians that God had "appointed a day, in which he will judge the world in righteousness" (Acts 17:31). In that day — which is certainly longer than any twenty-four hour day — Jesus Christ will return to judge the nations, the false church, and individuals. And everyone will meet Him. You will meet Him. Will you meet Him as one judged righteous on the basis of our Lord's death for sin and His gift of righteousness? Or will you meet Him as one who trusts in his own human goodness and is therefore cut off from God's presence forever?

It is my experience that people react in one of two ways to Christ's judgment. Some simply disbelieve it, for they think (or wish to think) that judgment is incompatible with the character of God. I mentioned something about the judgment of God on the Bible Study Hour once and received a letter from a woman who seemed greatly offended at the thought that a loving God could ever pronounce a judgment on anything. I wrote back asking her what she would think of a God who would let a murderer go on murdering throughout eternity, a thief go on stealing throughout eternity, a sexual pervert continue to violate other men and women throughout eternity, and other sinners to go on sinning. Certainly it is in the character of a loving and righteous God to stop such things. And He will stop it. It may help some persons if they think of the final judgment in this light and begin to find out what the Scriptures say concerning it.

The second reaction to the fact of God's judgment comes from the unbeliever who has heard the offer of salvation by grace through the Gospel but who prefers to deal with God's justice. God's justice! Oh, pity the man who wants nothing from God but God's justice! Justice will send a man to hell. It will condemn him. The only hope for any man lies in God's mercy.

The result of seeking nothing but justice from God is seen clearly in a story from the life of Abraham from the Old Testament. Abraham had been told by God that He was about to destroy the cities of Sodom and Gomorrah for their great wickedness, and Abraham had immediately begun to think about his nephew Lot and his family who lived there. He knew that they would also be destroyed in God's judgment, so he began to reason with God. He said, "Will you also destroy the righteous with the wicked? Suppose there are fifty righteous in the city; will you also destroy and not spare the place for the fifty righteous that are in it? Shall not the Judge of all the earth do right?" "Well," God said, "if there are fifty righteous persons in the city, I will spare it." Abraham began to get a little worried at this point because he only knew of four righteous persons himself. They were Lot, Lot's wife, and Lot's two daughters. And Abraham began to doubt that there were fifty. So he said, "Suppose there are only forty-five? Shall not the judge of all the earth do right?" And God said, "I will spare the city for the sake of forty-five." "Well," said Abraham, "Suppose there are forty?" God said, "I will not destroy Sodom and Gomorrah for the forty." "Suppose there are thirty?" "No, not for the thirty." "Twenty?" "No, not for twenty." "Now please don't get angry," Abraham said, "but suppose there are only ten? Shall not the judge of all the earth do right?" And God said, "I will not destroy the city for the sake of the ten." Abraham stopped talking. But, you know, even then Abraham had not reduced the figure far enough. And after God had removed Lot and his family from Sodom, His judgment fell upon the cities.

That is what happens when the Judge of all the earth does right! Men are condemned by God's justice. And if you seek nothing from God but justice, you will be condemned at Jesus Christ's return. Fortunately there is no need to meet the Lord Jesus as Judge. For the One who is coming in judgment is also the One who once came as the Savior, to die for your sin, to bear your judgment, and to meet you thereafter as your Lord, your friend, and your bridegroom. How will you meet Him? You must decide. The decisions of this life affect the issues of eternity.

38.

You Shall Live Again

(Philippians 3:21)

ONCE I DISCUSSED THE relative importance of the two most significant Christian doctrines with one of my friends. They were the death and the resurrection of Jesus Christ. And I came to the conclusion (I believe rightly) that although the death of our Lord is the heart of the Gospel both doctrinally and in terms of the evangelistic message, the resurrection is of at least equal importance with it historically in terms of the evidence for Christ's claims.

The evangelist Reuben A. Torrey called the resurrection of Jesus Christ "the Gibraltar of Christian evidences, the Waterloo of infidelity." And Torrey was entirely right. The resurrection of Jesus is the great historical fact upon which all of the Christian doctrines are suspended and before which all honest disbelief must waver. If it can be shown that Jesus of Nazareth actually rose from the dead, as the Scriptures claim and as Christians have always confessed, then the Christian faith rests upon an impregnable foundation. If it stands, they stand. If the resurrection falls, the other truths fall also. It was a recognition of this truth that caused Paul to write to the Corinthians, "If Christ be not risen, then is our preaching vain, and your faith is also vain. Yea, and we are found false witnesses of God, because we have testified of God that he raised up Christ, whom he raised not up, if so be that the dead rise not" (I Cor. 15:14, 15).

The resurrection of Jesus Christ is a bit like a clothesline that supports the clean wash. If the line falls, the doctrines of the faith fall. Where the resurrection stands, everything else stands with it.

THE OTHER DOCTRINES

What does the resurrection prove? The answer is: It proves all that needs to be proved. It proves the essential doctrines of Christianity.

In the first place, it proves the deity of our Lord. When He lived upon earth Jesus claimed to be equal to God and that God, this God,

253

would raise Him from the dead three days after His execution by the Jewish and Roman authorities. If He was wrong in this, His claim was blasphemy. If He was right, the resurrection would be God's method of substantiating it. Did Jesus rise from the dead? Yes, He did. And the resurrection is God's seal on Christ's claims to divinity. This is why Paul, who knew that Jesus had been raised, writes that Jesus was "declared to be the Son of God with power, according to the spirit of holiness, by the resurrection from the dead" (Rom. 1:4).

Then, too, the resurrection proves our justification before God. For the book of Romans states that Jesus "was delivered for our offenses, and was raised again for our justification" (Rom. 4:25). How does this happen? Well, Jesus had claimed that His death would atone for man's sin. He had said that He had come "to give his life a ransom for many" (Matt. 20:28). He died as He said. But the question remained: Could it be true that the death of this one man would be acceptable to God for others? Three days pass. Christ rises. His claim is established. And, thus, by the resurrection God shows that He has accepted Christ's atonement forever.

The resurrection also proves that the believer in Christ can have a supernatural victory over sin in this life, for Christ lives to provide the supernatural power for it. The author of Hebrews says, "Wherefore, he [Christ] is able also to save them to the uttermost that come unto God by him, seeing he ever liveth to make intercession for them" (Heb. 7:25). In the same way Jude says that "he is able to keep [them] from falling" (Jude 24).

The resurrection of Jesus Christ is also the unshakable evidence for our own resurrection. Because He lives we shall live also. That is why Paul says, in the verse to which we have now come in our study of Philippians, "Christ . . . shall change our lowly body, that it may be fashioned like his glorious body, according to the working by which he is able even to subdue all things unto himself" (Phil. 3:21).

This verse teaches several important things. It teaches that: 1) Jesus is living, 2) because He lives we shall live, and 3) because He was transformed we shall be transformed. Moreover, we know all of these things through the fact of His own resurrection.

Jesus Is Living

In the first place, Jesus is living. This great fact first gripped the disciples and friends of Jesus. During the days following the resurrection all of them moved from blank and enervating despair to firm conviction and joy. Thereafter this unshakable truth transformed their life and ministry.

During the last century the well-known critic of the gospels, Ernst

Renan, wrote that belief in Christ's resurrection arose from the passion of an hallucinated woman; that is, of Mary Magdalene. He meant that Mary Magdalene was in love with Jesus and deluded herself into thinking that she had seen Him alive when she had actually seen only the gardener. But this idea is preposterous. The last person in the world that Mary (or any of the others) expected to see was Jesus. To their minds Jesus had died forever, and all of their hopes had died with Him. The only reason Mary was in the garden on that Easter morning was to put spices around His dead body.

Moreover, even if Mary had believed in some sort of resurrection through the force of love, there is no evidence that the disciples could have been similarly deluded or that they anticipated anything of the kind. Many despaired; some, like the Emmaus disciples, were scattering. Thomas, for one, was adamant in his disbelief. And yet, we find that within a matter of days after the Lord's alleged resurrection all of them were absolutely convinced of what beforehand they would have judged entirely impossible. And they went forth to tell about it, persisting in their conviction even in the face of threats, persecution, and torture.

Torrey summarizes the evidence like this. "The most significant fact of all is the change in the disciples — the moral transformation. At the time of the crucifixion of Christ we find the whole apostolic company filled with blank and utter despair. We see Peter, the leader of the apostolic company, denying his Lord three times with oaths and cursings. But a few days later we see this same man filled with a courage that nothing could shake. We see Peter standing before the very council that had condemned Jesus to death, and saying to them: 'Be it known unto you all, and to all the people of Israel, that in the name of Jesus of Nazareth, whom you crucified, whom God raised from the dead, doth this man stand before you whole' (Acts 4:10). A little further on, when commanded by this council not to speak at all nor teach in the name of Jesus, we hear Peter and John answering: 'Whether it be right in the sight of God to hearken unto you more than unto God, judge ye. For we cannot but speak the things which we have seen and heard' (Acts 4:19, 20). . . . Something tremendous must have happened to account for such a radical and astounding moral transformation as this. Nothing short of the fact of the resurrection, of their having seen the risen Lord, will explain it." *

Certainly Paul was at one with this first great conviction of the

---

* R. A. Torrey, *The Bible and Its Christ* (Old Tappan, N.J.: Fleming H. Revell, n.d.), pp. 91, 92.

disciples when he made the resurrection of Jesus the basis of the Christian's own faith and spiritual confidence.

WE SHALL LIVE ALSO

The second important thought in our text is: because Jesus lives we shall live also. Jesus had said, "I go to prepare a place for you. And if I go and prepare a place for you, I will come again, and receive you unto myself, that where I am, there ye may be also" (John 14: 2, 3). In I Thessalonians Paul wrote, "For if we believe that Jesus died and rose again, even so them also who sleep in Jesus will God bring with him" (I Thess. 4:14).

At this point two truths must be made perfectly clear. 1) Apart from the resurrection of Jesus Christ there is no certainty of life beyond the grave for anyone. And 2) on the basis of the resurrection of Jesus Christ the believer can have a perfect confidence. The writings of philosophers and the men of letters have many arguments for immortality, but at best they offer only a speculation that such things may be so. One philosopher has called the doctrine of immortality "a candle flickering at the end of a dark tunnel." Another has called it "a star shining dimly on the blackest of nights." This is the philosophical hope of immortality, but it does not give confidence. It is a probability but not a certainty. The only sure evidence of our resurrection is the resurrection of Jesus Himself, who said, "Because I live, ye shall live also" (John 14:19). His resurrection makes the difference.

In the year 1899, two famous men died in America. The one was an unbeliever who had made a career of debunking the Bible and arguing against the Christian doctrines. The other was a Christian. Colonel Ingersoll, after whom the famous Ingersoll lectures on immortality at Harvard University are named, was the unbeliever. He died suddenly, his death coming as an unmitigated shock to his family. The body was kept in the home for several days because Ingersoll's wife could not bear to part with it; and it was finally removed only because the corpse was decaying and the health of the family required it. At length the remains were cremated, and the display at the crematorium was so dismal that some of the scene was even picked up by the newspapers and communicated to the nation at large. Ingersoll had used his great intellect to deny the resurrection. When death came there was no hope, and the departure was received by his friends as an uncompensated tragedy.

In the same year the evangelist Dwight L. Moody died, and his death was triumphant for himself and his family. Moody had been declining for some time, and his family had taken turns being with him. On the morning of his death his son, who was standing by the bedside, heard him exclaim, "Earth is receding; heaven is opening; God is calling." "You are dreaming, father," the son said. Moody answered, "No, Will, this is no dream. I have been within the gates. I have seen the children's faces." For a while it seemed as if Moody was reviving, but he began to slip away again. He said, "Is this death? This is not bad; there is no valley. This is bliss. This is glorious." By this time his daughter was present, and she began to pray for his recovery. He said, "No, no, Emma, don't pray for that. God is calling. This is my coronation day. I have been looking forward to it." Shortly after that Moody was received into heaven. At the funeral the family and friends joined in a joyful service. They spoke. They sang hymns. They heard the words proclaimed, "O death, where is thy sting? O grave, where is thy victory? The sting of death is sin; and the strength of sin is the law. But thanks be to God, who giveth us the victory through our Lord Jesus Christ." Moody's death was a part of that victory.

Now I do not mean to imply that the death of every Christian is equally glorious. Not all feel the force of these doctrines and live them in the moment of their homegoing. But many do. And death is still partially transformed even for those who do not. For a Christian death can be victorious. There is no hope apart from our Lord's resurrection. In the light of this resurrection, as we go out to the cemeteries to look at the graves of our parents, sisters, brothers, wives, husbands, friends, and children, we hear the Lord Jesus say, "Your parents shall live again; your brother shall live again, your son shall live again." And we know that even now they live in the spirit in Christ's presence.

> Jesus lives, and so shall I.
> Death! thy sting is gone forever!
> He who deigned for me to die,
> Lives, the bands of death to sever.
> He shall raise me from the dust:
> Jesus is my Hope and Trust.
>
> Jesus lives and death is now
> But my entrance into glory.
> Courage, then, my soul, for thou
> Hast a crown of life before thee;
> Thou shalt find thy hopes were just;
> Jesus is the Christian's Trust.

To Be Transformed

The last teaching of our text is that we shall be transformed. Because Jesus was transformed, we shall be transformed. Thus, Paul says that Jesus "shall change our lowly body, that it might be fashioned like his glorious body, according to the working by which he is able even to subdue all things unto himself."

I am often impressed by the way Paul builds word upon word in a statement like this so that there might be no doubt about what he is saying. In the first part of the sentence he speaks of the change that shall come in our bodies, and the word he uses in that expression is *schema*. This is the same word used in Romans 12:2 where the Christian is encouraged not to be conformed to this world. It speaks of an outward conformity.

But Paul also says that our bodies are to be "fashioned" like His glorious body. And here the word *morphe* is used. It also occurs in Romans 12:2. It points to an inward transformation. Paul uses both terms and by them teaches that our transformation will not only be external but internal also, so that we shall be conformed both inwardly and outwardly to the image of our blessed and glorified Lord. In that day we shall be like Him in body, soul, and spirit.

This is a great comfort to those who have lost believing loved ones. There is always a horror to death as we know it. It is connected to sin. And even the Bible knows it as the ultimate enemy of man. In death, and often before it, the body of a man is destroyed. Sometimes it is wasted by sickness; sometimes it is crushed in the abrupt terror of an accident. Often the last sight we have of a Christian friend is of a wasted body caught by the grim hands of death. And yet, in none of these grim experiences have we heard the end of the story. The last reel has not been shown. For we know that we shall meet again in Christ's presence. We shall meet in transformed bodies. And the former sadness will fade to a small and insignificant thing in the light of the unending joy of eternity.

Apart from the resurrection of Jesus Himself there are only three resurrections recorded in the four gospels — the resurrection of the son of the widow of Nain, the resurrection of the daughter of Jairus, and the resurrection of Mary's and Martha's brother Lazarus. Each began in mourning and sorrow; each ended in exuberant joy. What made the difference? Nothing but the coming of Jesus! Jesus said of Himself, "I am the life," and where life meets death, death is vanquished. Death was vanquished. And it will be abolished forever for us when Jesus Christ returns.

Perhaps you are saying, "But can I really believe that is possible? Is Jesus really able to do the things claimed for Him?" Of course, He is! Just think of the things for which the Bible tells us He is able. It says that "he is able to keep that which I have committed unto him" (II Tim. 1:12), "he is able to help them that are tempted"

(Heb. 2:18), "he is able to keep you from falling" (Jude 24), he "is able to do exceedingly abundantly above all that we ask or think" (Eph. 3:20), "he is able also to save them to the uttermost that come unto God by him" (Heb. 7:25). Can He do these things? Of course, He can. We have experienced them in part. In the same way He is certainly able to raise up our bodies, transforming them "according to the working by which he is able to subdue all things unto himself."

39

Therefore — Stand

(Philippians 4:1)

THE FINAL CHAPTER OF Paul's letter to the Philippians begins: "Therefore, my brethren dearly beloved and longed for, my joy and crown, so stand fast in the Lord, my dearly beloved." These words are a glorious bridge between the chapter just ended, with all of its great doctrinal statements, and the intensely practical chapter that is coming. And they sum up the preceding doctrines in one great practical issue. Because of what Jesus Christ has done for us — because of His life, death, and resurrection, and the resulting victory over sin and the devil — we are now to stand fast in Him, united as God's soldiers against a spiritually hostile environment.

STANDING

It is a remarkable fact that at several crucial junctures in Paul's letters the practical outcome of the Christian's warfare against the world and Satan is defined as a matter of "standing"; and this is the more remarkable because it is part of a military metaphor. In the final chapter of Ephesians, for instance, Paul writes of the life of the Christian as warfare. But even as he writes of the Christian's warfare, Paul says that the practical outcome for the Christian is not so much to advance into battle as to stand. He writes, "Put on the whole armor of God, that ye may be able to *stand* against the wiles of the devil. . . . Take unto you the whole armor of God, that ye may be able to with*stand* in the evil day, and having done all, to *stand*. *Stand*, therefore" (Eph. 6:11-14). If we were writing the passage and were using Paul's image, we should most likely speak of invasion, marching, or conquest. But Paul does not do that. Instead he speaks correctly of standing.

The reason is that God does not tell us to march into battle or to conquer, in spite of our great hymn "Onward, Christian Soldiers." He tells us to stand. And the implication of the command is that God has already done or is doing the conquering. We are only to hold the ground He conquers.

I suppose the difference between marching and standing is the difference between offensive and defensive warfare. Watchman Nee, the Chinese evangelist, says of this passage in Ephesians, "The difference between defensive and offensive warfare is this, that in the former I have got the ground and only seek to keep it, whereas in the latter I have not got the ground and am fighting in order to get it. And that is precisely the difference between the warfare waged by the Lord Jesus and the warfare waged by us. His was offensive; ours is, in essence, defensive. He warred against Satan in order to gain the victory. Through the cross he carried that warfare to the very threshold of Hell itself, to lead forth thence his captivity captive (4:8, 9). Today we war against Satan only to maintain and consolidate the victory which he has already gained. By the resurrection God proclaimed his Son victor over the whole realm of darkness, and the ground Christ won he has given to us. We do not need to fight to obtain it. We only need to hold it against all challengers." *

The words are also true in regard to Philippians. For when Paul writes in the fourth chapter, "Therefore, my brethren dearly beloved and longed for, . . . stand fast," he is pointing back to the great statements of what Jesus Christ has done for us in chapter three. And he is teaching, as Nee says, that it is on the basis of these conquests that the Christian warrior must stand.

The Victorious Christ

What are these conquests? What has Jesus Christ done for those who trust Him? The first one is certainly that referred to in chapter 3, verse 9, for the verse tells us that Christ died to bring us salvation. In Paul's terms salvation is to "be found in him, not having mine own righteousness, which is of the law, but that which is through the faith of Christ, the righteousness which is of God by faith."

According to the New Testament Christ's death on the cross accomplished two things. Negatively, it was the means by which our sins were removed and punished. Christ bore our punishment. And as a result, because there is no such thing as punishing the same crime twice with God, we need no longer fear anything at God's hand. The Bible says that God has removed our sins from us "as far as the east is from the west" (Ps. 103:12) and that He will remember them against us no more (Isa. 43:25). Positively, the cross is the means

---

* Watchman Nee, *Sit, Walk, Stand* (Ft. Washington, Pa.: Christian Literature Crusade, 1957), pp. 43, 44.

by which God offers us Christ's righteousness in place of our own inadequate righteousness.

If you were a contractor and were asked to construct a large office building upon a lot where a building already stood, you would have two ways of going about your assignment. You could build over the building that is already there, just as contractors in New York city have built over the old Grand Central Station. Or, you could tear the old building down and start anew. However, if the foundations of the old building were too weak to bear the weight of the new building, as is the case generally, then you would no longer have an alternative. You would simply have to clear away the old structure to make room for the new. So it is with God and His righteousness or goodness. The righteousness that God requires of you is too great to be constructed over the top of your righteousness. Your own righteousness cannot bear its weight. Therefore, God has asked you to allow Him to clear away all attempts you might make to please Him by your own righteousness and, instead, allow Him to construct the goodness of Christ. The Gospel teaches that God put Christ to death that you might be able to be found in Him, not having your own righteousness, "but that which is through the faith of Christ." This is the first great truth of Christianity.

Christ Lives

The second achievement of the Lord Jesus Christ is to be found in the fact of His resurrection. For Christ conquered death in order to live to be known by His followers. Paul speaks of this experiential knowledge in verses 10 and 11 as he writes, "That I may know him, and the power of his resurrection, and the fellowship of his sufferings, being made conformable unto his death, if by any means I might attain unto the resurrection of the dead."

There is a vast difference between being saved from something impersonally and coming to know the Savior. If you are a girl drowning in the ocean off the coast of Atlantic City, it would be wonderful to have a handsome lifeguard come and save you. But it would be quite another thing (and something much more wonderful) to have that same lifeguard fall in love with you and marry you. In that case you would know him, not only impersonally as your savior, but personally and intimately as your husband. And you would love him. In the same way, Jesus lives to know and to be known by His followers.

Knowing the Lord Jesus Christ does not mean that life will always be smooth. Christ was a man; as a man He knew temptations and suffering too. Even as Paul wrote these words to the Philippians he was experiencing suffering. But he was experiencing something else also. He was experiencing Christ's power in the midst of his sufferings. And he knew that the trials had entered his life not to depress or defeat him but to be an opportunity in which the supernatural power of the Lord Jesus Christ could be seen.

It should be true of us also. And we should look to the power of Jesus' resurrection as the ground of our own victories for Him.

Our Guide and Counselor

The same chapter of Philippians also suggests three more things that Jesus does for us. First, Jesus has promised to reveal His will to us. Paul says, "Let us, therefore, as many as be perfect, be thus minded; and if in anything ye be otherwise minded, God shall reveal even this unto you" (verse 15). This verse teaches that God has marked out a path for us to follow in life and promises to warn us if we deviate from it.

Jesus has also given us a rule of conduct, and this is set forth in the Scriptures (3:15-19). The Bible contains the principles that we should follow if we would live a godly life. It contains words that will speak to us directly as we seek God's will in particular matters. It is the food by which our spiritual natures should grow. It is the ammunition with which we should fight against Satan. Do you use it? Do you read it daily and memorize it? You should, for it is one of the great weapons that Jesus has given in order that we Christians might stand.

A final thing that Jesus does for us is to live within us to lead us in the upward way. Paul writes that it is for this that he has been seized by Christ Jesus (verse 12), and we have been seized for this too. How thankful we must be that the Lord Jesus did not merely give us the Bible to show us the way in which we should go, or merely set forth His life as the great example of holiness. We need more than an example. A gifted writer might be able to sit down in a garret somewhere and turn out a masterpiece of literature in spite of the noise about him, the debts, despair, or ill health. But unless we have the genius of the writer within us we cannot match his performance. Fortunately, when Jesus called us to Himself, He also provided the genius; for He came to live with us Himself through His Holy Spirit. In His strength we can press on toward the mark of God's calling.

The God of Elijah

In the same book mentioned earlier, Watchman Nee tells a wonderful story that illustrates many of these truths. In the early days of his work in China before World War II, Watchman Nee led a team of Chinese Christians on a preaching mission to an island off the south coast of China. There were seven workers: Nee, five experienced workers, and young brother Wu, a new and impetuous Christian who was eager to be included.

The island was a fairly large one, according to Nee, with perhaps 20,000 or 30,000 people. Throughout the New Year's holiday when they were on the island, Nee and the others worked hard, but with little success. At length the impetuous brother Wu asked the people of the island bluntly, "Why is it that none of you will believe?" And someone answered immediately, "We have a god — one god — Ta-wang, and he has never failed us. He is an effective god." "How do you know that you can trust him?" asked Wu. The people answered, "We have held his festival procession every January for 286 years. The chosen day is revealed by divination beforehand, and every year without fail his day is a perfect one without rain or cloud." "And when is the procession this year?" asked Wu. "It is fixed for January 11 at eight in the morning." "Then," said Wu impetuously, "I promise you that it will certainly rain on the eleventh." At once there was an outburst from the crowd, and the villagers cried out, "That is enough! No more preaching! If there is rain on the eleventh, then your God is God."

Nee himself was away in another part of the village when this verbal exchange occurred. But as soon as he heard of it he recognized that it was serious. The news was spreading like wildfire. And although Wu's challenge may have been a mistake, it was made and it was too late to change it. Everyone would soon know about it. What were the evangelists to do? Were they wrong? Had they made a mistake? Did they dare ask God for a miracle?

The Christians began to pray. And as they prayed, not yet daring to ask for rain, Wu said that like a flash the word came to him: "Where is the God of Elijah?" It came with such clarity and power that he knew that it was from God. He announced, "I have the answer. The Lord will send rain on the eleventh." Together they thanked Him and then went out to announce an acceptance of Ta-wang's challenge.

That evening as they returned to the hut in which they were staying, its owner, their host, made two very astute observations. First, he said, there was no doubt that Ta-wang was an effective god, for it really had not rained on his day in all those years. The devil was with that statue. Or, second, if you preferred a rationalistic explanation, you could remember that the village was a village of fishermen, and they of all people should know whether or not it would rain two or three days ahead. This was disturbing.

Nee writes, "As we went to our evening prayer, we all began once more to pray for rain — now! Then it was that there came to us a stern rebuke from the Lord: 'Where is the God of Elijah?' Were we going to fight our way through this battle, or were we going to rest in the finished victory of Christ? What had Elisha done when he spoke these words? He had laid claim in his own personal experience to the very miracle that his lord Elijah, now in the glory, had himself performed. In New Testament terms, he had taken his stand by faith on the ground of a finished work."

The workers went to bed and awoke on the eleventh. Nee says, "I was awakened by the direct rays of the sun through the single window of our attic. 'This isn't rain!' I said. It was already past seven o'clock. I got up, knelt down and prayed. 'Lord,' I said, 'please send the rain!' But once again, ringing in my ears came the word: 'Where is the God of Elijah?' Humbled, I walked downstairs before God in silence. We sat down to breakfast — eight of us together, including our host — all very quiet. There was no cloud in the sky, but we knew God was committed. As we bowed to say grace before the food I said, 'I think the time is up. Rain must come now. We can bring it to the Lord's remembrance.' Quietly we did so, and this time the answer came with no hint whatsoever of rebuke in it." *

Even before the "Amen" the evangelists heard a few drops of rain on the tiles. There was a steady shower as they ate their rice. As they began their second bowl they asked God for a heavier downpour, and it came in buckets full. By the time they had finished their breakfast the streets were flooded, and the bottom three steps of the house were covered with water.

Soon they heard what had happened in the village. At the first drops of rain a few of the younger men began to say, "There is God; there is no more Ta-wang! He is kept in by the rain." But he was not. They carried him out on a sedan chair to begin the procession. Surely he would stop the shower. But the downpour grew worse. After a few steps the coolies who were bearing the chair slipped and fell. When they fell, Ta-wang fell. He broke his jaw and his left arm. Repairs were made, and the statue was again brought out and dragged around half of the village. At last the rain and the mud defeated them.

The statue was taken inside, and the elders came to the conclusion that the eleventh of January was the wrong day. "The festival is to be held on the fourteenth at six in the evening," they said. Immediately the Christians accepted the challenge for the fourteenth. And on the fourteenth of January at six in the evening the skies that had previously

* Watchman Nee, *Sit, Walk, Stand* (Ft. Washington, Pa.: Christian Literature Crusade, 1957), pp. 57-64.

cleared once more filled with rain. The procession was again defeated by torrents. From that day forward the power of Ta-wang was broken, and the island of Ta-wang became an open field for the preaching of the Christian Gospel.

Do you see the force of the illustration? Standing upon the work of the Lord Jesus Christ and upon His promises does not mean that there will not be work for us to do. There will always be testing. There will often be much strenuous activity. It does not mean escape. But it does mean that even in the activity and even in the testing there can be an overriding confidence in God and in His promises. We shall know that we are merely standing upon the ground that He has already won and given to us. And by His grace we shall expect at the end of the battle still to be standing with Him victorious and in triumphant possession of the field.

40.

How to Get Along With Other Christians

(Philippians 4:2-5)

HAVE YOU EVER TRIED to tell someone something but have found it difficult either because you feared it might be offensive or because you knew the person might not understand? If so, you can well understand Paul's position as we consider the fourth chapter of Philippians, verses 2-5. For Paul was trying to say something to the Philippians that was difficult for him to say. And he was afraid that the persons involved might resent it.

Apparently there had been trouble at Philippi. And although it was not terrible trouble, it was a situation serious enough to make Paul worried. Two of the Christian women had been at odds with one another — Euodia and Syntyche — and the disagreement had grown to the point where it could hinder the unity and effectiveness of the church. Paul wished to warn them of the danger. He wanted to urge a more cooperative spirit. But these women were his friends. And every time he approached the subject of unity in the letter he seemed to come short of a direct application. At the beginning of chapter 1 he had spoken of his prayer that their love might "abound yet more and more" (verse 9). He closed the same chapter with the admonition, "only let your conduct be as it becometh the gospel of Christ . . . that ye stand fast in one spirit, with one mind" (verse 27). In chapter 2 he had urged the Philippians to be "of one accord, of one mind" (verse 2). In chapter 3 he had written, "Let us walk by the same rule, let us mind the same thing" (verse 16).

Now at last he returns to the theme in chapter 4 and this time tells what it is that is disturbing him. He writes, "I beseech Euodia, and beseech Syntyche, that they be of the same mind in the Lord. And I entreat thee also, true yokefellow, help those women who labored with me in the gospel, with Clement also, and with other my fellow workers, whose names are in the book of life. Rejoice in the Lord always; and again I say, Rejoice. Let your moderation be known unto all men. The Lord is at hand" (4:2-5).

How tactful this section of the letter is! Paul has finally pointed directly to the lack of harmony within the church. But he does not elaborate on the problem; he does not even reprove or command those involved. Instead he quietly points to the means by which the breach can be healed. In doing so he gives us the means by which unity may be restored among us and other Christians.

God's Children

We must recognize at the outset, however, that the unity referred to here is a Christian unity, and this means a unity only among those in God's family. Paul says that Euodia and Syntyche are to be "of the same mind *in the Lord*." And who are those "in the Lord"? Only those who are believers in the Lord Jesus Christ. Indeed Christian unity is only possible for them.

It is a matter of being a born-again member of God's family. I know that some who read these words may say, "Oh, but aren't all men members of God's family?" But the answer to that question is, "No, they are not." I know that there are some who teach this, that all men are God's children. But although it is true that all men are part of God's creation and all are His offspring, it is not true that all are His children. In fact, Jesus told some of the men of His day that they were actually of their father the devil.

In the eighth chapter of John's gospel we have an account of this in a conversation that Jesus had with the Jewish leaders. In the course of the conversation Jesus spoke of His teaching as that which would set men free. This set off a reaction. There is an old expression that says, "Never speak of rope in the house of a hangman." And it might well have been said, "Never speak of freedom to a first-century Palestine Jew." For freedom was a touchy subject in Judaea under Roman rule. The people reacted to it, and said, "What do you mean, free? Why do you say this to us? We are Abraham's children, and we have never been in bondage to any man."

Now this was either an outright lie, or it was self-delusion. The Jews had been slaves in Egypt for 400 years. They had been in bondage to the Philistines, the Ammonites, the Syrians, and the Babylonians. And even as they spoke to Jesus they were actually under the bondage of Rome and were carrying coins in their pockets with the image of Caesar stamped upon them. And yet they said, "We have never been in bondage to any man."

Jesus answered them by raising the conversation to the spiritual level

He had intended when He first referred to their bondage. He explained that the bondage He meant was a bondage to sin and that as sinners they were actually children of the devil. They could only become God's children through faith in Him.

We need to see that also. Are you a believer in the Lord Jesus Christ? Do you belong to God's family? You need to ask yourself that question, if you have never done it. For everything in the Christian life flows from it. There must be a moment in your life when you stand before God and say, "Lord God, I confess to You that I am a sinner and am barred from Your presence because of my sin. I am not of Your family and I have no claim to it. And yet I believe that Jesus died for my sin and that You have offered to take me into Your family and to give me new life through Him. I ask You to do that now. Amen." If you will do that (or have already done it), then God will make you a member of His spiritual family, the invisible Church, and you will experience new life in Him.

For all who have done this, for His children, God now commands a visible, earthly unity. As in the epistle to the Philippians, God commands that His children live in harmony with each other.

Maintaining the Bond

There are some practical ways in which the harmony that exists initially among God's children is to be expressed and maintained. And Paul tactfully lists them in his brief remarks to Euodia and Syntyche.

First, Paul says that Christians are to be like-minded, and this means that they are to have the mind of Christ. It is the same thing that Paul had in mind earlier when he wrote, "Let this mind be in you, which was also in Christ Jesus" (2:5). He is not speaking of the doctrines that Christ taught, although they are important. He is speaking of the attitude that Jesus had in relation to others. This is made clear in reference to the verse just quoted, for the mind of Christ there is the humble mind, the lowly mind. It is the mind of one who did not consider equality with God something to be retained at all costs but who emptied Himself to die for the salvation and well-being of others. It is evident that in this context Paul's plea to be "of the same mind" is a plea for the operation of humility and self-sacrifice among Christians.

This will never occur apart from a personal and intimate walk with God, for in ourselves we do not like humility. And we cannot achieve it without Him. If you are far from the Lord, then frictions will inevitably spring up between yourself and other Christians. The things they say will irk you. The things they do will get under your skin and fester. If this is not to happen, then you must maintain a close and personal fellowship with the Lord.

You see, Paul wanted his admonition to the women at Philippi to come down to the personal level. For he knew, as we all should know, that the effectiveness of the Christian warfare depends upon the conduct of the individual Christian soldier. As the Church impinges upon the world it is a little like a triangle. It has a broad base composed of many believers and many doctrines. But the impact point is the apex; and the apex is the individual Christian. The individual is what the world sees. The individual is the one who either promotes or hinders harmony. And who is the individual? You! And I! If there is to be Christian unity, you and I must maintain our walk with the Lord.

WORKING TOGETHER

Then, too, we must work with other Christians. Paul calls attention to this aspect of unity by referring to his fellow workers at Philippi and to the one who was a "true yokefellow" in that ministry. By these references he suggests that it is not enough for Christians merely to be thinking in a spirit of unity. They must be working in a spirit of unity also.

There has been much debate among some commentators on Paul's letter about who this "true yokefellow" is. Some, like Clement of Alexandria, one of the earliest commentators, think that the yokefellow was Paul's wife. But this is an odd suggestion since the Greek word is masculine in form. It is the least likely of all possibilities. Others have taken the word as a popular name, *Syzygus*, which is at least possible. I am inclined to think that those commentators are right who see the word as a reference to Epaphroditus, who has already been described as a "brother and companion in labor, and a fellow soldier" and who was now about to carry the letter back to Philippi from Rome. If this is the case, it means that Paul merely incorporated his charge to Epaphroditus into the letter, thereby giving him an official charge to help restore harmony at home. Epaphroditus in his conduct would himself be an example of true harmony.

Paul was looking back to the glorious days that he had spent in Philippi among the Christians. And he was thinking of the great joy he had had as he worked with them for spiritual ends. Now that unity is threatened. And he says to them, "Keep on. Do not let your unity be ruined by friction between your members. Work together. Make sure your unity can be seen in your actions."

Joy and Moderation

The third thing that the Philippians must do is to rejoice in the Lord. Paul says that in verse 4: "Rejoice in the Lord always; and again I say, Rejoice." Paul knew that if a Christian is rejoicing in God's mercy and goodness to him, he is not so likely to be nitpicking with his fellow Christians.

The word "rejoice" is in itself an interesting one, for it is only a variant form of the word "joy," which is one of the great Christian virtues, the fruit of God's Spirit. Consequently rejoicing, like joy, is supernatural. Joy is the Christian virtue; happiness is the virtue of the world. And there is all the difference in the world between them. Happiness is entirely external. It is circumstantial. We have all seen the Charlie Brown cartoon that defines happiness as a warm puppy. But suppose there is no puppy. Well, then, there is no happiness. Happiness depends on the things we have or can acquire. For some it is money. For some it is fame. For some it is power or good looks. But these are all external. And when these things go, happiness goes with them.

It is not that way with joy. Joy issues from the nature of God, and it is intended to well up within those in whom God's Spirit dwells. It is not external; it is internal. And it does not hinge upon chance. Things may happen to the Christian that no one, including the Christian, would be happy about. But there can still be joy. And the Christian who is filled with this supernatural, abounding joy will not be finding grounds for disagreement with his fellow Christians.

Finally, Paul says that Christians are to let their "moderation be known unto all men" (verse 5). Moderation here is not the same thing as temperance, which is mentioned as a fruit of the Spirit in Galatians 5. It is a different word from that. In fact, it is an unusual Greek word and one that does not even occur in the classical Greek before Paul's time. He may have coined it. Literally, it means "reasonableness" or "being reasonable." The sentence is a warning not to be unduly rigorous about unimportant matters.

Now it does not mean that Christians are to be compromising in their doctrinal beliefs. Paul is not talking about doctrine here any more than he was talking about doctrine when he referred to the mind of Christ in verse two. And he is not talking about compromise with the world's standards of conduct either. He has already written that Christians are to live as "blameless and harmless, children of God, without rebuke, in the midst of a crooked and perverse nation, among whom [they are to] shine as lights in the world" (2:15). He wrote to the Roman Christians that they were not to be "conformed to this world" but to be "transformed by the renewing of [their] mind" (Rom. 12:2). Actually, he is merely saying that those who profess the name of Christ should be a bit bending in their attitudes, especially where other Christians are concerned. They should not be brittle. Neither you nor I are to have a personality so inflexible that people bounce off it like a tennis ball bouncing off a stone wall. We are to listen to them, even to tolerate their errors for a time, if you will, in order that God in His time might use us better to encourage them in their walk with the Lord.

This should be especially applicable in Christian families. Often children rebel against the Gospel and against their parents; and they do so many times (I am convinced) simply because the parents have been too rigid and too doctrinaire in their training. Here, too, there must be moderation. And it must be an aspect of that yieldingness with one another to which Christians are called.

In the Lord

None of these high standards of conduct is easy. And the difficulty of doing them and living them is where the problem of unity lies. It is one thing to say to each other, "Well, let us be of the same mind and work together. Let us rejoice. Let us show moderation." But it is quite another thing to put the words into practice. Fortunately, Paul knew the difficulty also. And as a result he has given us the solution to the problem. Have you ever noticed how many times he speaks of being "in the Lord Jesus Christ" in the first four verses of this chapter? Three times! And once he reminds them that "the Lord is at hand." The solution is the Lord Jesus Christ. It is He who will do in the lives of yielded Christians what we might judge impossible.

Christian unity will occur only as we surrender ourselves to Him and seek His will, as His Holy Spirit enters our lives and begins to make us into the kind of men, women, children, and young people that He would have us be.

41.

The Meaning of Prayer

(Philippians 4:6, 7)

FOR MOST PEOPLE FEW doctrines associated with Christianity are more generally misunderstood than that of true prayer. It is totally misunderstood by non-believers, and it is misunderstood by many who profess the name of Jesus. The problem may be traced to the fact that so few persons know God well enough to be closely associated with Him in prayer. And since none of us is as closely associated with Him as we ought to be, prayer is at least partially confusing to us all. Does prayer change things? Or does prayer change people? Does God change His mind as the result of believing prayer? Or does God move us to pray? What does it mean to pray without ceasing? Who can pray? How do you pray? And why should a person pray anyway? In any gathering of God's people many of these questions will receive different and sometimes even contradictory answers.

In our study of the fourth chapter of Philippians there are two verses that are an exceptionally fine statement of the Christian doctrine of prayer. Paul says, "Be anxious for nothing, but in everything, by prayer and supplication with thanksgiving, let your requests be made known unto God. And the peace of God, which passeth all understanding, shall keep your hearts and minds through Christ Jesus" (Phil. 4:6, 7).

FOR CHRISTIANS ONLY

What is prayer? Prayer is talking with God. And the place to begin in any true definition of prayer is with the fact that prayer is for believers only. Paul did not write his words about prayer to the pagan world at Philippi or to the world at large. He wrote them "to . . . the saints in Christ Jesus" at Philippi. This means that prayer is exclusively for Christians. It is the means by which an empty soul that has been touched by Jesus Christ can be thrust beneath the life-giving fountain of God's grace, can bask in God's goodness, and can be supernaturally refreshed for life's tasks. Prayer is the Christians's antidote for anxiety.

273

I know that something that is called prayer is offered a billion times daily by millions of people who are not Christians, but this is not prayer in any real sense. Scores of non-Christian people in the East spend the better part of a day spinning prayer wheels. Savages chant prayers in many jungle clearings. Hippies finger prayer beads. Many poor souls cry out a prayer in the midst of some calamity. Many non-Christians give themselves to a life of meditation. But this is not true prayer, if the person involved is not himself a Christian. Prayer is talking with God, and the only prayer that God hears and answers is one that is made through His Son, our Lord Jesus Christ, who alone provides access to His presence.

This is taught in the Bible in the fifth chapter of Romans, verse two. Here Paul is beginning to talk about the results of justification. And he says that one of these results is access to God's presence. Before he believes in Jesus a man has no access to God's presence. After belief he is given an access similar to that which a child has to his earthly father. He writes, "Therefore, being justified by faith, we have peace with God through our Lord Jesus Christ, by whom also we have access by faith into this grace in which we stand" (Rom. 5:1, 2). First comes faith in Jesus; then comes access.

The same truth was taught in other words by Jesus. Jesus said, "I am the way, the truth, and the life; no man cometh unto the Father, but by me" (John 14:6). Jesus did not say that He was one of several ways to come to God, that He was a prophet who pointed out the ways to God; He said that He was *the* way to come to God. And He added, lest anyone misunderstand Him, "No man cometh unto the Father, but by me." This means that no prayer offered to God apart from faith in the Lord Jesus Christ has ever reached God His heavenly Father.

There are more passages in the Bible that tell when God will not answer prayer than there are passages in which He promises to do it. And God definitely says that He will not answer the prayer of anyone who does not come through faith in His Son.

Let me ask this question. Have you tried to pray and have you found God distant and unreal? And have you gone away without any real hope that God has heard you? It may be that you have never done the first thing God requires. Your sin divides you like a wall from God's presence, and it will only be removed by Jesus Christ. You need to come to Him. You need to say, Lord Jesus Christ, I recognize that I am separated from You by my sin; but I believe that You died for me to remove that sin for ever. Remove it now. And accept me as Your child. Amen." If you do that, God will remove your sin, and He *will* accept you as His child for ever.

BARRIERS TO PRAYER

Now we must also add that although it is true that God does not hear the prayer of non-Christians, it is also true that He does not hear the prayers offered by many Christians. In fact, the Bible says that God will never hear a Christian's prayer so long as the Christian is clinging to some sin in his heart. David said, "If I regard iniquity in my heart, the Lord will not hear me" (Ps. 66:18). And Isaiah wrote, "Behold, the Lord's hand is not shortened, that it cannot save; neither his ear heavy, that it cannot hear. But your iniquities have separated between you and your God, and your sins have hidden his face from you, that he will not hear" (Isa. 59:1, 2).

Do these verses describe your prayer life? If so, you must confess your sin openly and frankly, knowing that God "is faithful and just to forgive us our sins, and to cleanse us from all unrighteousness" (I John 1:9). We can only pray if our lives are open books before Him.

In normal life we must know a person well before the conversation flows freely. There are many people I know casually to whom I would speak about the weather, about their work, about their families, but to whom I would never speak about more personal things. There are others I know better; to these I would speak about some problems in my own life or about the concerns of others. Certain things I share only with my immediate family. And there are special things I share only with my wife. How easily I can speak depends upon how well I know the person. It is the same in our relationship to God. If we do not know God well, if our sin keeps us from Him, if we do not recognize His characteristics and how He operates with men, then He is like a stranger to us and the prayer flows slowly, even though we have come to faith in Jesus. Instead, we must confess our sin and learn to spend time alone with our heavenly Father. When we do that our prayer will become the kind of communion that we have in conversation with an intimate friend.

PRAYER FOR OTHERS

Everything that I have noted up to this point has ourselves as the center; but if you have begun to see what prayer is, you will also have begun to see that prayer necessarily involves other people. No matter how intimate the conversation may be between a husband and wife, it does not always center on their own affairs exclusively. They share news about their acquaintances and their concerns for them. So it is in prayer. The Bible calls such prayer "intercession." I Timothy 2:1 says, "I exhort, therefore, that first of all, supplications, prayers, intercessions, and giving of thanks, be made for all men."

As we meet with God in prayer — at the beginning of a day, at its end, or in any moment throughout it — these concerns should also be a part of our conversation with Him. And we should have great boldness as we present the concerns of others.

That great Bible teacher, Dr. Harry Ironside, tells a story in one of his books about intercessory prayer. He had been preaching in the mid-west and had held meetings in a church that contained a most unusual group of believers. They had Sunday services. They had mid-week meetings. But they did not come together for prayer. He spoke to them about this lack. They said, "Oh, we don't need to meet for prayer. We have no spiritual needs, for the Bible says that we have all spiritual blessings in Christ Jesus. And we have no need of material things, for we are well provided for. So we don't pray." Ironside said, "Well, that is unfortunate. At the very least, you should pray for me that God will give me freedom of speech as I go about preaching the Gospel."

Well, they could not seem to understand his point, and Ironside left. Some time later he collapsed while in the pulpit. It was found that he had typhoid fever with a temperature of 106 degrees. In time he recovered, and during the next year he was back with this strange group of Christians. They said to him, "You know, when we heard that you were sick with typhoid fever we began to pray for you. We prayed for you twice a week, but after we heard that you had recovered we stopped." Ironside said, "Well, that is unfortunate also. As long as I was in the hospital room I was all right. All I had was typhoid fever. But now that I am out preaching the Gospel, I am faced with all of the spiritual temptations that come to a Christian minister. Now I need your prayers more than ever."

Now I know someone is going to say, "Do you mean to teach that God will only take care of another Christian if we pray?" No, I do not think intercession means that. But it does mean that God allows us to share in the blessings He gives to others and that He delights in using our prayers as a means through which He operates.

Let me illustrate this thought by a story. More than a generation ago a man named Hotchkiss went to Nigeria where he spent over forty years as a missionary. One day he received a pith helmet in the mail, and he lost so much time in showing it to his native friends that he became late for a service he was to have in a village located across a large plain. There was a rule in Nigeria in those days that no one ever crossed a large open space for fear of stampedes by the herds of wild game that roamed at large in the country. A safe path always passed within a short run of the trees. Well, Hotchkiss was late, and he knew he would only be on time if he went directly across the plain. So he started across it. Halfway across the worst happened. He heard the thunder of rhinoceros hoofs, and as he looked up he saw a herd of the monstrous animals headed toward him. It was too late to run. There was nowhere to go. So Hotchkiss knelt down in the middle of the plain, clasped his Bible to his chest, and prayed, "Lord, here I come." An eternity passed as the roar grew louder and then faded away into the distance. At last all was quiet. Hotchkiss arose. He was standing in the midst of the plain marked with the hoof-prints of a hundred or more rhinoceros. But he was alive. And he went on to his meeting in the village.

Years later, a couple visited this man in Nigeria. They had come from Ohio. And in the course of their conversation the husband said to Hotchkiss, "You know, I had a most unusual experience once that concerned you." Hotchkiss asked what it was. The man said, "Well, one night I woke up suddenly with an irresistible urge to pray for you. And I did, committing you to God's safekeeping." Hotchkiss asked, "And do you remember when it was?" The man said, "Yes," because he had written it down that night in his Bible. When they compared the times, it was on the same day and at the same hour that Hotchkiss had been spared from what had seemed a certain death on the Nigerian plain.

Now someone will argue, "Oh, but God would have saved Hotchkiss anyway, even if the man had not prayed." I think that is probably right. Yes, God would have saved him. But the point is that in God's marvelous working He moved a man halfway around the world to pray for Hotchkiss in that hour. And thus, years later, the man was able to share in the blessing of his friend's supernatural deliverance. In the same way we have the privilege as God's children of committing others into His hands for His blessing — our friends, neighbors, acquaintances, and family. And as we do, we are permitted to share in His blessing on them. Our Christian life holds few joys greater than this one.

SUPPLICATIONS

There is one other point about prayer that comes directly from this passage. Not only is prayer talking with God. Not only is prayer intercession for others. Prayer is also an opportunity to present our requests to Him. Paul calls them supplications, and he says, "Be anxious for nothing, but in everything, by prayer and supplication with thanksgiving, let your requests be made known unto God." What does supplication mean? It means "an earnest request." God invites us to place our earnest requests before Him.

This is God's cure for anxiety. Christians are often troubled about many things. Perhaps you are also. You may be troubled about your work, your family, the future, money, sex, or happiness. God invites you to place your requests about these things before Him. The promise of the verse is that the peace of God will keep your heart and mind through Christ Jesus.

Have you ever noticed that the verse does not say that we shall necessarily receive the things we ask for? You would expect the verse to say, "Be anxious for nothing, but in everything, by prayer and supplication with thanksgiving, let your requests be made known to God, and God will fulfill your requests." But it does not say that. It says "Be anxious for nothing, but in everything, by prayer and supplication with thanksgiving, let your requests be made known unto God, and *the peace of God, which passeth all understanding, shall keep your hearts and minds through Christ Jesus.*" Our prayers are often in error, and we pray for things that are not good for us. God does not promise to give us these things. All things work together for *good* to them that love God. However, God does promise to give a supernatural peace to those who share their real needs with Him.

We must not think that Paul was recommending something for others that he had not found true for himself. Paul, too, had had this experience. Do you remember the prayer that Paul wrote as part of the fifteenth chapter of Romans? Paul was in Corinth and was about to go on to Jerusalem with the collection from the Gentile churches. After that he had planned to travel to Rome as an ambassador of the Christian Gospel. He prayed for three things: 1) "that I may be delivered from them that do not believe in Judaea"; 2) "that my service, which I have for Jerusalem, may be accepted by the saints"; and 3) "that I may come unto you with joy by the will of God, and may with you be refreshed" (Rom. 15:31, 32).

How were Paul's requests answered? Well, we do not know every aspect of God's answers, but we do know that Paul's first request was not fulfilled literally. Paul fell into the hands of the unbelievers and spent two years in prison in Caesarea as a result, although his life was spared. We have no information about his second request — that his collection might be received willingly by the saints in Judaea — but there is no reason to think that Paul received a warm welcome from anyone. Finally, we know that Paul's third request — for a joyous journey to Rome — was fulfilled, if it was fulfilled, only after long delays and through much hardship. When Paul arrived in Rome at last, he arrived as a prisoner in chains.

God certainly did not answer Paul's requests as Paul intended. But

God did answer. And He answered exactly as Paul indicates in his words about prayer to the Philippians. How did God answer? He answered by giving Paul peace. Paul knew God's peace even in the most difficult of earthly circumstances, and he writes out of these circumstances to tell us also to make requests of God, our heavenly Father.

42.

God's Rule for Doubtful Things

(Philippians 4:8, 9)

THESE VERSES ARE A STATEMENT of one of God's great rules for doubtful things. They introduce us to the general problems of regulating our conduct in areas of life where the Bible is not entirely explicit. Should a Christian drink alcohol or not? Will it be harmful to his testimony if he plays cards? Can he enter politics? Can he work for a company that manufactures war materials? To what extent can a believer adopt the standards of his times and society? The answers to such questions must be given in their broadest possible scope; accordingly, we shall range through Scripture, returning at last to these verses in Philippians.

VARYING STANDARDS

We need to recognize first that although many of the issues that trouble Christians are silly and do not deserve much attention, not all of them are. Consequently we must not make the mistake of avoiding all serious thought about such matters.

For instance, in this country there are often many "don'ts" in Christian circles that I am convinced have in themselves little or nothing to do with Christianity: should I or should I not go to the movies? should I wear make-up? should I play cards? In some circles these behavioral patterns are almost a badge of a person's commitment to Jesus Christ. And yet in England, among believers who are entirely as conservative and equally committed to the Lord, these things often mean nothing at all. Instead, the touchstone of real commitment is thought to lie in observing Sunday as a day of rest free from normal activities. In Switzerland women are noted for their piety if they wear long hair; if it is short in line with modern fashions, many will think that they are backsliding in their Christianity.

The funniest story I ever heard along these lines came from Germany. A congregation in Germany had invited an American preacher for a series of meetings, and he had been a great blessing to them. Afterward, however, one woman commented to another that it was a puzzle to her how he could be the channel of such blessing when he was apparently such an unspiritual man. The other woman said, "What do you mean? Why not?" She answered, "Well, the whole time he was talking to us he had a white handkerchief showing in his breast pocket." We laugh at that, of course. But it is not entirely funny, for it is only an example of the many silly things that sometimes shift the thinking of Christians away from much more significant matters.

Some doubtful things, then, are silly, but there are also doubtful items that deserve more serious attention. Elisabeth Elliot Leitch has written on one of these problems in a little book called *The Liberty of Obedience* which is based on her experiences. She had always had the idea, perhaps as the product of her Christian upbringing, that there was a certain type of clothing that was right for a Christian to wear. And conversely, there was clothing that was wrong. But then she went to Ecuador, and she found herself in the midst of a tropical people who wore little or no clothing at all. What did her standards have to do with them? Should she dress new converts? Should their standards prevail? She said the problem became even more complex when she realized in time that, although the women in the tribe wore almost no clothing, they were nevertheless conscious of the proper ways to walk, sit, and stand that they thought modest. The entire problem forced her to ask herself if there is anything inherently Christian or non-Christian in the way we dress in America.

Another problem with an uncertain answer is alcohol. Should a Christian drink? Does the level of society in which a Christian finds himself matter? I tend to think that something as obviously harmful as alcohol has been in many instances should automatically be avoided; and I admire men, such as the many Christian business men I know who do not drink. But what happens to this conviction when you go to France, as I did as a young boy, and see the leading deacon of an evangelical Protestant church going around a large ring of children at a Sunday school picnic pouring wine? Oh, I know that part of the reason he did it was to prevent their getting sick on the water in a rural area, but the main point is his attitude toward alcohol. And this was obviously quite different in France from America, even among people who believed all that the most conservative Christians believe about the Gospel in the United States. Comparisons such as this defeat any approach to the problem through legalism. And any such comparison throws the student back once more upon the important principles of Scripture.

What are they? I should like to suggest three great principles that will at least help any Christian in 99 percent of his difficulties. All of these are found throughout Scripture, but they are summarized in three important verses: Romans 6:14; I Corinthians 6:12 (also 10: 23); and Philippians 4:8. They tell us that we are to live (as we have been saved) by grace; that we are to think first, last, and always of others; and that we are to pursue the highest things. The last verse is our text in Philippians.

Not Law, But Grace

The first principle, then, is that we are not under law; we are under grace. And the text is Romans 6:14: "For sin shall not have dominion over you; for ye are not under the law but under grace." This verse teaches that whatever the answer may be to the problems with doubtful practices, it is not legalism. That is, the way will never be found by organizing any body of Christians to declare whether or not movies, cigarettes, alcohol, cards, the Masons, war, or whatever it may be, are proper.

Historically, this problem was fought to a decisive conclusion in the first generation of the Church. We must remember that, because of the wide dispersion of Jews through the Roman world in the centuries before Christ, there was hardly a congregation of believers during the first Christian century that did not consist of a mixture of Jews and Gentiles, even in the most Gentile cities of the empire. Somehow, probably because of their own religious and social training, the Jewish Christians got the idea that the Gentile believers should submit to the ceremonial laws of Israel. And the result was a tremendous battle in which for a time the apostle Paul fought almost single-handedly against them. For a time even Peter was carried away with the error. But Paul resisted him (Gal. 2:11-14). And Paul later defended the case for Gentile (and Jewish) liberty before the other apostles in Jerusalem. On this occasion Peter sided with Paul and said, "Now, therefore, why put God to the test, to put a yoke upon the neck of the disciples, which neither our fathers nor we were able to bear? But we believe that through the grace of the Lord Jesus Christ we shall be saved, even as they" (Acts 15:10, 11). In the early Church the battle against legalism was won for pure grace.

It is also true, however, that the same verse that speaks against legalism also speaks against another error that is likewise a wrong approach to the problem. This error is the error of license, the teaching that because we are not under law but under grace the Christian can therefore go on doing as he pleases. That is to say, "Let us sin that grace may abound." This error pretends to be logical, but it is not. It is infernal. And Paul does not hesitate to say so. The very next verse says, "What then? Shall we sin, because we are not under the law, but under grace? God forbid" (Rom. 6:15). And he adds, "But now being made free from sin, and become servants to God, ye have your fruit unto holiness, and the end everlasting life" (verse 22).

Paul's argument is that life by grace actually leads to holiness and, hence, we should not fear to abolish legalism as an answer to the problems of Christian conduct. The way it works may be illustrated by two types of marriage. There is the type of marriage that is founded on law. In this marriage the wife says something like this, "Now I know that you are going off to that office party tonight, and I know that dozens of those young secretaries will be there. Don't you dare look at any of them. Because if you do and I hear about it, I'll really lay into you when you get home. And be back by ten-thirty." Well, if the wife says that, the husband is likely to go off saying to himself, "So that's what she wants, is it? Well, I'll just stay out as long as I please and do as I please." And there will be no end of friction. Legalism does not promote happiness or fidelity in marriage.

The other type of marriage is one in which there is love rather than law. Each partner knows the faults of the other, but they know that they love each other anyway and have forgiven the faults in advance. Are they happy? Certainly they are happy. And they are faithful in the relationship. In a similar way, the grace of God never makes us rebels; it makes us men and women who love God and desire to please Him.

ALL THINGS ARE NOT EXPEDIENT

The second principle for determining God's will in doubtful matters is that although all things are lawful for the Christian — because he is not under law but under grace — yet all things are not expedient. And that is true for two reasons: first, because the thing itself may gain a harmful control over him or have a harmful effect on him physically and, second, because through him it may hurt other Christians.

The first reason is given in I Corinthians 6:12: "All things are lawful unto me, but all things are not expedient; all things are lawful for me, but I will not be brought under the power of any." Paul knew that God had not set him free from sin and from the law in order for him to become captive to mere things.

The guiding principle here is whether you as a Christian are using things or whether things are using you. Take food for an example. Nothing can be as obviously good for a person as food; it is necessary for bodily strength as well as mental health. But it is possible for a person to become so addicted to over-eating that the good end is thwarted and the person's health is endangered. Hence, certain eating habits should be avoided (verse 13). The second of Paul's examples is sex (verses 13-20). This too is good. It is a gift of God. Within the bonds of marriage it is a force for strength in the home as well as an expression of close union. But it too can be destructive. It can control the person instead of the person controlling it. And in this form sex can destroy the very values it was created to maintain. The Bible teaches that the Christian must never use things — food, sex, drugs, alcohol, cars, homes, stocks, or whatever it may be — in such a way that he actually falls under their power. In some of these cases, such as the case of habit-forming drugs, I would think that I Corinthians 6:12 is an unequivocable warning to avoid them.

Later on in I Corinthians Paul gives another reason why all things should not be expedient: the freedom of one believer may hurt the spiritual growth of another. Here Paul says, "All things are lawful for me, but all things are not expedient; all things are lawful for me, but all things edify not" (I Cor. 10:23). The verses that follow show that he is thinking of the edification and growth of fellow Christians.

I do not believe that this verse means that you are going to have to take your standards of conduct entirely from what other Christians say or think. If you do that, you are either going to become hypocritical, schizophrenic, or mad. Miss Ethel Barrett, who is well known for her Bible-story work among children, tells of her early experiences with matters of dress as she first began to travel about the country. Originally she came from California, and her standards of dress were formed by the climate and style of California. Hence, her clothes were bright, and she wore make-up and large hats. When she went east and began to work there she soon met some for whom her standards of dress were unspiritual. They said, "Why does she look like that? That is no way for a Christian to dress." Well, being young and less experienced then, she took it to heart. She changed her clothes, and she stopped wearing make-up. It was not long, however, before some new remarks got back to her: "Why does she have to look so drab and unpleasant? She would have a much more effective and spiritual ministry if she would brighten herself up a bit." Ethel Barrett learned through experience that you cannot take all of your standards of conduct from other Christians. And she was right. The verse does not mean that you are to allow the prejudices and viewpoints of others to dictate your pattern of behavior.

And yet the verse does mean something. For it says that there are situations in which we must avoid certain things, even if they are right in themselves, lest they be detrimental to others. Let me give you an example. Suppose you have been witnessing to a young man who has been having a hard time overcoming a disposition to sexual sins. He has become a Christian, but the lure of the flesh is still with him. Well, this verse means that you had better not take him to see or encourage him to see certain of our modern films. And what is more, you had best not go yourself, for he may be harmed by your freedom. In the same way, we are not to serve alcohol to anyone for whom it may be a problem; and for his sake, we are to avoid it also.

Moreover, we are to be consistent in our abstinence, for we must not appear double-faced or hypocritical. And we must sometimes be consistent over a long period of time. Paul wrote, "Wherefore, if food make my brother to offend, I will eat no meat while the world standeth, lest I make my brother to offend" (I Cor. 8:13). Just think: "While the world standeth!" And this from the same apostle who defended the cause of Christian liberty successfully before the Jerusalem apostles! We must remember that it will be costly if we are to be careful of the effect of our conduct upon others.

THE BETTER THINGS

The final principle of the three that I think best helps to direct our conduct in doubtful areas is Philippians 4:8 — "Finally, brethren, whatever things are true, whatever things are honest, whatever things are just, whatever things are pure, whatever things are lovely, whatever things are of good report; if there be any virtue, and if there be any praise, think on these things." According to this verse the Christian is to decide between doubtful things by choosing the best.

Moreover, this does not exclude the best things in our society, whether explicitly Christian or not. For the meat of the verse lies in the fact (not always noticed by commentators and Bible teachers) that the virtues mentioned here are pagan virtues. These words do not occur in the great lists of Christian virtues, lists that include love, joy, peace, long-suffering, and so on. On the whole they are taken from Greek ethics and from the writings of the Greek philosophers. What does this mean? It means that in using them Paul is actually sanctifying, as it were, the generally accepted virtues of pagan morality. And he is saying that although the pursuit of the best things by Christians will necessarily mean the pursuit of fellowship with God, pursuit of the will of God, pursuit of all means to advance the claims of the Gospel, and other spiritual things also, it will not mean the exclusion of the best values that the world has to offer. The things that are acknowledged to be honorable by the best men everywhere are also worthy to be cultivated by Christians. Consequently, a Christian can love all that is true, honest, just, pure, lovely, and of good report,

wherever he finds it. He can rejoice in the best of art and good literature. He can thrill to great music. He can thrive on beautiful architecture. And he should do it. You should do it. And you can thank
God as a Christian for giving men the ability even in their fallen state
to create such things of beauty.

Moreover, as you use this principle for determining God's will in
doubtful things, you can also take confidence from the promise of God's
presence that accompanies it. Paul often writes parenthetically in his
letters, and he does so here. The result is that the first half of verse
nine seems partially to distort the meaning of the sentence. The first
half says, "Those things which ye have both learned, and received,
and heard, and seen in me, do." And as the verse stands we would
tend to think that the promise of God's presence is attached to it.
Actually, it is attached to verse 8, and the promise is: "Whatever things
are honest, just, pure, and lovely, think on these things . . . and the
God of peace shall be with you."

When we pursue the highest things in life, both spiritually and
secularly, then the God of peace will be with us. And we shall have
the confidence that He will bless and guide us as we seek to please
Him.

43.

The Church That Remembered

(Philippians 4:10-18)

THROUGHOUT THE HISTORY OF Christianity individual churches have been remembered for different things, some good and some bad. In the first chapter of the book of Romans there is a picture of a church that was conspicuous for its faith and that is remembered even today because of it (Rom. 1:8). The church at Ephesus was known for its hard work, and it is remembered for that (Rev. 2:2, 3). Corinth is remembered for its division and moral laxity, the church at Laodicea for its apostasy, the congregation at Thessalonica for its doctrinal disputes centered on Christ's second coming.

In Philippi we have a picture of a church that is remembered because *it* remembered. It remembered the apostle Paul in his moments of great financial necessity. And we remember it for its example of true Christian compassion and stewardship.

GENUINE INTEREST

When Paul first came to the city of Philippi in Macedonia there were no Christians, for he was the first missionary. And it was only as Paul began to preach and to teach the Old Testament that a small group of believers gathered around him. These Christians were attached to Paul, because through him God had called them to faith in Jesus Christ and through him God had brought great blessing. These Christians loved Paul and wished to help him. And they continued their interest in him even after he had moved on to other cities. For a short time after he had left Philippi, Paul worked in Thessalonica. And since this was near Philippi the Philippians sent messengers to find out how Paul was doing. Word came back that Paul was in financial need. They took a collection and sent it to him. Later when they had heard that the need continued they did the same thing again. Paul refers to this in his letter to them saying, "For even in Thessa-

287

lonica ye sent once and again [that is, twice] unto my necessity" (Phil. 4:16).

After a short period of time a riot drove Paul out of Thessalonica, and he went south to Berea and then moved on to Athens. While in Athens his companions from the north went back to Macedonia and sent on Silas and Timothy whom he had left there; these caught up to him in Corinth. For a time during these journeys the church at Philippi must have lost track of Paul, and they must have asked themselves questions about him. "Where is he now? The last we heard of him he was in the little town of Berea, but they say that he left there and went south. I wonder where he stopped? Is he in Athens? Did he go on to Corinth? Perhaps he has left Greece entirely?" The questions continued until a traveler, who had seen Paul recently, finally came to Philippi. Now the questions changed. "Is Paul all right? Does he have a place to stay? Is he without money? Is he forced to take care of himself by tentmaking? Or are Christians taking care of him?" The questions would have come forth like a torrent.

When the answer came that Paul was again in need, the Philippians once more sent money. This happened at least once after Paul had left Thessalonica, for the letter says that the Philippians had cared for him in the beginning of the Gospel after he had left Macedonia. II Corinthians says that when he was in Corinth "that which was lacking to me the brethren who came from Macedonia supplied" (II Cor. 11: 9). These were presumably Philippian Christians. When the answer came back from the visitor that Paul was all right and well cared for, then the Philippians rejoiced and used their money elsewhere.

Eventually the believers at Philippi lost touch with Paul entirely, for Paul was constantly on the move and communications were uncertain and almost always slow. He left Greece and returned to Judaea. There was a third missionary journey; again they had contact; again Paul moved on. At last Paul was imprisoned in Caesarea and then after two years was dispatched in chains to Rome.

Many years had now passed since Paul had first visited Philippi and had founded the church there, but the love of the Philippians for Paul was still strong and the church had not forgotten his service among them. At length news of Paul came to them from Rome, and they learned that he was now in prison there and lacked everything. Many had left him. He could not work. He was not even warm enough during the long months of the damp Roman winter. Immediately the Philippians began to collect funds. And when they had them they sent the gift to Rome as quickly as possible in the care of Epaphroditus.

Paul was overjoyed. And as a result he wrote the closing verses of Philippians to express it. "But I rejoiced in the Lord greatly that now at the last your care of me hath flourished again; of which ye were also mindful, but ye lacked opportunity. Not that I speak in respect of want; for I have learned, in whatever state I am, in this to be content. I know both how to be abased, and I know how to abound; everywhere and in all things I am instructed both to be full and to be hungry, both to abound and to suffer need. I can do all things through Christ, who strengtheneth me. Notwithstanding, ye have well done, that ye did share with my affliction . . . Not because I desire a gift; but I desire fruit that may abound to your account. But I have all, and abound. I am full, having received of Epaphroditus the things which were sent from you, an odor of a sweet smell, a sacrifice acceptable, well-pleasing to God" (Phil. 4:10-14, 17, 18) To Paul's mind the gift from the Philippians was a shrub that had flowered, as it were, in spring after a long winter. And it was a sacrifice to God for which Paul was thankful.

Fruit That Abounds

Paul's pleasure at the gift that the Philippian Christians had sent was not merely for his own sake, however. He was pleased for their sake also. For he knew, as we should all know, that a gift actually benefits the giver more than it benefits the one who receives it.

This is true on the human level. But it is even more true spiritually, for Paul writes that in God's sight the gift would appear as fruit credited to their personal account (verse 17). We often think of the fruits of Christianity only in terms of character, primarily as the fruit of the Spirit listed in Galatians 5:22, 23. But other things are said to be fruits of the Christian life also. Converts are the fruit of our labors for the Lord Jesus Christ. And here money given to help another Christian is called fruit also. According to this text we may say that our gifts to others are encouraged by God, noticed by God, and much desired by Him.

Unfortunately, much proper Christian giving is hindered by the deep conviction in some believers' minds that security is really dependent on having things or money. Some girls think that security consists in being able to capture a husband. And many husbands think that their security consists in amassing a fortune. If they are able to save a thousand dollars, they feel that they would be a bit more secure if they had two. If they earn two thousand, they think of ten. Ten leads to twenty. And pretty soon they have their eyes on even more. Against this misplaced desire God says that if the believer is not trusting Him he is no more secure with a million dollars than just one. And if he trusts God, he is secure without any.

From my own observation of the various patterns of Christian giving today I believe I would say that one of the best things that could happen to many believers would be for them to be led to give away, all at one time, a substantial part of their savings. That is, they should give a substantial part of their capital. Why? Because there is some-thing about giving away a sizable percentage of one's money — and, of course, the amount would vary entirely from one individual to an-other — that is spiritually invigorating. And there is seldom a case in which a large gift does not throw the Christian back on the Lord and increase the feeling that He is all wonderful and that He is more than able to care for the one who trusts Him. I have seen this happen in many instances. And I have never known a true Christian to be sorry for even the most sacrificial giving afterward.

Perhaps someone is going to ask at this point, "Well, what about tithing? Doesn't the Bible say that we are to tithe? And doesn't that mean that we are only required to give a tenth of all earned income?" Well, the answer to that question is that the Bible does speak about tithing; but that was for Jews under the Old Testament laws. "Well then," you say, "doesn't that mean that we are released entirely from the requirement to give?" Yes, in a sense we are; for we are not under law. We are under grace. But if you understand what it means to be under grace rather than under law, then you also understand that under grace the standard does not go down — it goes up. For instance, the Sermon on the Mount is not law as the Ten Commandments are law; it is an ethic to be lived out by God's grace in the lives of re-generate men. But because it is by grace, the standard goes up. And instead of being told only that we shall not murder, we are also told that we shall not hate. And not only should we not commit adultery, we are not even to lust after another person mentally. It is the same with stewardship. Instead of owing God ten percent of our income, we are now told that all that we have belongs to Him.

We are not under law as regards percentages. But we do have a high level of responsibility for the support of other Christians and Christian work, and we are responsible for determining God's will where our own individual stewardship is concerned.

If God tells you that you are to give ten percent of your income to Christian work in any one year, then you are to give ten percent. If you have abnormally high and valid commitments one year, perhaps in regard to the medical care of your family or the education of your children, and God tells you that ten percent is too high, then you are to give less. If God tells you to give twenty percent, give twenty per-cent. If He says fifty, give fifty. Just be sure that you know inside that it all belongs to Him and that He has the final word on how you spend it.

THE ONLY ONES

Finally, let me call your attention to another phrase in this section that also deserves to be noticed. It should encourage us in a special form of stewardship. It occurs in verse 15: "Now ye Philippians know also that in the beginning of the gospel, when I departed from Macedonia, no church shared with me as concerning giving and receiving, *but ye only*. For even in Thessalonica ye sent once and again to my necessity." Ye only! Not only were the Philippians distinguished by the fact that they had remembered Paul in his need — that was significant — they had also been the *only* ones to remember him. And that was significant indeed.

There is always a special aura about someone who does something for you when only that one has remembered to do it. In his vastly successful book *How to Win Friends and Influence People* Dale Carnegie has a section in which he tells of some of the devices he developed for pleasing business acquaintances. One of them was this. Whenever he would meet a man for the first time, Carnegie would ask at some point in the conversation under which sign of the Zodiac the man had been born. In 99 cases out of 100 the person would not know, so Carnegie was able to ask the day of his birth so as to be able to tell him. This was only a gimmick, however. For as soon as Carnegie had found out the date of his birth, he would tuck it away in his memory and then would write it down at the first opportunity he found to do so. Later, the date was entered on a calendar along with other significant birthdays. And each year on that date the acquaintance would receive a birthday card from Carnegie. The famous author then says that he imagined, and generally learned later from experience, that in most cases he was the only one outside of the immediate family who had remembered the man's birthday. And the resulting warmth and good will were staggering.

I believe that if Dale Carnegie could do that for secular ends to win friends and influence people, Christians ought to be able to do the same type of thing for spiritual ends and to do so sacrificially to win them for Christ.

Do you want real joy in this world, and real fruit in your Christian ministry? If so, let me suggest this. Instead of wondering to yourself, as you often do, why people do not treat you better or remember things that are important to you, seek for the ways in which you can help them, particularly in those areas in which only you know the problem. God will show you how. The other person will think that no one understands his need or no one is aware of his problem. And then your gift or your word of encouragement will come. He will be overjoyed; and if he is a Christian he will see it as another way in which God uses men as channels of His faithful provision and blessing.

I cannot tell you who the person is whom you could help. I cannot tell you what the circumstances will be or even what you can do. That will vary, and you will have to find it out for yourself. It might be a person in your own family with a unique need, perhaps one of your children who desperately needs someone to do something special for him or for her, or your wife or husband who needs understanding. It might be someone at work who thinks (and rightly) that no one cares about him. It might be someone at church. It might be a stranger. It might be a Christian work or worker. It might be a financial need. It might be a word of encouragement. Whatever it is, God will help you to find it if you ask Him. He will show you what to do. And He will give you great joy in being the one who (like the Philippians) did not forget, but remembered.

44.

The God Who Provides

(Philippians 4:19)

I AM FREQUENTLY ASKED what I consider to be the best cure for mental and spiritual depression. And I answer that the best cure for spiritual depression is to feed on the promises of God. Are you depressed or discouraged? Has life gotten you down? If so, somewhere in the Bible there is a promise of God to cover it. I am convinced there is no need, no anxiety, no worry, no dismay for which God has not made dozens of encouraging and uplifting promises.

GOD'S PROMISES

Years ago now a delightful old French woman told me a story from her own life that illustrates this principle. In her youth in France she had been taught to make a little box of Bible verses containing a selection of the promises of God from Scripture. Each verse was written on a small piece of paper about the size of a piece of chewing gum, and each was then rolled up to make a miniature scroll. After there were forty or fifty of these small scrolls they were placed on end in a tiny open box so that the tops were even and each one was visible. This was the promise box. And she had been encouraged as a child to pull out one verse each morning and read it. One day during the Second World War (when she was much older) she was feeling terribly discouraged by many things that had happened. In her depression her mind turned to the little box of promises that had been long since forgotten. She went to the drawer of the dresser where she had kept the box, and she took it out. She prayed, "Lord, You know how depressed I am, and You know that I do need a word of encouragement. Isn't there a promise here somewhere that can help me?" She finished praying and stepped over to the window where the light was better for reading. As she did she tripped over a loose edge of the rug and all the promises went spilling out onto the carpet. And she said, "Lord, how foolish I have been to ask for one promise when there are so many glorious promises in your Word!"

Just think of the breadth and the scope of God's promises. There is John 3:16, a promise of everlasting salvation: "For God so loved the world, that he gave his only begotten Son, that whosoever believeth in him should not perish, but have everlasting life." Romans 8:28 says, "And we know that all things work together for good to them that love God, to them who are the called according to his purpose." John 10:9 points out, "I am the door; by me if any man enter in, he shall be saved, and shall go in and out, and find pasture." John 10:27, 28 says "My sheep hear my voice, and I know them, and they follow me. And I give unto them eternal life; and they shall never perish, neither shall any man pluck them out of my hand." Some promises concern prayer. Philippians 4:6, 7 says, "Be anxious for nothing, but in everything, by prayer and supplication with thanksgiving, let your requests be made known unto God. And the peace of God, which passeth all understanding, shall keep your hearts and minds through Christ Jesus." I John 5:14, 15 tells us, "And this is the confidence that we have in him, that, if we ask anything according to his will, he heareth us; and if we know that he hear us, whatever we ask, we know that we have the petitions that we desired of him."

We come now to what is perhaps the greatest promise in the entire Bible. And it is great because it includes all of the other promises in itself. What is the promise? It is Philippians 4:19, "But my God shall supply all your need according to his riches in glory by Christ Jesus." Do you stand in need of salvation? God will supply salvation. Do you need strength for life's trials? God will supply strength. If you are lonely, God can meet you and comfort you in your loneliness. If you are discouraged, He can lift you up. No need is left out, for the verse says that "God shall supply *all* your need according to his riches in glory by Christ Jesus."

The God of Israel

A verse like this needs to be savored in each of its phrases. And the place to begin is with the two most important words in the sentence, the subject. The words are "My God." Who is the one who Paul knew was able to supply the needs of the Philippian Christians? It was not any god, for he did not say "a god" or merely "the god in whom you may happen to believe." Paul was not referring to the gods of the Greeks, Egyptians, Assyrians, or Romans. When Paul said, "My God," he was being specific and personal. Paul's God was Jehovah, the God of Israel who had revealed Himself to men personally in Jesus Christ. This God was a great God. He was a gracious and effective God. In fact, to the biblical writers all other gods were "no-gods" (idols); they were idols only, and they were entirely ineffective.

The God of Philippians 4:19 is the God who called Abraham out of Mesopotamia when he was an idol worshiper like all of his contemporaries and who sent him on his way to a new land promising that he would be blessed and that there would be greater blessing to all men through his descendants. The God of Philippians 4:19 is the God who called Israel out of Egypt, who took her through the Red Sea, who preserved her for forty years in the wilderness, and who finally enabled her to conquer the land of Canaan. He is the God of David, of Elijah, of Jeremiah, of all the prophets. And He is the God and Father of our Lord Jesus Christ who as Christ died for our salvation and then triumphed over the tomb. This is the God who stands behind His promises.

This is important. And it is important for the simple reason that the value of a belief depends entirely upon the effectiveness and fidelity of the thing or person believed. Once I was talking to someone about faith, and he asked whether the faith of Christians is any different from the kind of self-delusion that many persons practice to escape reality. He wanted to know if faith was not purely subjective. I admitted in reply that there is a subjective element to faith. Faith is individual. Emotionally there probably is very little difference between this type of conviction and delusion. But that is only half of the picture. Although there is little or no difference between the two kinds of faith psychologically, there is all the difference in whether or not the object of the belief corresponds to the things believed about it. For instance, there is no difference at all in the belief of a man who leans against a papier maché column, thinking it is marble and able to hold him up, and the belief of a man who leans against a real one. But the real column will support the man while the artificial one will collapse and let him fall down. The God of whom Paul speaks is a God who will support His people and who will not let the one who believes in Him down.

Is He your God? You need to face this squarely. Because if He is not your God, if you have never come to Him through faith in the Lord Jesus Christ, then the promises of God's care in the Bible are not for you. On the other hand, if you do believe in Him and wish to obey Him, then you will find Him strong in your need. And you will find Him entirely and consistently faithful.

Man's Need

The emphasis of the first part of the verse is upon God, but the second part speaks of man's need. And we must think of this also. What is our need?

First, there is our need for forgiveness. God provides that abundantly, for He offers forgiveness of sins that are past, present, and future. Forgiveness is made possible for us through the death of the Lord Jesus Christ, and we receive it personally by acknowledging our sin before God and accepting Christ's sacrifice. The apostle John wrote, "If we say that we have no sin, we deceive ourselves, and the truth is not in us. If we confess our sins, he is faithful and just to forgive us our sins, and to cleanse us from all unrighteousness" (I John 1:8, 9).

The doctrine of forgiveness through Christ is never taught but that some people imagine that a promise of forgiveness is actually an invitation to wrongdoing. For the argument goes, "If we know that God will forgive us, why can't we do as we want to beforehand?" Fortunately, it does not work that way. I know of a Christian family who raised two fine boys in the midst of one of our large cities. Because they were in the midst of the city the boys were often tempted to join one of the gangs that roamed through the neighborhood and destroyed property. The parents might have said, "Look here, George, if you ever get mixed up in one of those gangs and get hauled in by the police, don't come running to me for help. Just take your medicine and remember that I warned you about it beforehand." But if they had done that, the boys would likely have taken up bad company in self-defense. Instead, the father called them to him and said, "Now look, I know about the temptations that you will be facing in the city. But I want you to know this. If you ever get into trouble with the gang, never keep it to yourself. Come back here. This is your home. You belong with me and your mother, and we'll face everything that happens together. Never doubt that we love you and that we'll forgive you." Well, in that home the boys grew to be strong Christian men and were kept pure and honest. How glorious, that God our heavenly Father treats us in an identical manner!

Forgiveness is not our only need, however. Our second great need is for fellowship with God. For without God we are spiritually hungry, empty, and miserable. That is why Saint Augustine said, "Thou hast made us for thyself, and our hearts are restless until they find their rest in thee." We do not need to be miserable and spiritually hungry, however. For God longs to be known by us, to fill the spiritual vacuum of our hearts, to commune with us personally, and to meet us in our deep longings. Moreover, He is able to do so abundantly "according to his riches in glory in Christ Jesus."

Do we also need God's defense against enemies? Yes, at times. And is God able to supply that? Of course, He is! David, the first great king of Israel, had enemies. He had enemies within and without, in his own family and in other nations. But when he came to the end of his life and was able to look back thankfully over the years of God's deliverance from his enemies he said, "The Lord is my rock, and my fortress, and my deliverer, the God of my rock; in him will I trust: he is my shield, and the horn of my salvation, my high tower, and my refuge, my savior; thou savest me from violence" (II Sam. 22:2, 3). God is also able to meet your need against enemies.

A NEED FOR TESTING

I must add one other thing, however, for it is sometimes true that in God's sight we have a need for that which is not so pleasant. We need to be disciplined, taught, or tested. And if that is the case, then it is also true that Philippians 4:19 is a promise of God to supply the unpleasant discipline and testing.

Early in his ministry that great Bible teacher Dr. Harry Ironside had an experience that perfectly illustrates this provision. On one occasion he had acted on faith, as he often did, to preach for two weeks in Fresno, California. And the time came, surprisingly to him, when he was entirely out of money. He had begun with a small amount, but this was used up. And he now had no funds with which to eat. He was even forced to check out of his hotel room and leave his suitcase at a drugstore to be picked up later. There was some complaining and bitterness, according to Ironside. And when the thought of Philippians 4:19 crossed his mind — "But my God shall supply all your need according to his riches in glory by Christ Jesus" — his spirit rebelled. "Why then doesn't He do it?" he questioned. It seemed that God had promised, but that He was no longer keeping His word.

That night, as he settled down under a tree on the lawn of the Court House in Fresno, God spoke to Ironside concerning many things about which he said he had grown careless. And in his prayer and meditation he experienced a great spiritual awakening. From that time on the work went better. Old friends appeared, first to invite him to lunch and later to provide accommodation. And the church to which he was ministering took a collection at last to help him out on his return journey.

At the end he went to the post office and found a letter from his father, much to his surprise. He opened it. And there staring him in the face was a postscript that said, "God spoke to me through Philippians 4:19 today. He has promised to supply all our need. Some day He may see that I need a starving! If He does, He will supply that." Ironside says, "Oh, how real it all seemed then! I saw that God had been putting me through that test in order to bring me closer to Himself, and to bring me face to face with things that I had been neglecting." * He wrote later that he wished to share the experience with others, like you and me, who may be going through similar times of testing.

GOD'S RICHES IN GLORY

The final phrase of our text speaks of the measure of the supply of God for our need. And the measure is this: "according to his riches in glory by Christ Jesus."

Every so often now the world is witness to some new space spectacular. I suppose that every time an astronaut goes off into space there are millions of people who wish they could share his experience. Suppose that one of these persons would ask one of the astronauts to bring back a sample of space. Well, he could take up a small canister, seal it in space, and bring it back. And there is a sense in which the sealed canister would contain a sample. It would be perfectly empty. But it would not even begin to capture the immensity and grandeur of space. If it were to hold more, it would be necessary to enlarge the container. But even then it could never even begin to exhaust that immensity.

In a parallel sense God has promised to fill the need of the believer in Jesus Christ out of His infinite wealth and resources. He will expand us as time goes on, and we shall come to hold more. We shall become more and more like Jesus Christ. But even at the greatest extent of our enlarged capacity we shall only touch His resources slightly. And there will always be infinite resources beyond the ones we then experience.

Do not think that you can ever exhaust the grace and the riches of God by your needs, however great they may be. Can the finite exhaust the infinite? Can that which is corrupt exhaust that which is incorruptible? Can the part exhaust the whole? Can man exhaust God? It is impossible. In this life, as in the next, God shall supply all our needs, according to His riches in glory by Christ Jesus, and still there will be inexhaustible resources beyond.

---

* H. A. Ironside, *Random Reminiscences* (Neptune, N.J.: Loizeaux Bros, n.d.), pp. 73-85.

45.

Grace and Glory

(Philippians 4:20-23)

As EDWARD GIBBON APPROACHED the end of writing *The Decline and Fall of the Roman Empire,* a project that had taken nearly twenty years of his life, he returned to the city of Rome and made his way to an outcropping of the Capitoline hill from which he could look out upon the forum, made desolate by the passing of the centuries. It was the point from which many famous men and many writers have surveyed the ruins of the Roman city and from which many persons do today. As Gibbon looked at the forum and began to compose the final words of his history, his mind went back over all he had written and he expressed the wish that those who should read his masterpiece should come to appreciate, not so much the detail of the narrative, but the great themes of the work and its general conclusions.

I believe that something similar happens to any author as he draws near the end of his work. It has happened to me, to some extent, as I come in this chapter to the close of my exposition of the book of Philippians. And it happened to Paul as he completed his remarks to his Philippian friends. Few of Paul's books end abruptly. And none of them ends without thought. I believe that in this book, as in others, Paul's thoughts ran back over the work he had written, and his final remarks were added to impress his most important themes upon his readers. He writes: "Now unto God and our Father be glory forever and ever. Amen. Greet every saint in Christ Jesus. The brethren who are with me greet you. All the saints greet you, chiefly they that are of Caesar's household. The grace of our Lord Jesus Christ be with you all. Amen" (Phil. 4:20-23).

These last verses contain a twofold doxology interspersed with a few brief words of greeting. The doxology has the glory of God and the grace of the Lord Jesus Christ as its theme.

GOD'S GLORY

What is the glory of God mentioned in these last verses of Philippians? Well, it is not exactly the same thing as the glory mentioned in verse 19, although the words are identical. In verse 19 Paul says, "But my God shall supply all your need according to his riches in glory by Christ Jesus." Here he is thinking of glory in the sense that God's glory expresses God's character. God's glory is the outward expression of what God is internally. Hence, Paul is really saying that God shall continue to supply the need of the Christian out of His inexhaustible might, wisdom, love, holiness, truth, and other perfections. However, when Paul prays in verse 20 that glory might be *given* to God, he is thinking of glory in another sense. Here glory is praise. And he is really looking forward to the day when God shall be praised and honored as He should and must be forever.

There is a picture in the fourth and fifth chapters of Revelation of how this will happen. In the earlier chapters of the prophecy we learn of the vision John had on the island of Patmos, and we read the messages of the exalted Christ to His churches. In chapter four the scene changes. Here the heavens are opened, and John rises to catch a glimpse of heaven.

What does John see? He sees God on His throne. And the description of what he sees is meant to convey a sense of God's glory and of the glory given to Him by the redeemed creation. First, God is praised as the author and agent of redemption. This is symbolized by the sea of glass, like crystal, which John sees before the throne. It parallels the great laver of water for the purification of the priests that stood before the Jewish temple in Solomon's day. But here it is not filled with water; it is solid, turned to crystal. For, thanks to God's great work of redemption, there is now no further need for washing from sin. All is sinless in heaven. The four living creatures who stand near this crystal laver sing, "Holy, holy, holy, Lord God Almighty, who was, and is, and is to come" (Rev. 4:8).

Second, God is praised in His kingship. Here the entire idea of kingship in Israel is summed up with God as king and the Lion of the tribe of Judah as the heir of David's throne forever. The elders sing to the king, "Thou art worthy, O Lord, to receive glory and honor and power; for thou hast created all things, and for thy pleasure they are and were created" (Rev. 4:11).

Finally, just as the kingship theme of the Old Testament and the theme of redemption are caught up in this great picture of the glory of God in heaven, so also is the prophetic theme brought to its high and praiseworthy conclusion. For Christ, the author of prophecy, opens the scroll of prophecy for the final time, after which the whole of creation cries out, "Blessing, and honor, and glory, and power be unto him that sitteth upon the throne, and unto the Lamb forever and ever" (Rev.

5:13). And the elders and the living creatures bow down and worship Him that lives and reigns forever.

When Paul closed his letter to the Philippians he was looking forward to the day when God should be praised in this way and when all honor should be given to the Lord Jesus Christ, before whom every knee should bow. In this desire the first part of his doxology sums up much of the teaching of Philippians.

BROTHERS AND SAINTS

At this point in his final remarks Paul inserts two verses of personal greeting. I do not believe that this is accidental. Too often Christians deal in abstract things when they should think of persons. And they find it easy to disassociate theological ideas from real life. Paul never does this. And, what is more, he does not do that here. Paul had been speaking of the glory of God, which is certainly an exalted theological concept, but he no sooner speaks of this concept than his mind immediately runs to those who would actually give God glory. And that means that he was thinking concretely of Christians.

Of whom did he think? Well, in these two short verses Paul's thought runs to four distinct bodies of believers. First, there are the Christians at Philippi. He is writing to these, and he refers to them when he says, "Greet every saint in Christ Jesus." Second, there are the Christian leaders who are in Paul's immediate company: Timothy, Epaphroditus, and others. Paul calls them "the brethren who are with me." Third, there is the vast company of believers in Rome. He refers to these when he says, "All the saints greet you." Finally, there is the special body of Christians who were employed in the various services related to the imperial court. Paul thinks of these Christians when he writes, "Chiefly they that are of Caesar's household." Paul knew that it was these very human brothers and saints, some of whom had been sharply critical of him, who would one day join in the great heavenly chorus to sing God's praise. And he rejoiced that they would give God glory.

Do you think that way about the Christians with whom you are associated? Some of them are objectionable, I know that. And some are extremely critical of you. Some have experienced very little sanctification. But God is going to use them to acknowledge His glory. And they, just like yourself, will be part of the heavenly chorus. Perhaps it will help you to live with them (and them to live with you) if you will think of them in terms of their destiny instead of their objectionable characteristics and conduct.

GRACE BE WITH YOU

The final verse of the letter to the Philippians says, "The grace of our Lord Jesus Christ be with you all. Amen." God's grace! The grace of our Lord Jesus Christ! There is nothing more significant that Paul could have used to end his epistle.

Have we understood anything at all about this letter? If we have, we must have understood that the message of Christianity from the beginning to end is of grace, God's unmerited favor to men. Do we deserve anything from God? Do you? Do you deserve life or health or happiness? Do you deserve God's love or the salvation purchased for you by Jesus Christ on Calvary? Do you deserve the Scriptures? Do you deserve the gift of God's Holy Spirit? Or His keeping in your daily life? Or the fact that you are made God's heir in the Lord Jesus Christ and will one day share in all of the riches of God's nature? Do you? Not at all! You deserve nothing. I deserve nothing. You and I have run from God, and still, even after we are born again, we run from Him. Yet, when we were far from Him, God came to us dying for our sin, rising for our justification, and now living to enter the life of those who believe on Him and to guide them in holiness. He loves us. He will love us forever. That is grace. It lies at the heart of the Gospel.

Finally, Paul does not only mention the word grace. He also mentions the Lord Jesus Christ. And that is significant, for it is only through the Lord Jesus Christ that we know God's grace and indeed continue to experience it. In fact, it is only through Jesus Christ that we experience any spiritual blessing.

Think how many times the name of the Lord Jesus Christ is mentioned in this Philippian letter. The letter begins with the name of Jesus; it ends with His name. And He is mentioned in every conceivable relationship. As I have thought on these themes I have been greatly blessed by some words written by Bishop Handley C. G. Moule:

> The mere number of mentions of the Savior's name is remarkable. More than forty times we have it in this short compass; that is to say, it occurs, amidst all the variety of subjects, on an average of about once in every two or three verses. This is indeed perfectly characteristic, not of this epistle only but of the whole New Testament. What the apostle preached was not a thing but a Person; Christ, Christ Jesus, Christ Jesus the Lord.
>
> But let us not look only on this frequency of mention. Let us gather up something of what these mentions say "concerning the King."
>
> The writer begins with describing himself and his associates as the servants, the absolute bondmen, of Jesus Christ. And truly such servants witness to the worthiness of their Master.

He addresses those to whom he writes as saints, as holy ones, *in Jesus Christ*. Their standing, their character, their all, depends on Him; on union with Him, on life in Him. Without Him, apart from Him, they would not be saints at all.

The writer speaks of his imprisonment at Rome; the subject is full of Jesus Christ. "My bonds *in Christ*" is his remarkable description of captivity. And the result of that captivity was, to his exceeding joy, just this, amidst a great variety of conditions in detail, including some exquisite trials to patience and peace: "*Christ* is being preached"; "that *Christ* may be magnified in my body, whether by life or death." He is kept absolutely cheerful and at rest; and the secret is Jesus Christ.

He has occasion to speak of his trial, with its delays, and its suspense between life and death. The whole is full of Jesus Christ. "To me to live is *Christ*"; He fills, and as it were makes, life for me. "And to die is gain" — why? Because "to depart and to be with *Christ* is far, far better." . . .

He dwells, in various places, on the life and duties of the Philippians. His precepts are all this, in effect — Christ applied to conduct. "Let your life-walk be as it becometh the gospel of *Christ*"; "Filled with the fruit of righteousness which is through *Jesus Christ*"; "It is granted to you not only to believe in *Christ* but also to suffer for His sake."

In particular, he has to press on them the homely duty of practical self-forgetfulness. He takes them for model and motive to the heaven of heavens, and shows them "Christ Jesus" there, as for us men and for our salvation He prepares to come down, and comes. "Let this mind be in you," as you contemplate the original glory, the amazing incarnation, the atoning death, of *Christ Jesus*.

He expresses hopes, intentions, resolutions, as to his own actions. All is still "in Jesus Christ"; "I trust in *the Lord Jesus* to send Timotheus"; "I trust in *the Lord* to come myself shortly."

Does he speak of the believer's joy? "We rejoice in *Christ Jesus*"; "Rejoice in *the Lord* alway, and again I say, Rejoice." Does he speak of pardon and of peace? "I counted all things but loss that I might win *Christ*, and be found in Him, having the righteousness which is of God by faith." Does he speak of knowledge, and of power? "That I might know *Christ*, and the power of his resurrection, and the fellowship of His sufferings, being made conformable unto His death"; "I can do all things in *Christ* which strengtheneth me."

He speaks of a holy immortality, of eternal glory, and of pleasures for evermore. It is no vague aspiration; it is a sure and certain hope; and it is altogether in Jesus Christ. "Our home, our citizenship, is in heaven, from whence also we look for the Savior, the Lord *Jesus Christ*, who shall change the body of our humiliation into likeness to the body of His glory, according to the working whereby He is able to subdue all things unto — Himself."

He bids his beloved converts stand fast; it is in *the Lord*." He bids them to be of one mind; it is "*in the Lord*." He bids them be always

calm, always self-forgetting; *"the Lord* is at hand." He assures them
of an all-sufficient resource for their every need; "My God shall supply
all, according to His riches, in glory, in *Christ Jesus."*

His last message of blessing brings together their inmost being and
this same wonderful Person; "The grace of our *Lord Jesus Christ* be with
your spirit. Amen." . . .

What a witness it all is to the glory of our beloved Redeemer; to
the majesty of His Person; to the fulness and perfection of His Work;
to the solidity, the sobriety, the strength, of the faith which is in Him!
There is no inflation or rhetoric in the language of the epistle about Him.
Glowing with love, it is all clear and calm. Yes, for Christ Jesus is not
a phantom of the fancy; a hope floating on the thick waves of a wild
enthusiasm. He is an anchor, sure and steadfast. Blessed are they who
ride secure on the deep, held fast by Him.

The epistle witnesses to Him as to a treasure worth all our seeking,
at any cost; infinitely precious to our joyful finding; infinitely deserving
of our keeping, of our holding, our "apprehending," as He in His mercy
has laid hold of us, and will keep hold of us, even to the end; "unto the
day of Jesus Christ." *

As I read these words of Bishop Moule my own heart was warmed,
as I trust yours is also, thinking of the pre-eminence, honor, and great
glory of our Lord Jesus Christ. He is our life; He is the hope, prayer,
song, and joy of Christians in all ages — of Paul and his friends at
Philippi, of the Roman Christians, of Bishop Moule and his congregations, and now of us also. May this great theme — the Lord Jesus
Christ and His grace — bless your heart today and may it continually
do so until that day when we shall know Him perfectly even as we
are known.

* H. C. G. Moule, *Philippian Studies* (Glasgow: Pickering & Inglis, n.d.), pp.
255-260.

SUBJECT INDEX

Abraham, 32, 37, 59, 212, 221, 251, 252, 268, 295
Access to God, 274
Adam, 165
Ahab and Micaiah, 109-111
Albright, W. F., 25
Alcohol, 280, 281
Ambition, 226
American culture, 82
Amos, 250
Andrew, 91
Angels, 157, 158
Anxiety, 189, 278
Apathy, 226
Apostles' Creed, 251
Ark of the Covenant, 146
Assets and liabilities, 193-199
Athens, 288
Auca Indians, 50, 51
Augustine, Saint, 244

Bacon, Francis, 93
Barnhouse, Donald Grey, 45, 70, 107, 120, 121, 234
Barth, Karl, 112, 113
Basilica of St. Peter, 87
Beare, F. W., 14
Belief, see Faith
Berea, 288
Bethany, 90
Bible, see Word of God
Bishops, 24, 25
Blessed Hope, our, 247-252
Boasting, none in heaven, 43
Borden of Yale, 225
Born again, 241, 242, 268
Brotherhood, 47, 181, 301

Caesarea, 288
Cain and Abel, 69
Calvin, John, 38
Carnegie, Dale, 194, 195, 291
Christ Jesus, acknowledged, 157-159; coming again, 153, 154, 247-252; condescension of, 127, 128; consolation in, 114, 115; cross of, 261, 262; David's Lord, 156; death of, 122, 143-148; divinity of, 131-136, 151,

152, 253, 254; doctrine about, 126, 127; exaltation of, 155-160; example of, 144, 145; faith in, 88, 89; fellowship with, 89-91; following after, 91, 92, 220-225; glory of, 128, 129, 133-136; guide and counselor, 263; humanity, 137-142; humility of, 17, 121-128; incarnation of, 137-142; Jehovah, 22, 23, 149-151; known by Christians, 214-219; Light of the World, 108; like us in disappointments, 141, 142; lives, 214, 254-256; looking to, 238, 239; Lord, 149-151, 156, 157; love of, 97; magnified in believers, 77-85; man and God, 126, 127; mark of, 112-117; mind of, 16-18, 70; names of, 149-154, 160, 302-304; obedience of, 17, 18; power of, 166, 167; pre-eminence of, 127; redemption by, 22; resurrection of, 253-256, 262, 263; righteousness of, 198, 199, 261, 262; satisfies, 198; seen in Scripture, 136; sin-bearer, 145, 146; sovereignty of, 152, 153; striving for, 226-232; suffering, 141; truth about, 131-136; union with, 217; victorious, 139-141, 261-263; walking with, 240-246; way to God, 274
Christian, and doubtful things, 280-286; becoming a, 188, 189; citizenship, 101-103; fellowship, 34-39, 47-52, 116; formerly a slave to sin, 21, 22; giving, 289-292; joy, 271; love, 52, 54, 55, 115, 116; made like Christ in death, 96-98; saint, 23, 24; servant, 20-22; shares Christ's glory, 136; slave to Jesus Christ, 21, 22; transformation of, 258, 259; unity, 103, 104, 112-117, 267-272; walk of a, 240, 241; warfare, 104, 105
Christian life, 100-105; examples of, 174-179; following Christ, 220-225; goals of, 168-173; growth in, 173; hope in suffering, 249-251; know-

305

SCRIPTURE INDEX

NOTES

NOTES

NOTES

NOTES

NOTES

NOTES